College Success:

A Concise Practical Guide

Seventh Edition

David L. Strickland, MA

Carol J. Strickland, PhD, RN

BVT Publishing

Better textbooks, better prices

www.BVTPublishing.com

College Success: A Concise Practical Guide

Seventh Edition

Publisher and Director of Development: Richard Schofield

Product Development Manager: Shannon Conley

Senior Designer: Esther Scannell

Designer: Tim Gerlach

Managing Editor: Anne Schofield

Associate Content Developer: Chad Peterson

Proofreader: Tara Joffe

Permissions Specialist: Logan McDonald

Production and Fulfillment Manager: Janai Bryand

Photo Credits: Media Bakery, Shutterstock

Some ancillaries, including electronic and print components, may not be available to customers outside the United States.

Textbook^Plus (Loose-Leaf Bundle) ISBN: 978-1-62751-866-6

eBook^Plus ISBN: 978-1-62751-864-2

Loose-Leaf ISBN: 978-1-62751-855-0

Softcover ISBN: 978-1-62751-860-4

Instructor Resource Edition ISBN: 978-1-5178-0110-6

Chapter Roadmaps

Table of Contents

Chapter 3   63

Learning and Grades: Why Am I Really in College?

Chapter 4   95

Learning Preferences: How Do I Learn Best?

Chapter 5   131

Getting Organized: Plan Your Work and Then Work Your Plan

Chapter 6   177

Listening and Taking Notes: Do You Hear What I Hear?

Chapter 7   207

Reading Textbooks: What They Never Taught You in Kindergarten!

Chapter 8   239

Writing College Papers: I Have a Paper Due!

Chapter 9   265

Psychological Balance: Walking the Tightrope

Chapter 12   371

Planning Your Future: What Courses Should I Take?

Appendix   403

References   407

Index   417

Figures & Tables

Assignments

Preface

TO THE STUDENT

Welcome to College! *College Success: A Concise Practical Guide* is especially designed to help you succeed in college. It contains twelve brief—but rich—chapters on topics proven to make a difference for academic success. This book is written by two professors who have over forty-six years of combined teaching experience. They have taught in small two-year colleges as well as in large public and private universities. The book can be used alone or in conjunction with a course that focuses on student success in college.

Following are ways in which you will benefit from reading this book and completing all of the assignments:

- You will learn to approach the challenge of college with a **perspective** and **attitude** that will help you be successful—not only in college but in life after graduation.

- You will learn **techniques** that will help you plan, organize, listen, learn, read, and write in college.

- You will learn how to connect with **people** on campus who will support your success.

- You will learn how to connect with **resources** on campus that will support your success.

If this book is used while you are taking a course about being successful in college, read the chapters thoughtfully before your instructor discusses them in class. You will be glad you did.

How This Book Works

College Success includes exercises and assignments that you can complete on your own or as part of a course. The classroom is a great place to discuss techniques for success and your new college experiences with your instructor and your peers. A student success class can be like a support group for new college students.

The Chapter Roadmap

Each chapter begins with the *chapter roadmap* page. The chapter roadmap includes a brief abstract or summary of the chapter, a list of the learning goals for that chapter, and a checklist to help you work through the chapter.

<u>The Learning Goals</u>   One of the most important features of this textbook, and possibly any textbook, is the list of learning goals. The learning goals are a series of statements that describe what you should be able to do after you have read and studied the chapter. These goals help you identify what aspects of the chapter are most important; therefore, if used properly, they can help you sharpen the focus of your study. In a well-designed course, the learning goals and the questions you see on exams will be linked—that is, the exam questions will be specifically designed to measure whether you have successfully achieved the learning goals. Thus, you could use the learning goals to develop a study guide that would enable you to efficiently prepare for exams. We will describe how to do this in more detail under the section titled "How to Use the Study Guide." The checklist will help you connect the learning goals to the study guide pages found at the end of each chapter. The study guide pages, if used properly, will help you identify and learn the important concepts of the chapter. Those concepts are the same ones that you can expect to see represented on exams.

<u>The Checklist</u>   The checklist presents a series of activities to complete as you study the chapter. You will benefit most if you *complete the activities in the order in which they appear* since they are deliberately ordered to give you the best learning experience. For example, the first item on the list is the "Critical Thinking Activity." This should be done before you read the chapter, because if you have completed it prior to reading, you will better understand the chapter. The same principle applies to the second item on the checklist: compiling a series of questions about the learning goals that you can reference as you read.

Critical Thinking Activity

As mentioned earlier, immediately following the chapter roadmap page is a critical thinking activity. Remember that college-level study is more about thinking and understanding than about memorization. Some memorization may still be necessary—especially when you encounter concepts that are completely new to you; however, thinking critically about and analyzing those concepts are central to a college education. Please note that the critical thinking activity is the first item on the checklist and is designed to be completed before you read the chapter.

Reading Comprehension Questions

As you read, you will periodically come across *reading comprehension questions*. There are four types of these questions in each chapter. When you encounter one of these questions, pause from your reading and try to answer it. When you finish the chapter, check your answers for all four questions against the answer key located in the back of the book. If you missed any of the questions, go back and review that section of the chapter and try to figure out why.

This activity is designed to help you improve your reading comprehension in four areas: 1) knowledge, 2) literal comprehension, 3) inferential comprehension, and 4) analysis. The answer key is not just for checking your work—you can also use it to assess your strengths and weaknesses. Simply count the number of questions you got correct in each of the four categories. This will give you a general idea of which types of reading comprehension you do best and which types you may need to work on.

Chapter Summary

The brief chapter summary can be used to quickly grasp the topics that will be covered. Reading it and the learning goals before you begin the chapter will create a framework for all the information to follow, so that you will learn and remember more.

Review Questions

Near the end of each chapter you will find a page of review questions with five true-false questions. You should mark your answer and then, in the space provided, write your rationale (reason) for selecting true or false. If you are using this book for a student success course, then your instructor will have the answer key for the chapter review questions.

Assignments

One or more practical assignments can be found at the end of each chapter (with directions provided). If you are taking a student success class, your professor may assign some of these for a grade.

How to Use the Study Guide

Each chapter has a *study guide,* designed to help you understand and discuss material from the chapter. As already mentioned, the learning goals for each chapter are listed at the beginning (on the chapter roadmap page). These goals are then repeated on the top of each study guide page. The learning goals tell you what is important in the chapter. If you want to seriously study the chapter and accomplish the learning goals, you will need to do more than simply read the learning goals. You will need to break them down into one or more questions. Below is a five-step method for using the study guide.

Step 1: Convert the Learning Goals into Questions Before You Read the Chapter

The learning goals are expressed as statements. Therefore, if you want to make sure that you thoroughly understand each goal, you will have to first convert them into questions. Do this *before* you read the chapter in the space provided for you on the study guide pages. Simply *write the questions in the left-hand column* of the study guide page. Look at Figure 1 as an example. The fictional student, Sharon Cooper, has converted Learning Goal 1 for Chapter 3 into five different questions. Each of these questions will help Sharon with a different aspect of the goal. Notice how the questions are broken down into the *smallest parts* possible. Thus, there are many questions covering just one goal. You should try to break down the goal into *as many questions* as you can. This will allow you to focus on the details of the goal, rather than just skimming the chapter's contents.

Figure 1

Example of Study Guide Page Based on a Lesson Objective

Name: *Sharon Cooper*

Study Guide | Goal 1

The student will be able to compare and contrast the focus-on-grades approach with the focus-on-learning approach.

Questions	Answers & Notes
1. What is the focus-on-grades approach?	*It is an approach to learning in which the student thinks of the grade as something separate from learning. Given this focus, he or she attempts to achieve the desired grade with the least investment possible.*
2. What is the focus-on-learning approach?	*It is an approach to learning in which the student seeks to learn as much as he or she can in the course.*
3. How are the focus-on-grades and the focus-on-learning approaches similar? (compare)	*These approaches are similar in that they are both ways in which students approach the way they learn in college. They both result in grades that are reflective of the approach taken.*
4. How are the focus-on-grades and the focus-on-learning approaches different? (contrast)	*These approaches are different in that the student is trying to learn at a different level, resulting in good grades if the student has learned but not necessarily a good grade if the student has not learned at a deeper level. The focus-on-grades approach involves focusing on what is on a test and on shortcuts that the student can use to learn quickly. The focus-on-learning approach involves focusing on learning the most a student can learn in the course and on what the most important material to learn is.*
5. What are at least two ways in which the focus-on-learning approach is more effective than the focus-on-grades approach?	*The focus-on-learning approach is more effective because it results in deeper learning than the focus-on-grades approach. Deeper learning means that the student will retain the information for the longterm, and not just for a short-term test. In addition, the focus-on-learning approach automatically results in higher exam scores because the student has learned the material he or she needs to know.*

Step 2:   Read the Chapter

Once you have clarified exactly what it is that you need to learn from the chapter, you are ready to *start reading.* As you read, *keep the learning goal questions in mind.* When you encounter information pertaining to one of your questions, you should make a note of it. Some students like to highlight the information and then write a note for themselves in the margin reminding them why it is highlighted.

Step 3:   Answer Your Study Guide Questions

Once you understand the answers to your study guide questions, you should record the answers in the right-hand column of the study guide (see Figure 1). Why? This will allow you to create a series of questions and answers that you can use as a study and regulation tool (see Step 5).

Step 4:   Read Your Study Guide Pages

With your study guide completed, you can now study simply by reading through it. It is often helpful to read the pages aloud as a study activity. Read and repeat. You should read your study guide on a regular basis throughout the semester.

Step 5:   Use the Study Guide to Test Yourself

Testing yourself as a part of your regular study routine is called **regulation**. This is a key to success, especially if you are going to have an exam based on the learning goals. Hold a blank piece of paper in your hand and use it to cover the right column (the answers). Then read the first question to yourself. Try to answer it. After you state your answer, slide the blank page down to reveal the answer and check your progress. Repeat this with the next questions, and so on, until you finish all the questions. Note any questions that you miss and spend additional time studying those before your next regulation session. Use this regulation strategy on a regular basis throughout the semester. Then, on the night before an exam, you will not need to stay up long hours cramming. By then, all you will probably need to do is read your study guide and regulate one last time. After a good night's sleep, you can wake up refreshed and go tackle the exam with confidence. If you regulate on a very regular basis, as we have described here, you will be so familiar with the most important questions of the course that by the time you take the exam, you are sure to score very high. What's more, the knowledge you have gained will be imprinted in your long-term memory, where it will serve you for years to come.

Student Resources

The following student resources are available for this textbook at www.BVTLab.com:

Practice Questions

Students can work through hundreds of practice questions online. Questions are multiple choice or true/false in format and are graded instantly for immediate feedback.

Flashcards

BVTLab includes sets of flashcards that reinforce the key terms and concepts from each chapter.

Chapter Summaries

A convenient and concise chapter summary is available as a study aid.

PowerPoint™ Slides

All instructor PowerPoints™ are available for convenient lecture preparation and for students to view online for a study recap.

From the Author

We hope this book will help you navigate through your first year of college as successfully as possible! Feel free to contact either one of us with questions or suggestions for improving this book.

David L. Strickland (dstrick@ega.edu) & Carol J. Strickland (ccornwel@gmail.com)

TO THE INSTRUCTOR

This book was written with the student in mind and has been developed as a comprehensive reading and study guide that both student and instructor can use in a course focusing on college success. The book is also written so that students can use it independently, in case they are not enrolled in a college success course. The book is learner centered and will hopefully capture the interest of students and keep them engaged throughout the semester.

This text has several features that we hope will provide additional resources and enrichment to assist the student in becoming a successful college scholar. Many of the features and resources can also be useful in the classroom as activities that will provide valuable experiences for your students. These include 1) chapter roadmaps (which comprise a brief chapter summary, chapter learning goals, and a study checklist), 2) critical thinking activities, 3) a comprehensive test bank, 4) reading comprehension questions, 5) links to websites that complement the chapter, 6) study guide pages for each chapter, and 7) learning activities and assignments designed specifically for each chapter— all in a student-friendly format.

Student-Friendly Format

This text is written in plain, everyday language that is designed to be student friendly and easily understood. Multiple features were designed to be helpful to the student as he or she progresses through the text.

Chapter Roadmaps

Chapter roadmaps are located at the beginning of each chapter. They include an overview of the entire chapter, along with learning goals and a checklist designed to help students focus on the most important concepts as they work through each chapter. The learning goals presented in the chapter roadmap are linked to the study guide (where they are repeated) and also to exam, quiz, and homework questions in the test banks.

Critical Thinking Activities

Immediately following the roadmap page is a critical thinking activity, which is intended to be completed by the student *prior* to reading the chapter. Note that this order is reinforced in the checklist. Each activity poses a problem or issue that will stimulate further critical thinking by students and will help mentally prepare them to get the most from the chapter. This feature was developed in order to engage the student in deeper thought about a topic; the critical thinking activities are also well-suited for use by the instructor in the classroom as a discussion starter.

Reading Comprehension Questions

Four questions have been included throughout each chapter so that students can self-regulate their reading comprehension. The questions have been designed to assess the following four major aspects of reading: 1) knowledge, 2) literal comprehension, 3) inferential comprehension, and 4) analysis. At the end of the book is a table that can be used by the student to record his or her answers and to check them against an answer sheet. The table then allows students to tally the number of questions they got correct in each of the four categories, giving them a general idea of their reading strengths and weaknesses.

Links to Websites

Links to relevant websites are included in each chapter. They are designed to provide additional information and to pique students' interest about the topic.

Study Guide Pages

At the end of each chapter are study guide pages based on the learning goals. Space is provided for student-generated questions and answers. Please refer to "How to Use the Study Guide" (in the section titled "To the Student") for more detailed information.

Learning Activities and Assignments

The learning activities and assignments include specific interactive exercises that encourage the student to apply concepts covered in each chapter.

Instructor Supplements

We have created the following teaching package for instructors:

BVTLab

An online lab is available for this textbook at www.BVTLab.com, as described in the BVTLab section below.

Instructor's Manual

The Instructor's Manual (IM) provides many resources for the instructor, including teaching suggestions and strategies for each chapter; instructor checklists; student handouts; a catalog of carefully evaluated, lesson-related videos for each chapter; and suggested "tweets" and blog posts for each chapter. New in the seventh edition are lesson plans for each chapter, including both a traditional lesson plan and a flipped class lesson plan for each chapter.

PowerPoint Slides

PowerPoint slides are provided for each chapter. New in the seventh edition are annotations with materials from each chapter to assist you in teaching the content.

Test Bank Files

Test questions were developed to reinforce chapter concepts and to measure progress toward the learning goals, as well as to verify that students have read the chapter. This test bank is available to the instructor for use in homework, quizzes, and/or exams, and can be found at the faculty ancillary website for this text. The test bank includes questions in multiple formats (including multiple choice, true/false, short answer, and essay) for each chapter, and they are linked to each learning goal. The test bank is available in three database formats: Respondus®, Microsoft® Excel®, and a comma-separated text file. The questions from the test bank are also available as a Microsoft® Word® or text document.

Course Management Software

BVT's course management software, Respondus, allows for the creation of tests and quizzes that can be downloaded directly into a wide variety of course management environments such as Blackboard®, WebCT™, Desire2Learn®, Canvas™, and others.

BVTLab

BVTLab is an affordable online lab for instructors and their students. It includes an online classroom with a grade book and chat room, a homework grading system, extensive test banks for quizzes and exams, and a host of student study resources. Even if a class is not taught in the lab, students can still utilize the resources described below.

Course Setup

BVTLab has an easy-to-use, intuitive interface that allows instructors to quickly set up their courses and grade books, and to replicate them from section to section and semester to semester.

Grade Book

Using an assigned passcode, students register for the grade book, which automatically grades and records all homework, quizzes, and tests.

Chat Room

Instructors can post discussion threads to a class forum and then monitor and moderate student replies.

Student Resources

All student resources for this textbook are available in BVTLab in digital form.

eBook

Students who have purchased a product that includes an eBook can download the eBook from a link in the lab. A web-based eBook is also available within the lab for easy reference during online classes, homework, and study sessions.

Instructor Resource Edition

Hopefully you are reading this from the preface of *College Success: Instructor Resource Edition* (IRE)! The IRE includes, for each chapter, a summary of the objectives, tips and advice from the authors, information on how to create a culture of learning and how that relates to the chapter's contents, a brief overview of the contents, and an Abridged Lesson Plan. (In the Instructor's Manual, we also have full-length lesson plans for both a traditional classroom format and a flipped class format for those instructors seeking more detailed guidance.)

From the Author

We hope this textbook will be valuable to you as you teach students the tools and strategies necessary to succeed in college and beyond. Please let us know if you have suggestions for improvement or other comments. We encourage you to contact BVT if you wish to obtain a copy of *College Success: Instructor Resource Edition* (IRE). Also, if you wish to adapt this book specifically to your own institution's needs, perhaps by adding or modifying portions, please contact BVT Publishing at 800-646-7782.

David L. Strickland (dstrick@ega.edu) & Carol J. Strickland (ccornwel@gmail.com)

TO THE ADMINISTRATOR

Some background information about how this textbook was developed may be of interest to administrators. The personalized, versatile, and cost-effective features of the book are of particular interest.

Our Experience

The institution where David teaches has a one-credit-hour orientation course that, in the past, was required for students who had tested into learning support classes (such as learning support math or learning support English). Typically, only underprepared students enrolled in the course (as the orientation course was not otherwise required).

However, administrators and faculty were seeking practical, effective, and cost-efficient ways to improve learning and to increase retention, completion, and graduation rates. It was clear that a majority of new students entering college had weak or nonexistent organizational skills and poor study strategies. The approach and strategies most commonly employed by students (such as cramming for exams as the primary or sole method of study) appeared to be ineffective and sometimes counterproductive. This was true for students in general—not just for those who had lower entrance exam scores.

We decided to create an orientation course similar to a first-year experience course that would be required for all new students. The instructor would serve as a mentor, and the students in the class would serve as a support group for one another during their first semester. Topics addressed by the course would include basic study skills as well as an orientation to campus policies and procedures. Initially, the course was taught by volunteer faculty as a part of their service to the college. For the first year, we adopted a textbook that was similar in design to the textbooks used in other courses and typical of those used for student success at that time.

Evaluation of the program after the first year revealed a few problems with the textbook. The cost of the book to students was prohibitively high (over $100), and we found that instructors used very little of the book in their classes (usually only about one chapter). So we began looking for a solution. The second year we tried to run the program without a book, but we found it ineffective and difficult to standardize around central objectives. Finally, I suggested that we produce our own textbook that would address a simple list of core competencies and that would be personalized to our institution and the specific needs of our students. I volunteered to write most of it, and we discovered that BVT could help us publish it for a lower cost than what we would pay to produce it in-house. We personalized the text to our institution, and we decided that it could serve as an orientation manual, a textbook for study skills, and a day planner that the student could use to organize his or her studies—not only for the first year of college but also every year until graduation. Important college events and deadlines were already printed on the calendar within the book.

One way in which we made the first edition of the college success book very cost effective was to include, within the book, approximately forty pages of handouts that were formerly distributed during new-student orientation. In this way we were able to capture the cost of paper, printing, copying, collating, and so on since those orientation handouts were included in our new textbook at no additional cost. The textbooks were distributed to students during orientation, and the portion of the text containing the information from the previous handouts was used for instruction during orientation. The students were told that the remaining pages of the same book would serve as the textbook for the required student success course during their first semester.

We completed a study examining the impact of the student success program on retention rates at East Georgia State College. Data from the institution's enrollment database were used to examine retention over a fifteen-year period (from 2000 to 2015). The study chronicled the retention rates for students who experienced the student success course since its inception. It also chronicled the retention rates for an equal number of years before the student success course became a requirement. Retention statistics were compared between the years when the student success program was in force and those prior to the inception of the program. While extraneous variables cannot all be accounted for—so causality cannot be inferred—it remains a fact that retention rates have increased for the years that the student success program has been in force. Students of all levels of college readiness who have taken the student success course have experienced higher retention rates than students in the same readiness category that did not have the course.

Customization for Your Campus

College Success: A Concise Practical Guide can be easily customized for your campus and even for different courses and disciplines on your campus. You can include an appendix with all of your printed orientation materials. These can be perforated pages in the bound book or color-coded pages in the loose-leaf format.

Other customizations that you might consider are:

- Rearranging the chapter order
- Deleting unwanted chapters
- Adding chapters with your own content
- Modifying any of the text or illustrations throughout the book
- Creating additional assignments or in-class exercises
- Creating additional lab content or student resources
- Making up your own cover with your university logo
- Including a welcome letter from your president

Please contact BVT Publishing at 800-646-7782 for further information on customization.

ACKNOWLEDGMENTS

We wish to acknowledge the input and contributions of many people who had a role or made a contribution to the preparation of this book. We extend our thanks to our colleagues at East Georgia State College, who have offered encouragement, inspiration, and many great ideas that we have attempted to include in the book. Special thanks to those instructors who have taught Student Success and have provided us with valuable feedback. Certain colleagues have been especially influential: David Altamirano, Ed Bayens, Larry Braddy, Alan Brasher, Carol Bray, John Bressler, Sally Cook, Val Czerny, Mark Dallas, Jeff Edgens, Raymond Hayes, Ken Homer, Pat Homer, Jeff Howell, Courtney Joiner, Bob March, Walter Mason, Dee McKinney, Caroline McMillan, Sandra Sharman, Tommy Upchurch, Raleigh Way, and Eric Wruck. A warm thank you goes out to Lee Cheek for his unwavering support of the student success effort at East Georgia State College.

We would like to give many thanks to our BVT family, without whose help and guidance this book would not have been possible. A special thanks to Richard Schofield (Publisher and Director of Development) for his support and keen vision and for providing a way for our projects to go forward. For their persistence and commitment to this project, we thank Shannon Conley (Product Development Manager), Esther Scannell (Senior Designer), Tim Gerlach (Designer), Tara Joffe (Proofreader), Logan McDonald (Permissions Specialist), and Janai Bryand (Production and Fulfillment Manager). Thanks especially to Chad Peterson (Associate Content Developer) for his hard work and diligence in marketing and "getting the word out"! An especially warm thanks goes out to Annie Schofield (Managing Editor), who has been our consistent and strong support in extensive editing with her patient, helpful, and ever-positive manner! Each of you has helped make our vision become a reality! Many thanks and congratulations to all of you!

ABOUT THE AUTHORS

David L. Strickland, MA, is the director of the Student Success Program and a professor of sociology at East Georgia State College. He is coauthor of an introductory sociology textbook, *My Sociology,* now in its second edition. He is the author of the freshman orientation course textbook at East Georgia State College, *College Success: A Concise Practical Guide* (seventh edition). In addition to writing, he has taught college courses full time for more than twenty years. During that time he also served for three years as the director of institutional research for the college. Prior to teaching sociology, he conducted grant-funded health-care research at the Center for Rural Health and Research at Georgia Southern University and published numerous articles and chapters on the sociology of health care. He has been a pioneer in the area of online instruction and served as a coauthor for the eCore version of *Introduction to Sociology,* which was used by the thirty-four institutions of the University of Georgia. Strickland credits some of his insights regarding orientation to college to the fact that he, like a large number of the students that he teaches, was a first-generation college graduate.

Carol J. Strickland, PhD, RN, is retired from teaching but served for seven years as associate professor of nursing and director of nursing research at Georgia Southern University School of Nursing in Statesboro, Georgia. She worked in nursing at the University of Rochester School of Nursing in Rochester, New York, for twenty-four years, where she received her PhD in nursing. Her interests and clinical experiences are in psychiatric mental health nursing, combining her knowledge of nursing with that of the neuropsychological and neuroimmunological functioning of the human brain. She has published numerous articles in the area of psychiatric mental health nursing practice, psychoneuroimmunology, and sociology. She was also recently appointed to the editorial review board of the *Journal of the First-Year Experience and Students in Transition.* Strickland states that her knowledge of first-year experiences comes both from having served as an instructor/mentor in a first-year experience course at the University of Rochester and from immersion in the literature. In addition, she was a first-generation college graduate. She has gained insights into the value of having a book designed to guide the mentorship process that is so essential to helping students transition from high school to college: "In this way, we pass on core competencies and the knowledge to facilitate educated, visionary, and dedicated scholars who will be the leaders, teachers, and mentors of tomorrow."

WHAT STUDENTS HAVE SAID ABOUT COLLEGE SUCCESS

To be honest, in the beginning of this course, I deemed it unnecessary for me to take this course. I thought the lessons in this course were things that I would already know, but I have honestly learned so much. My favorite and most informative lesson is Designing Your Long-Term Graduation Plan. I really got to see just how long it will take me to graduate, and it gave me the ability to view what classes I should take together and the ones I shouldn't due to the difficulty of each. I also liked the Focus-on-Learning Assignment because it gave me a sense of the difference between focusing on grades and learning. To be honest, I didn't know there was much of a difference between the two. I discovered that many students simply focus on grades because grades equal diplomas and students rarely become interested in actually learning the material. I also learned that memorizing material doesn't always guarantee actually grasping the material at hand. I have applied many of the online assignments to my daily use.

The Student Success course helped me in many ways. In high school I was the student who skimmed through text-books for answers, procrastinated down to the last second to complete projects, and did very little outside research once class was over. This semester (Fall 2013) actually is not my first college semester, but it is my first successful college semester. My first attempt at college was pathetic, to say the least. I was constantly behind, confused, and frustrated. I surely could have used a class like this back then, and now that I have taken Student Success, I feel far more confident and prepared to earn my degree.

[College Success] includes many easy-to-use templates and organizers to help students form and follow study plans. I have even mapped out every class I will take up until I earn my degree from East Georgia College. If you had told me I would be this organized and on-beat a year ago, I wouldn't have believed you, but here I am. I now understand that by trying to "just get by," I was being academically dishonest and doing a great disservice to myself.

Now I'm taking my time when I'm reading for class. I look up words I don't know. I plan out my projects the day I get them and stick to my plan. I do extra research on things we discuss in class. I am excited about earning my degree, and I am doing all that I can to utilize my resources and get the highest education I can. I am no longer trying to "make the grade"; I am trying to learn. That is what this class did for me, and I am very thankful for the change.

Student Success has helped me in one HUGE way. Over the last few chapters of the textbook, I have realized how I have cheated myself out of the joy of one of my classes. I owe that professor an apology. I have made B's in his class. I will not fail the course. I have not been bored. The honest truth is that I have been lazy and have procrastinated. I have a busy family life but I KNOW I could have done more! I could have made a very high A and left the course with such a better understanding than what I have.

This book made so many good points that new college students need to recognize immediately if they want to be successful in college, attain a degree, or further their education. The first thing would be to understand that it was a choice to come to college, but no one will hold your hand, as they did in High School, to guide you to a degree. Another big take-away is, once the decision has been made to attend college, you have to make college and your studies a priority—not just try and fit it into or around your already busy schedule.

Chapter Roadmap

1

Introduction

In this chapter you will learn about some of the ways in which college is different from high school, and you will gain a better understanding of what will be expected of you. This chapter also describes how this book is designed to help you do your best in college and ultimately reach your goal of earning a college education and a degree.

This chapter roadmap page presents the formal learning goals for this chapter and a checklist that you should follow as you read and study the chapter.

Student Learning Goals

After completing this chapter you should be able to do the following:

1. Describe the ways in which high school and college are different.

2. Anticipate many of the challenges associated with attending college.

3. Define success in college in terms of both certification and qualification.

Chapter Checklist

You will benefit most if you complete the activities in the order that they are listed.

❑ **Target Date/Deadline:** _____
Complete Critical Thinking Activity 1.1.

❑ **Target Date/Deadline:** _____
Convert the student learning goals to questions that you can answer as you read the chapter. Write your questions on the study guide pages near the end of this chapter.

❑ **Target Date/Deadline:** _____
Read the chapter.

❑ **Target Date/Deadline:** _____
Try to answer the reading comprehension questions as you come to them in the chapter. Check each answer by comparing it to the list of correct answers in the back of the book. If any answer was not correct, then review the passages preceding the question to see why you missed the question.

❑ **Target Date/Deadline:** _____
Answer the student learning goal questions you created. These answered questions will be your study guide.

❑ **Target Date/Deadline:** _____
Write down any questions, insights, or comments that you have as you read so that you can bring them up in class.

❑ **Target Date/Deadline:** _____
Complete Review Questions 1.1.

❑ **Target Date/Deadline:** _____
Complete Assignment 1.1 (Record of Grades).

❑ **Target Date/Deadline:** _____
Review what you have learned from this chapter.

Critical Thinking Activity 1.1

Before you read this chapter—and without looking anything up on the Internet or elsewhere—use the space provided on this page to write your own definition of success in college.

What is success in college?

_____

_____

_____

_____

_____

_____

_____

_____

_____

_____

_____

_____

_____

_____

_____

_____

_____

_____

_____

_____

_____

_____

_____

_____

_____

_____

_____

_____

Adjusting to College:

We're Not in High School Anymore!

1

"Some people dream of success while others wake up and work hard at it."
— Winston Churchill[1]

For many first-time college students, college is like a magical land filled with new wonders and experiences. Perhaps you, like most students, are experiencing greater autonomy and independence than you ever have before. Surely some adjustment will be necessary to keep your balance. Most students realize that this is true of their social lives—but they may not immediately realize how much college differs from high school academically.

This book will help you successfully transition from high school to college. It covers principles, attitudes, and behaviors that will help you maximize your college experience, reach learning outcomes, stay in your academic program, and graduate. Chapter 1 begins by describing some of the ways in which college is different from high school academically.

1.1 High School Is Not College

High school and college are different in many ways. This is not to say that high school is inferior but rather to help students identify and address the challenges unique to college. There is a misconception that college is like "Grade 13"; but students who believe that college is like high school do not perform as well as students who have more accurate expectations. High school may have prepared you academically for college, but the norms (the way things are done) in college are often very different from what you have experienced in high school. What, specifically, are the differences? Table 1.1 presents some of the most important ones.

Montgomery College's First Year Experience Program (http://cms.montgomerycollege.edu/edu/) offers the following five guiding principles based on the differences between high school and college:[2]

1. As a high school student, you were probably told what to do and were corrected if you did not do it, but in college "you are expected to take responsibility for what you do and don't do, as well as for the consequences of your decisions."[2]

2. In high school you were probably told what you needed to learn from the reading assignment in class, but in college it is "up to you to read and understand the assigned material [because the] lectures and assignments proceed from the assumption that you've already done so."[2]

3. High school was primarily about learning facts and skills, but "college is a learning environment in which you take responsibility for thinking through and applying what you have learned."[2]

4. High school focused on "the ability to reproduce what you were taught in the form in which it was presented to you, or to solve the kinds of problems you were shown how to solve."[2] In college, however, "mastery is often seen as the ability to apply what you've learned to new situations or to solve new kinds of problems."[2]

5. In high school you may have been rewarded for a "good-faith effort," but in college "results count … good-faith effort will not substitute for results in the grading process."[2]

You have probably begun to formulate a pretty good picture of how the college experience will be different from the high school experience after reading Table 1.1. Consider the practical implications of some of those differences. What are the implications of increased freedom and responsibility? What changes will you have to make to the way you study and prepare for exams or other assessments? How will your reading load be different? What will professors expect of you?

Table 1.1

High School Versus College*		
Characteristic	**High School Model**	**College Model**
Venue for Learning	Most learning occurs in class. Students may study outside class as little as one to two hours a week, and this may be mostly last-minute test preparation.	Most learning occurs outside of class. On average, students will need to study about two hours outside of class for each hour spent in class.
Schedule	The student attends classes back-to-back for about six hours each day (thirty to thirty-five hours per week).	The student must create his or her own schedule. Most classes do not meet every day. There may be many unscheduled hours between classes. Class times vary throughout the day and evening. The student spends only twelve to seventeen hours each week in class.
Role of the Instructor	Teachers are directive and nurturing.	Professors expect the student to be independent and to take personal responsibility for learning.

Characteristic	High School Model	College Model
Office Hours	Teachers do not keep office hours. Instead, they answer questions and offer help to students in class.	Professors schedule regular office hours in order to meet with students individually. Scheduled office hours are usually posted in the syllabus, on the professor's website, and on the office door. (The syllabus is a document that contains lots of important information about the expectations of the course.) You are not interrupting or bothering professors when you meet with them during their office hours. That time has been set aside especially for you. You could just drop by the office; however, if you have a serious question, you should make an appointment so that the time slot will be reserved for you.
Reading Requirements	The student seldom needs to read anything more than once, and sometimes listening in class is enough.	The amount of reading assigned by professors may be large. The student must review class notes and text material regularly. Preparation for exams typically requires multiple reviews of all course materials.
Presentation of Material	Teachers present the material at a slower pace, and the presentation is designed to support the textbook.	Professors present the material at a faster pace, and their presentation is designed to supplement the text. Professors often expect you to study the book on your own—and then they will add to or explain it.
Frequency of Testing	There is frequent testing. Therefore, the student is required to master only a small amount of the total course material for any single exam.	Testing is less frequent (often limited to a midterm and final). Therefore, the student must be prepared to demonstrate mastery of a much larger amount of material for a single exam.
Extra Credit	High school grades may be derived not only from exams but also from other assignments. Consistently good homework grades or extra credit assignments might be used to compensate for poor performance on exams and raise your course grade.	College grades are usually derived from exams and major papers. Typically, there is limited opportunity (or none) to earn additional points toward the semester grade. It is important that you determine how each of your courses will be graded. This information is provided in the syllabus.

* Information paraphrased from multiple sources

Sources: College Board (2009). *College survival tips: Making the transition.* Retrieved May 17, 2009, from https://bigfuture.college-board.org/find-colleges/campus-life; D. Thompson (2011). What's the best investment: Stocks, bonds, homes … or college? *The Atlantic.* Retrieved April 30, 2012, from http://www.theatlantic.com/business/archive/2011/06/whats-the-best-investment-stocks-bonds-homes-or-college/241056/; R. Hansen. Retrieved September 22, 2015, from http://www.mycollegesuccessstory.com/academic-success-tools/high-school-vs-college.html.

Reading Comprehension Question 1.1 (Knowledge)

Which of the following are ways in which college is different from high school?

a. In high school, teachers are directive and nurturing.

b. In college, the amount of reading assigned by professors can be very large.

c. In college, professors expect you to study the text on your own.

d. All of the above

1.2 College Involves Freedom and Responsibility

It is great to be an adult in college with the independence and freedom to make your own decisions about how you spend your time. The downside is that you are now the only person responsible for those decisions.

When you were younger, your parents may have taken responsibility for making sure you woke up and made it to school on time. Some of your teachers may have distributed study guides and prescribed exactly what you should do for homework. In order to be successful, you simply did as you were told.

In contrast, now that you are an adult in college you will have to take charge of managing your time and planning your homework. You have to set your alarm, take care of all of your personal needs, get to class on time, and be ready to learn. No one will make you do it, and no one will check to see what you do or don't do. If you don't get it right—if you don't make learning a personal priority—then you are likely to earn some failing grades.

Rarely do you hear college students use the term *homework*. Instead you might hear them use the term *study*, as in "I have to study this weekend for a history test on Tuesday." This is probably because college professors almost never assign homework. Generally speaking homework is a set of practice exercises assigned by a teacher; usually, it contributes to students' grades for the class. Unlike high school teachers, college professors leave it to students to decide for themselves how to go about learning the required information. So if college professors don't assign homework, does that mean you don't have to do work at home? No. It means that you will have to create your own reading, learning, and practice exercises, and assign them to yourself. That is the definition of studying.

Professors may not assign homework, but they definitely expect you to invest a lot of time and effort in studying. Students who practice good, regular study habits find it much easier to learn and earn high marks in college. Developing an effective study plan is one of the things that you will explore in this book.

In College, Studying Happens Outside of Class

Another important thing that you need to know about college is that most studying—and therefore most learning—will happen outside of class. Typically, the bulk of learning in school prior to college occurs in the classroom. In college, you will have to do a lot of reading and studying before you even go to class in order to be successful at learning. The figures vary from course to course, but as a general rule, about two-thirds of the learning in college takes place outside of class.

Figure 1.1 illustrates the phenomenon that the higher you go in college, the more studying and learning will take place outside of class.

Figure 1.1

Venues for Studying and Learning at Various Academic Levels

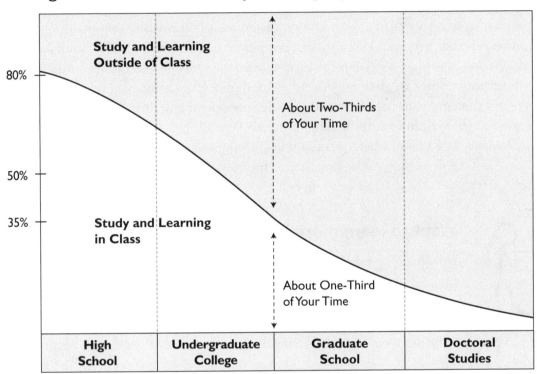

Higher levels of education require a larger percentage of outside study.

It is not the case that every college course requires two hours of study outside of class for every hour of class time. Each course that you take in college will be somewhat different. Some will require you to spend a lot time studying outside of class, and others not so much. Taken together, however, the average is about two hours outside of class for every hour spent in class. In order to be successful, you will need to determine how much time you will need to spend studying for each of your classes, and plan that study time as a part of your daily routine. One thing that can help you plan your time, and that every college course has in common, is a document called the *syllabus*.

The Syllabus Is Your Best Friend

In college, the syllabus will be your best friend. The syllabus is the main way in which professors assist you in planning your study regimen. The syllabus is a document that is distributed, or otherwise made available (sometimes online), on or before the first day of classes. It contains lots of important and useful information about the expectations of the course and often includes descriptions and deadlines for assignments and the dates of exams. You need to know this information to be successful in the course. Make reading the syllabus a top priority, and ask your professor to clarify any part of the syllabus that you do not understand.

Apart from providing the syllabus, professors typically do not give homework or tell you how to study for their classes. You now have to decide for yourself when, how long, and what to study. You have to make up your own homework. This skill takes practice and time to learn. This book will help you get it right.

However, if classes have already begun, you should not wait to read all of your syllabi—you should read them carefully as soon as you have access to them. One of the things you should do right away is find out how you will be graded in each course, so that you can start keeping a record of your progress. The successful student never has to ask the professor, "How many days have I been absent?" or "What is my grade in this class so far?" A successful student will keep a personal record of absences and grades on exams or other assignments.

The assignment that accompanies this chapter (Assignment 1.1) will help you get started with the process of keeping a record of your grades. Assignment 1.1 provides you with a single page on which to record your progress. You will need a separate page for each course, so make copies as needed. As soon as you get a syllabus for each course, immediately use the Assignment 1.1 form to list the exams or other assignments that will be required. Later, when you receive grades on the exams or assignments, you can record them in the space provided. Any time you are absent from a class session, you should record the date of the absence in the space provided on the form. In this way you will always know where you stand in the course; and if some of your early grades are poor, you can take steps early in the semester to improve. Constant monitoring of your progress and early intervention are keys to success in college.

Want to learn more? Try this resource.

How is college different from high school?
http://bvtlab.com/S77R8

Montgomery College's First Year Experience Program website offers the following advice on transitioning to college:[2]

- Take control of your own education: Think of yourself as a scholar.

- Get to know your professors; they are your single greatest resource.

- Be assertive. Create your own support systems, and seek help when you realize you may need it.

- Take advantage of academic and student support services on campus.

- Take control of your time. Plan ahead to satisfy academic obligations first, and then make room for everything else.

- Stretch yourself: Enroll in at least one course that really challenges you.

- Make thoughtful decisions: Don't take a course just to satisfy a requirement, and don't drop any course too quickly.

- Think beyond the moment: Set goals for each semester [or quarter], the year, and your college career.

Making a smooth transition into college is the first step on the road to success in college.

Reading Comprehension Question 1.2 (Literal Comprehension)

Which of the following is one of the major differences between college and high school?

a. In college, two-thirds of learning takes place outside of class.

b. In college, professors are nurturing and directive.

c. In college, professors have all the answers.

d. In high school, teachers are not as highly directive as college professors.

1.3 The Road to Success

What Is Student Success?

This student success book is designed to orient the new college student to the unique challenges associated with college life. The overarching goals of the book are to enable the student to avoid the pitfalls that often result in failure and to seize the opportunities that lead to success. This book will help you to problem solve as you go through your first year of college.

What is success? You may find a plethora of statements defining success in books and on the Internet. For example, consider these somewhat humorous success statements from the online *Quote Garden* (http://bvtlab.com/78P76):

> *"I couldn't wait for success ... so I went ahead without it."* Jonathan Winters

> *"Success is simply a matter of luck. Ask any failure."* Earl Wilson

> *"It's not that I'm so smart; it's just that I stay with problems longer."* Albert Einstein

> *"Don't be afraid to give your best to what seemingly are small jobs. Every time you conquer one, it makes you that much stronger. If you do the little jobs well, the big ones will tend to take care of themselves."* Dale Carnegie

Some of these statements about success are funny and even insightful, but they only address the topic of success in a general sense. How do you define success specifically with regard to your experience in college? In Critical Thinking Activity 1.1, which appeared at the beginning of this chapter, you were asked to think about and write a definition of success in college. So—what is success in college? Success in college ultimately means graduating (i.e., earning a degree); it also includes all of the quality milestones along the way, such as learning as much as you can and maintaining a high grade point average (GPA). Success in college means not only becoming better certified but also better qualified.

So—What Is Success in College?

There is no question that one of the main purposes of attending college is to acquire a credential. The college diploma is meant to signify that students have met certain academic and other requirements that have prepared them for any number of careers, generally, as well as careers associated with their discipline, specifically. The credential is supposed to represent a certain level of learning and mastery. Usually, the way that mastery is determined is through grades. If students make high marks or grades, it is assumed that they have learned what they need to know to master the discipline. However, it is important to distinguish between grades and learning, as they are not always the same.

In and of itself, a grade does not represent learning. For example, when students cram for an exam the night before a test and are able to score high enough on the test to pass the course—but literally forget 80 to 90 percent of what they studied within a short time thereafter—then those students will have acquired a passing grade but might not have really learned what they need to know. If too many of the grades they receive were acquired in this manner, then their diplomas are a misrepresentation of their actual learning. If passing without truly learning becomes ubiquitous at a particular college or university, then the status of a degree from that institution loses much of its value in the job market. In an extreme case, the diploma loses its meaning and is nothing but a piece of paper. Therefore, it's very important that as you are progressing through your academic program, you strive to make high grades through learning. If you truly learn the material, you will automatically make higher grades and you will be prepared for the career of your choice. While you must take care to always make good grades, never lose your focus on learning. The real reason you are in college is to learn and change and grow—and to become a person worthy of your credentials.

Success Means Becoming Qualified

If you focus on learning rather than grades, you will become qualified. If you focus on grades to the exclusion of learning, you may become certified, but you won't be qualified. You will be a fraud. No student enters college planning to be a fraud. Sadly, the structure of our educational system—with its focus on grades and credentials—pushes students in that direction. The wise student will not succumb to the path of least resistance; he or she will not focus on grades alone to the exclusion of learning. Instead, the wise student will design study plans that give him or her time to actually learn the material, to grow and to change, and, in the process, to attain high marks and a credential. In this way, the wise student will become both certified and highly qualified. The personal benefits of becoming both certified and qualified remain with you for years to come because you have been changed.

So the primary purpose of taking a course is not to simply pass the exam or get the credit—instead, the primary purpose is to learn something important. Every course that you take should change you in some way. Even though your beliefs, values, and personal goals may not change, your knowledge of the world, your ability to think critically, your ability to reason, and your ability to apply the sum of your knowledge to new challenges—all should be improved. Therefore, it is safe to say that a liberal arts education should change you. It should make you a better person. That is success.

What Is Failure in College?

Failure in college can manifest as flunking out, dropping out, or losing out. Flunking out happens when students accumulate too many failing grades and find it nearly impossible to raise their GPA to the level required for graduation. Dropping out occurs for many reasons. Sometimes students drop out due to factors beyond their control, but too many students drop out for academic reasons.

Losing out is what happens when a student graduates without having been challenged, without having changed for the better, and without being prepared for what lies ahead. This book aims to help you avoid all of these types of failure.

1.4 Attitudes and Resources for Success

This book is designed to help students connect to various resources and to develop attitudes and habits that will support their success. Table 1.2 illustrates these goals by listing some of the resources and attitudes that the book will address. As illustrated in the table, attitudes involve both perspectives (How do you view the task at hand?) and practices (How do you approach the task at hand?). Resources include knowledge (What things do I need to know to be successful?), tools (What tools will help me achieve success?), and helpers (Who is here to help me be successful?). Each of these items is very important.

Table 1.2

Examples of Attitudes and Resources for Success

Attitudes		Resources		
Perspectives	**Practices**	**Knowledge**	**Tools**	**Helpers**
Focus on learning	Maintain a study calendar	College policies and procedures	Library resources	Academic advisors
Embrace responsibility	Develop a study plan for each class	Expectations in college	The college website	Tutors
View academics as a top priority	Develop and maintain a long-term graduation plan	How to develop and follow a study plan	College catalog	Faculty
Hold realistic expectations for college	Attend cultural events that enhance learning	How to design a long-term academic plan	Student organizations	College counselors
Commit time and effort to college success	Participate in student organizations	How to prepare for early registration	Fitness facilities	College staff in various departments
Eliminate hindrances to success	Develop a fitness plan	How to manage your time	Planning calendar	Campus security
	Develop positive relationships with helpers	How to listen and take notes	Written study plan	
	Assess yourself		This textbook	
	Get help early			

Reading Comprehension Question 1.3 (Inferential Comprehension)

What is the main reason for this college success guide?

a. To enable the student to avoid the pitfalls that often result in failure and to seize the opportunities that lead to success
b. To keep track of new students in the system
c. To provide students with an easy book for their first semester
d. None of the above

Reading Comprehension Question 1.4 (Analysis)

Why is it important for the student to know what happens in his or her first year of college?

a. The student can be prepared for classes.
b. The student can achieve the intended benefit from college.
c. The student will be clear about what is required in college.
d. All of the above

1.5 Summary

This chapter discussed the transition to college and contrasted the expectations and experiences of students in college compared to high school. You were challenged to create your own definition of success in college and were informed that college success involves the acquisition of both a credential (earning the degree) and a quality education (becoming a changed person through learning). There was also a brief discussion about attitudes and resources that will help you to be successful. We will explore specific attitudes and strategies in more detail in other chapters.

Study Guide | Goal 1

The student will be able to describe the ways in which high school and college are different.

Questions	Answers & Notes

Name: _____

Study Guide | Goal 2

The student will be able to anticipate many of the challenges associated with attending college.

Questions	Answers & Notes

Study Guide | Goal 3

The student will be able to define success in college in terms of both certification and qualification.

Questions	Answers & Notes

Study Guide | Preparing for Class

Use this page to record questions or insights to discuss in class.

Name: _____

Review Questions 1.1

Instructions

Following are five true-false statements taken from the information in this chapter. First, try to answer them without looking back at the chapter. Then review the chapter to see how well you did.

Question & Answer	Rationale
Circle true or false for each of the following statements.	Write an explanation stating why each statement is true or false.
1. Tests are given more frequently in college than in high school. True or False	Your Rationale:
2. College is very similar to high school except that you live away from home and you have to study a little more. True or False	Your Rationale:
3. If you ask your professor to help you with time management, he or she will call you every morning to wake you up for class. True or False	Your Rationale:
4. Class meetings are very important in college because most learning occurs in class. True or False	Your Rationale:
5. The road to success involves your attitude toward learning, as well as your use of campus resources. True or False	Your Rationale:

Name: _____

Assignment 1.1

Maintain a Record of Your Progress

Goal

The purpose of this activity is to prepare the student to constantly monitor his or her grades for each course so that he or she will be able to remedy low or failing grades early in the semester.

Objective

The student will keep a record of his or her grades for each course and will use the record to evaluate his or her progress on a regular basis.

Instructions

The successful student never has to ask the professor, "How many days have I been absent?" or "What is my grade in this class so far?" because a successful student will keep his or her own record of absences and grades on exams or other assignments. You can use the **Record of Grades and Attendance** form provided on the next page of this textbook. *You will need a separate copy of the form for each of your courses, so make photocopies of the form before you write on it.*

Follow These Steps

Step 1: Consult the syllabus for each of your courses to determine how the semester grade will be calculated for that particular course. Use the form called **Record of Grades and Attendance** provided on the next page to list of all of the factors that contribute to the semester grade (e.g., exam scores, attendance, grades on essays, grades for discussions, and so on).

Step 2: Keep a record of the grades earned or points earned for each of these factors. Update it every time you receive a new grade or assignment feedback. If your grade is low or the feedback on other assignments suggests that you could do better, then think about ways that you can improve before the next graded assignment is due.

You will need to complete a separate record of grades for each of your courses. Recording your grades in one place will make it easier for you to monitor your progress throughout the semester.

Notes

Name: _____   Course: _____

Record of Grades and Attendance

Grades

What is the semester grade formula for this course?

Exam or assignment	Date Submitted	Grade/Score
1.		
2.		
3.		
4.		
5.		
6.		
7.		
8.		
9.		
10.		
11.		
12.		
13.		
14.		
15.		
Total:		

Attendance Record

What is the attendance policy for this course?

You should attend every class. However, if you are ever absent from this class, record the date of the absence here so that you can keep track of absences and calculate how they affect your grade.	1.
	2.
	3.
	4.
	5.

Chapter Roadmap

Introduction

In this chapter you will learn about the on-campus resources that can help make students successful. These resources include people, places, and things (technologies).

This chapter roadmap page presents the formal learning goals for this chapter and a checklist that you should follow as you read and study the chapter.

Student Learning Goals

After completing this chapter you should be able to do the following:

1. Understand and effectively use various technologies, including the college website, the college library website, and the college's course management system.

2. Practice an etiquette that will promote effective communication with professors and others.

3. List and describe what resources are available from the college library, counseling centers, and various offices on campus.

4. Identify, appreciate, cooperate, and coordinate with the various people on campus who can contribute in some way to your success.

Chapter Checklist

You will benefit most if you complete the activities in the order that they are listed.

❑ **Target Date/Deadline:** _____
Complete Critical Thinking Activity 2.1.

❑ **Target Date/Deadline:** _____
Convert the student learning goals to questions that you can answer as you read the chapter. Write your questions on the study guide pages near the end of this chapter.

❑ **Target Date/Deadline:** _____
Read the chapter.

❑ **Target Date/Deadline:** _____
Try to answer the reading comprehension questions as you come to them in the chapter. Check each answer by comparing it to the list of correct answers in the back of the book. If any answer was not correct, then review the passages preceding the question to see why you missed the question.

❑ **Target Date/Deadline:** _____
Answer the student learning goal questions you created. These answered questions will be your study guide.

❑ **Target Date/Deadline:** _____
Write down any questions, insights, or comments that you have as you read so that you can bring them up in class.

❑ **Target Date/Deadline:** _____
Complete Review Questions 2.1.

❑ **Target Date/Deadline:** _____
Complete Assignment 2.1 (Identifying Resources).

❑ **Target Date/Deadline:** _____
Review what you have learned from this chapter.

Critical Thinking Activity 2.1

In this chapter you will learn some simple, but important, things that will help you be successful. Consider the following questions. Can you answer all of them without looking up the answers? These are practical things that you need to know as a college student; you are likely to experience situations in which ignorance of these simple things could keep you from being successful.

1. What are four things that you should include in every email message that you send to your professor?

2. Describe what a special collection is in a college library. Why might it be useful to you?

3. What is a course management system, and how does it work?

4. How does your college website work?

Connecting to Resources:

People, Places, and Things

2

""The Internet is becoming the town square for the global village of tomorrow."
— Bill Gates[1]

"A library is not a luxury but one of the necessities of life."
— Henry Ward Beecher[2]

"A university is just a group of buildings gathered around a library."
— Shelby Foote[3]

One of the most important things that new students can do to make success in college a reality is to discover and take advantage of the many campus resources available to them. In this chapter we will highlight a few of those resources, which include people, places, and technologies.

2.1 People

Following are brief descriptions of some of the people on campus that, in some way, contribute to your success as a student. You are literally surrounded by these helpers every day. You will interact often with some of these people, whereas others seem to work behind the scenes. Reading about them in this chapter will encourage you to do the following:

1. Realize that they are there, working every day, ultimately for your benefit.

2. Cooperate with them in their efforts.

3. Take advantage of the service that they offer to you.

4. Show appreciation for what they do.

Table 2.1

Successful Students Connect to Campus Resources		
People	**Places**	**Things (Technologies)**
Advisors	Learning center	College website
Coaches	Computer labs	College email
Counselors	Counseling center	College catalog
Faculty	Financial aid office	Course management system
Grounds and building staff	Fitness center	Faculty webpages
Librarians	Library	College library site
Office staff	Registrar's office	Your personal college portal
Other students	Student organizations	
Security	Auditorium	
Academic tutors		

Advisors

An academic advisor is someone assigned to help you develop a class schedule, register for classes, develop your short- and long-range plans and explain the degree program requirements to you, assist you with dropping or adding classes, and answer specific questions that you may have about your program of study. Check with your academic department or division to find out the name of your advisor. Some colleges have an advisement center with full-time employees devoted entirely to advisement. You would be wise to seek their advice. Sometimes students are inclined to take the advice of other students on these matters. Be careful because some rules or policies change from year to year. Your student friends might not be aware of changes to programs, prerequisites, and so on; your advisor, however, will know the most accurate information.

Coaches

Coaches head athletic teams and serve student athletes in many ways. If you take the time to talk to any one of them, you will quickly discover that they are not concerned merely with the success of the team (winning games) but that they also strive to help the students under their leadership to develop and to succeed academically.

Counselors

The vast majority of colleges provide a counseling office or counseling center of some type. Counselors can help with a variety of personal issues, disability issues, and issues with the transition to college. Keep in mind that counseling is not just for those with special problems; rather, counseling is beneficial to all students. The services that most counseling centers offer are described in detail later in this chapter.

Faculty (Office Hours)

Of course, in class you interact with instructors several times a week—but don't forget about office hours. As has already been mentioned, each faculty member has designated certain hours each week during which he or she plans to be in the office so that students can visit and receive assistance. If you need help with a course, you should not hesitate to make an appointment to visit your instructor. It is easy to find out when these office hours are because they are usually listed in the syllabus and posted on each faculty member's office door. Usually, the department or division secretaries also have a list of the office hours for everyone in the division. You will find that faculty members are very busy with research, writing, paperwork, grading, committee meetings, and so on. However, you should also know this: helping students is a top priority for college faculty.

Staff

Before most students are even awake, the grounds and building crews are already hard at work at your college making the grounds and buildings beautiful, comfortable, and accessible to students. The food service staff arrives early and starts preparing to serve the campus community. Much of what we do on campus would come to a screeching halt were it not for the long-suffering labor of the computer services staff working, mostly behind the scenes, to keeping everything running. Secretaries and other office staff spend many hours each day helping students connect with the right people, fill out the correct forms, and solve other problems. All of these people take pride in the fact that they are there to help you. You should demonstrate gratitude and cooperate with them whenever possible because, after all, you are helping them help you.

Librarians

A library is not merely a hollow room lined with books; it is, instead, a hive of information driven by a staff that works diligently to design, manage, and continually update the library as a resource for students. Most students would earn much higher grades and get a lot more out of college if they used the library more. The library staff is ready to help you do just that. The library staff can help you understand the library and make use of its resources. Using the library will help you with classroom assignments and papers. Additional information about the library appears later in this chapter.

Other Students

One of the best resources available to you in college is other students. People are greatly influenced by the groups to which they belong. That is why it is very important that you make meaningful connections to other students who care about success in college as much as you do. Your grandmother was correct when she advised you to avoid friends who just want to party all the time, waste time goofing off instead of studying, and participate in nefarious activities like excessive alcohol and drug use. You need to find partners in each of your classes who can help you study for that class and fill you in on what you need to know if you ever have to miss a class. Seek out student organizations that reflect both your interests and your anticipated career. Student clubs should not take away from your study time, but in proper balance, they can offer you networking opportunities, orient you to the norms of your chosen career, help you develop valuable work-related and communication skills, and provide you with opportunities to simply have fun. Your college website probably has a page or area devoted to various clubs and student organizations, and you should look into them as soon as you can. Table 2.2 provides just a few examples of typical student organizations and clubs you might find in college.

Table 2.2

Examples of Student Organizations	
African-American Union	The Robert Feline Playmakers (Theater)
Alpha Sigma Psi (Anthropology, Sociology, & Psychology Club)	SGA (Student Government Association)
Art Mania Club	SIFE (Students in Free Enterprise)
Chess Club	SNEA (Student National Education Association)
EARTH Club	Tennis Club
International Club	STEMMEGA (Math and Science Club)
Music Makers Club	Video Gamers Association

Security

Campus security personnel are not there merely to give you a parking ticket if you park in a restricted zone. Campus police are active around the clock, keeping a watchful eye in order to protect you. Help them serve you better by cooperating with posted speed limits and other laws and by reporting emergencies or suspicious activities to them. If an emergency situation, such as a natural disaster or school shooting, occurs on your campus, campus security are likely to be the first on the scene. Cooperate with them and follow their instructions because that may just save your life.

Academic Tutors

Some of the most appreciated helpers on campus are the academic tutors who work in learning centers. These tutors help students with math and writing challenges. You will be surprised how much easier success will come if you visit your college's learning center. Few students realize what a huge benefit it is when tutors are provided on your campus for free (or included as a part of your regular student fees). If tutors were not provided, and you found yourself seeking the services of a private tutor, you would most likely pay a hefty price for the service.

Years ago, one of my students lamented to me that she had failed a required beginning-level math course twice. She said, "I fear that I will never be able to graduate because I can't get past this required math class, and I just can't understand Professor Smith." The student had good grades in her other classes. When I looked at her schedule, I noticed that she had a free hour after her math class and that the tutoring lab was in the same building as her math classroom. I suggested that she simply go to the tutoring lab after each math class, sit in the lab, and practice the math that was covered in class that day. Then if she came upon a problem that she did not know how to solve, she could ask a tutor to explain it. In this way she could learn the parts of the math lesson that she had difficulty with, one problem at a time, and she would never fall behind in class. She followed my advice. During the next semester, she stopped me in the hall one day to tell me, with excitement, that the plan had worked and that she had earned an A. That student learned just how valuable the campus tutoring service can be.

2.2 Places

Following are brief descriptions of some of the places on most campuses that, in some way, contribute to your success as a student. This is not an exhaustive list. It is a bit humbling to realize that the entire campus infrastructure exists to help you as a student. A lot has been invested in your success.

Learning Centers or Academic Centers

These can be some of the most important locations on campus because centers often provide free tutoring for English, math, and other subjects. Try to visit your college's learning center as soon as you can during the semester to acquaint yourself with all that the center has to offer. Take note of the contact information, such as the telephone number, email address, and web address, and of the hours of operation. Then, return any time you need help.

Computer Labs

Computer labs are located in various buildings across most campuses. Students should make a note of which computer labs are located near them and what times those labs are open. Wireless Internet access is also available on most campuses for students who wish to use their own laptop computers, tablet computers, or other wireless devices. Check the college webpage or the information technology (IT) department to find out how to connect.

Counseling Center

Counseling centers exist to enable students to achieve their goals and to reach their fullest potential by offering personal, career, and academic counseling services. Many colleges offer individual and group therapies, stress management seminars, and other types of psychologically educational seminars throughout the year, as well. Table 2.3 shows some of the services that counseling centers typically offer. Do not hesitate to use their services when you need help.

Most colleges have a webpage for the counseling center (CC) that offers information on a wide variety of issues and links to additional sources. Table 2.4 shows some of the topics that might be addressed by your college CC webpage. Take time to browse your college's CC webpage so that you will be aware of what resources are available to you when you need them.

Table 2.3

Services Offered by Most Counseling Centers (CCs)	
Service	**Description**
Personal Counseling	CCs can help you cope with life changes (relationships, adjustment to college, relocation) and with personal problems (stress management, depression, anxiety, and, more specifically, test anxiety).
Career Counseling	Most CCs offer a career resource library and a computerized career guidance program. They can provide access to information about occupations, schools, financial aid, and job-seeking resources. They can also help you 1) assess your career interest, abilities, and job values; 2) explore occupations, majors, and schools; and 3) develop a résumé and conduct a job search.
Academic Counseling	Academic counseling includes assessment of your learning preferences, counseling on test preparation techniques, and counseling on test anxiety.
Disability Services	This service is provided for students who need help with classroom or other accommodations due to a disability.
Outreach Programs	Upon request, most CCs will provide workshops on stress management, test anxiety, eating disorders, sexual assault awareness and prevention, time management, depression, diversity awareness, communication, and so on.
Group Counseling	Assertiveness training, test anxiety, stress management, single parenthood, healthy relationships, nontraditional student support are all topics covered in group counseling.
Consultation Services	Most CCs will also meet with individuals, small groups, organizations, and departments to assist them in defining issues and developing strategies to deal with concerns.

Table 2.4

Topics Addressed by Many CC Websites
Accommodations for disabilities policy
Career resources
Crisis intervention protocol
Conflict resolution and mediation
De-escalation techniques
Disability resources
Disability services manual
Mental health
Confidentiality statement
Self-help

The Library

This chapter began with an engaging quote by Shelby Foote that expressed the prominence of the library on campus: "A university is just a group of buildings gathered around a library."[3] If the library were a person, she might appear to the casual observer to be quiet and unassuming; yet to the serious college student, the library is revealed as an incredible hulk of academic power.

Students on college campuses can access thousands of books, journal articles, and other resources online through their library. To make the most effective use of the library during your time in college, you need to understand how it is organized, what resources are offered, and what policies are in effect.

Organization

In most colleges and universities, the books in the library are arranged on the shelves according to the Library of Congress Classification System, which separates all knowledge into twenty-one classes. Each class is identified by a letter of the alphabet, subclasses by combination of letters, and subtopics within classes and subclasses by a numerical notation.

Locating Materials and Information

In most libraries, there are computer labs that provide all of the information you need to locate books, videos, periodicals, and thousands of other resources. In many cases you can search the holdings of the library online. Libraries provide services to link you to thousands of reference materials that will assist you in being successful in your college studies. Usually, libraries have a main hub that provides access to multiple databases, which in turn hold thousands of articles in periodicals and chapters in books. Many articles are full text. Students who need periodical articles that are not available in their library can often obtain those materials through an interlibrary loan system. Ask the library staff about requesting materials.

Research Help

A series of studies called the ERIAL project[4] found that many students, even when they struggled to find good sources, did not seek help from the librarians. These studies also found that students who had attended library orientations or tutorials showed more proficiency than those who had not. You will be more successful in college if you attend library orientations and make it a point to ask the librarians for help when you need it.

Most librarians have created subject-specific research guides and course-specific guides to help you with any research project you may have. These guides are crafted to help you when you do not know where to begin your research in a certain subject area or are produced to help you with a specific course. Be sure to ask your librarian about any library guides that might be available to you.

Atmosphere

College libraries strive to accommodate both group and individual study. They often have several, small study rooms available for group study as well as quiet areas in which to study alone. These provide excellent places to study if your home environment is noisy or distracting (as is often the case for students who live in dorms or shared apartments). If you ever need help accessing any of these study areas in the library, a library staff member will be happy to assist you.

Special Collections

Most campus libraries house special collections about specific topics or people. These collections can house print items, images, manuscripts, maps, artifacts, microforms, and digital and audio-visual materials. Many of these collections relate to the specific college, local history, regional and state history, and genealogy. As such, collections typically include many items that are unique, historical, rare, and/or irreplaceable.

Campus Athletic Fitness Center

Almost all colleges have a campus athletic fitness center. This is a place where you can participate in physical exercise and various sports. The activity center can be an excellent resource for all things related to maintaining physical health throughout college. There are often many groups and teams that you can join, meaning this can also be a source of social networking and friendship. When you arrive on campus, check out what your college has to offer in regard to athletic and other fitness opportunities.

Reading Comprehension Question 2.1 (Knowledge)

How are the books in the library arranged?

a. In alphabetical order by title
b. In groups and categories, according to the Dewey Decimal System
c. In accordance with the Library of Congress Classification System
d. In no particular order at all

The Campus Bus System

(It is not a place, but your campus bus system will *take you* places.) Forrest Gump's mama told him that a good pair of shoes could take him anywhere. If Forrest were a student in college, however, he might appreciate knowing that many colleges have a campus bus system that would take him places faster.

In order to reach some locations, you may have to transfer from one route to another. You should check the bus schedules and include that information in your calendar planner. If you can, plan how you get to and from classes *before* you register for them and certainly before the semester gets underway.

2.3   Things (Technologies)

The Internet and related technology are now ubiquitous in higher education, but which technologies and which practices are most likely to help you be successful in college? What practices might thwart your success? How is your use of technology for success in college different from the use of technology in other capacities?

This chapter addresses electronic technologies and physical resources that will help you to be successful in college. Simply knowing how to use these programs is not enough to make you successful. You must know how to use them effectively in the college environment. There will be times when you need to turn technology off so that you can spend time thinking and focusing exclusively on your studies.

Your College Portal

Some colleges have a web portal that you will be able to use to access many resources online. In this case, you would log on to the web portal with a username and password (usually obtained during registration). Once you have logged on, you may have access to a number of different accounts: your campus email account, your campus financial account, your campus records, and/or your campus course delivery system. If you do not know your username or password, be sure to ask a staff or faculty member how to access your college's web portal. You will find that, usually, there is a "forgot your username" or "forgot you password" link on the website, so you may wish to check that first.

College Webmail

The vast majority of colleges have an email program similar to your personal email. It is very important to check your college webmail on a regular basis since it is usually the official email system of your college—the method by which information and important announcements will be delivered to you throughout the semester and your career at college. Look for links regarding webmail on the college home page. (Sometimes there is an option to have your college email forwarded to your personal email address—but you should still log on to your college email periodically to clean out your inbox so there is enough room for new messages.)

Anatomy of an Email to Your Professor

Email messages that you send to your professor, or to other college staff, should not be as casual in style and content as those messages that you might send to a friend. Your professor may teach hundreds of students in five or more classes. Therefore, when you send an email to the professor, it is very important that you identify yourself and indicate specifically which class you are taking. Be sure to use the following guidelines every time you write to a professor:

1. Always include your full name as part of the message.

2. Always identify about which class you are writing. Specify the name of the class (e.g., SOC 1101 Sociology), the section (e.g., Section B), and class meeting particulars (e.g., meeting TH at 9:30 a.m.).

3. Always include your contact information (such as your email address and/or phone number) so that the professor may respond to your message if necessary.

4. Always use complete sentences and correct grammar.

Following are three examples of email messages: one that has the correct characteristics and two that do not and which are not appropriate. The names have been changed to protect the innocent (or guilty), but these are *actual emails* that have been received from students. Can you identify what is wrong with the poorly written messages? How many problems can you find in the poorly written messages?

Example of a Really, Truly, Undeniably Horrible Email Message

From:	cgriffin3@college.edu
Date:	3/11/2014 11:18:29 am
To:	bsmith@college.edu
Subject:	(no subject)
Attachments:	

wht up when is r test

Example of a Poorly Composed Email Message

From:	cgriffin3@college.edu
Date:	3/11/2014 11:18:29 am
To:	bsmith@college.edu
Subject:	Test Date
Attachments:	

When is our next test?

Chris

Example of a Well-Written Email Message

From:	cgriffin3@college.edu
Date:	3/11/2014 11:18:29 am
To:	bsmith@college.edu
Subject:	Social Problems Assignment from Chris Griffin
Attachments:	**Chris_Griffin_Assignment1.doc (112 k)**

Professor Smith,

Per your instructions in the syllabus, I have attached writing assignment #1 for Social Problems (Section B, 12:30 pm, MW) to this email.

Please send a reply to confirm that you have received it as I do not wish for the assignment to be late.

Sincerely,

Chris Griffin

cgriffin3@college.edu

478-455-4123

Social Problems 1101; Section B; MW 12:30 pm

Reading Comprehension Question 2.2 (Literal Comprehension)

Which of the following is true according to this chapter?

a. Emails to a professor should always identify you by your name and your class and should include your contact information.

b. Emails to a professor are very similar to texting, except that you may have to use the college webmail system to deliver them.

c. Emails to your professor should be casual and friendly.

d. Emails sent through the campus webmail system automatically identify you and provide your contact information, so you never need to do so.

Things You Should Know About Most College Webmail

There are usually links on your college's home page from which you can discover the webmail addresses and telephone numbers of your professors, advisor, and staff members for the various departments and offices on campus.

You can usually locate policies regarding your college's webmail on the college website. You should make sure that you are aware of those policies. If your college, like many, sends important college correspondence to your college webmail account instead of using paper mail (snail mail) or any other email accounts that you may have, then it is vital that you check your college webmail on a regular basis.

Reading Comprehension Question 2.3 (Inferential Comprehension)

What is the main idea of the passage entitled, "Things You Should Know About Most College Webmail"?

a. Colleges have certain policies and established norms about the correct and incorrect way to use webmail in college.

b. Webmail is very complicated and difficult to use.

c. Webmail can be used to publicize a personal business.

d. None of the above

Course Management Systems

A course management system (CMS) or learning management system (LMS) is a software program that your college uses to manage online courses or the online components of face-to-face (F2F) courses. Examples of course management systems include Blackboard®, D2L® (formerly known as Desire2Learn), Moodle™, and Canvas™. There are others. Your college may use one of these, a different CMS, or one of these called by a name unique to your institution.

The CMS is used to deliver online courses and hybrid courses (courses that meet partly online and partly in a classroom) and to enhance F2F classes. Even if you are not enrolled in an online or hybrid course, your professor may use a CMS to post information for your class, such as the syllabus or grades. In some cases the professor of an F2F class may use a CMS for much more—such as email, discussions, quizzes, surveys, handouts, instructional videos, a calendar, announcements, and so on. Ask your professor about this at the beginning of the semester so that you will know what to expect and so that you will not miss out on any resources that might help you succeed in the course. Look for tutorials on the college website to help you learn to navigate your college's particular CMS.

It would be wise to check your college webpage for the technical requirements of the CMS *before* you get started accessing your courses online because you may need to adjust your computer or use certain programs on your computer to make it compatible with the CMS used at your college. For example, the CMS may not work properly in all Internet browsers and may specify which browsers or versions of particular browsers you should use. Examples of browsers include Google Chrome™, Mozilla® Firefox®, Microsoft® Internet Explorer®, and Apple® Safari® to name a few. Also, the CMS may require that you set your browser to allow cookies, pop-ups, or Oracle® Java™. Some of the courses that you access through the CMS may also require plug-ins, such as Adobe® Reader®, Adobe® Flash® Player, Apple® QuickTime®, or Microsoft® Windows® Media Player®, for your browser.

Using Your College Database Software

Colleges often use database software systems for administrative applications. Your college database software program is probably connected to the database where student enrollment and grade information are stored. Usually, you can access your college's database software program from the college home page. You should find out what your college's software database program is called so that you can locate and make full use of the system. As a student, you can usually use your college database software to manage many aspects of your college experience. Following are examples of some of the things for which you can usually use your college database software:

- You can check your own records at the college—such as registration status, financial aid status, and registration holds.

- You can view the course schedule for current and future semesters.

- You may be able to register yourself for classes online.

- You may be able to check your midterm grades.

- You can view your official grades at the end of the semester.

Reading Comprehension Question 2.4 (Analysis)

What is the primary purpose of the parts of this chapter dealing with technology?

a. To show the student how advanced the technology is at college

b. To demonstrate to the student that there are rules about using email in college

c. To assist the student in becoming familiar with various Internet technologies in order to increase the student's chances for success in college

d. To point out the deficiencies in college Internet technologies

Want to learn more? Try these resources.

"See You Online! Tips for Using College Library Resources and the Web"
http://bvtlab.com/68JBN

The *Back to College*® website presents this article by Sylvia DeSantis, in which she describes college and university online databases, using search engines for college research and university electronic catalogs.

Library Survival Skills for New College Students
http://bvtlab.com/b57T7

This webpage, prepared by Nancy Guidry and Dawn Dobie of the Bakersfield College Library, presents and describes fourteen library skills that new students need to succeed.

"Top 10 Ways Your College Library Can Help You"
http://bvtlab.com/r2aUW

This short article by Courtney Brunch appears in the *Front Range Community College Blog: Writing the Front Range* and lists ten ways that the college library can help students.

2.4 Summary

This chapter discussed many of the people, places, and things that will help you succeed in college. People include advisors, coaches, counselors, faculty, buildings and grounds staff, librarians, office staff, security, and other students. Places include learning centers, computer labs, counseling centers, financial aid offices, fitness centers, libraries, registrar's offices, and student organizations. With regard to technology, you learned some basic information about your college's webmail, course management system, and college database software systems. A simple—but very important—topic of this chapter was the discussion of the anatomy of an email to your professor. If you make the extra effort to make sure that your email messages have the characteristics described in this chapter, you will enjoy much more successful communication with your professors. Improving your communication skills will contribute to your overall success in college and your subsequent career.

Name: _____

Study Guide | Goal 1

The student will be able to understand and effectively use various technologies, including the college website, the college library website, and the college's course management system.

Questions	Answers & Notes

Study Guide | Goal 2

The student will be able to practice an etiquette that will promote effective communication with professors and others.

Questions	Answers & Notes

Name: _____

Study Guide | Goal 3

The student will be able to list and describe what resources are available from the college library, counseling centers, and various offices on campus.

Questions	Answers & Notes

Name: _____

Study Guide | Goal 4

The student will be able to identify, appreciate, cooperate, and coordinate with the various people on campus who can contribute in some way to the student's success.

Questions	Answers & Notes

Study Guide | Preparing for Class

Use this page to record questions or insights to discuss in class.

Name: _____

Review Questions 2.1

Instructions

Following are five true-false statements taken from the information in this chapter. First, try to answer them without looking back at the chapter. Then review the chapter to see how well you did.

Question & Answer	Rationale
Circle true or false for each of the following statements.	Write an explanation stating why each statement is true or false.
1. Students should always use their personal email account to check their official college mailbox. True or False	Your Rationale:
2. Using your college's database software program is important because it will allow you to access your grades and assess your progress in college. True or False	Your Rationale:
3. Counseling centers help with a very limited number of psychological issues for college students. True or False	Your Rationale:
4. When sending an email message to a professor via webmail, there is no need to mention the class about which you are writing. True or False	Your Rationale:
5. If the library were a person, she might appear to the casual observer to be quiet and unassuming; however, to the serious college student, the library is revealed as an incredible hulk of academic power. True or False	Your Rationale:

Name: _____

Assignment 2.1

Identifying Campus Resources

Instructions

This assessment provides you with a worksheet to help you to identify campus resources and to always be prepared to take advantage of their services.

Follow These Steps

Step 1: Use the form on the following pages to record some information about the different resources available on your campus. Examples of resources include the library, your academic advisor, the tutoring center, computer labs, faculty and teaching assistants, departmental offices for your major, coaches, and so on. The information should include contact information, office hours or hours of operation, location, and how the resource can help you. Record the information in the space provided.

Step 2: Insert or copy these pages into your calendar/planner so that you will always have the information when you need it. If you use an electronic calendar/planner, then copy the information to your electronic planner so that you will have access to it when you need it. Remember to update the information any time the details, such as hours of operation, change.

Notes

_____
_____
_____
_____
_____
_____
_____
_____
_____
_____
_____
_____
_____
_____
_____
_____
_____
_____
_____
_____
_____
_____
_____

Directory of Campus Resources

Resource:	How can this resource help you?
Phone/Fax:	
Email:	
Webpage:	
Location:	
Hours of Operation:	

Resource:	How can this resource help you?
Phone/Fax:	
Email:	
Webpage:	
Location:	
Hours of Operation:	

Resource:	How can this resource help you?
Phone/Fax:	
Email:	
Webpage:	
Location:	
Hours of Operation:	

Resource:	How can this resource help you?
Phone/Fax:	
Email:	
Webpage:	
Location:	
Hours of Operation:	

Resource:	How can this resource help you?
Phone/Fax:	
Email:	
Webpage:	
Location:	
Hours of Operation:	

Directory of Campus Resources (Cont.)

	How can this resource help you?
Resource:	
Phone/Fax:	
Email:	
Webpage:	
Location:	
Hours of Operation:	

	How can this resource help you?
Resource:	
Phone/Fax:	
Email:	
Webpage:	
Location:	
Hours of Operation:	

	How can this resource help you?
Resource:	
Phone/Fax:	
Email:	
Webpage:	
Location:	
Hours of Operation:	

	How can this resource help you?
Resource:	
Phone/Fax:	
Email:	
Webpage:	
Location:	
Hours of Operation:	

	How can this resource help you?
Resource:	
Phone/Fax:	
Email:	
Webpage:	
Location:	
Hours of Operation:	

Chapter Roadmap

Introduction

In this chapter you will learn about the types of attitudes and approaches to learning that help make students successful.

This chapter roadmap page presents the formal learning goals for this chapter and a checklist that you should follow as you read and study the chapter.

Student Learning Goals

After completing this chapter you should be able to do the following:

1. Compare and contrast the focus-on-grades approach with the focus-on-learning approach.

2. Explain why the focus-on-learning approach is most effective.

3. Explain why long-term learning is more productive than cramming for an exam.

4. Describe the characteristics of a responsible learner.

5. Explain how failure to take responsibility for learning—both on the part of students and on the part of professors—can be detrimental to both individuals and society.

6. Explain the difference between deep learning and surface learning.

Chapter Checklist

You will benefit most if you complete the activities in the order that they are listed.

❑ **Target Date/Deadline:** _____
Complete Critical Thinking Activity 3.1.

❑ **Target Date/Deadline:** _____
Convert the student learning goals to questions that you can answer as you read the chapter. Write your questions on the study guide pages near the end of this chapter.

❑ **Target Date/Deadline:** _____
Read the chapter.

❑ **Target Date/Deadline:** _____
Try to answer the reading comprehension questions as you come to them in the chapter. Check each answer by comparing it to the list of correct answers in the back of the book. If any answer was not correct, then review the passages preceding the question to see why you missed the question.

❑ **Target Date/Deadline:** _____
Answer the student learning goal questions you created. These answered questions will be your study guide.

❑ **Target Date/Deadline:** _____
Write down any questions, insights, or comments that you have as you read so that you can bring them up in class.

❑ **Target Date/Deadline:** _____
Complete Review Questions 3.1.

❑ **Target Date/Deadline:** _____
Complete Assignment 3.1 (Form a Study Group).

❑ **Target Date/Deadline:** _____
Review what you have learned from this chapter.

Critical Thinking Activity 3.1

Consider the following questions; select the answer that most closely matches your personal preference for each situation described.

1. You have been rushed to the hospital after an auto accident. Which would you prefer?

    a. To be treated by a nurse who earned her credentials by cheating on the final exam in nursing school

    b. To be treated by a nurse who, thanks to her excellent negotiating skills, was able to graduate nursing school by bargaining with the professor after failing the final exam

    c. To be treated by a nurse who earned her credentials not only by learning enough to pass her exams, but also by making sure that she understood everything that she was supposed to learn

2. You are an elementary school principal who is interviewing applicants to teach a second-grade class at your school. Your child is in that second-grade class. Which would you prefer?

    a. To hire an applicant who passed her math class by taking the class online and having a friend who was good at math take all of the exams for her

    b. To hire an applicant who says in the interview, "I only want to teach at the first-, second-, or third-grade levels because I don't like math"

    c. To hire an applicant who struggled with math initially, but who passed the class because she spent extra time doing practice questions and getting help from the tutoring lab until she mastered the subject

3. You have won the lottery and are now $100 million richer than you were yesterday. You don't know how to properly manage this large amount of money or how to deal with the tax issues associated with it, so you decide to hire a CPA to help you. Which would you prefer?

    a. To have your finances managed by an accountant who earned his credentials by cheating on the final exam in college

    b. To have your finances managed by an accountant who believes in investing as little effort as possible to get the most benefit possible (When he was in college he used ratemyprofessor.com to figure out which professors were easy and took only easy classes. This way he was able to get his degree without having to invest very much time in studying or learning.)

    c. To have your finances managed by an accountant who is good at his job because when he was in college he took responsibility for his own learning and researched topics deeply until he gained a clear understanding of everything he needed to know to earn his degree and to do his job well

Is there a pattern to your answers for these three questions? If so, why? Make some notes about what you think, and be prepared to discuss this in class.

_____
_____
_____
_____
_____
_____
_____
_____
_____
_____
_____
_____
_____
_____
_____
_____
_____
_____
_____
_____
_____
_____
_____
_____
_____
_____
_____
_____
_____
_____
_____
_____
_____
_____

Learning and Grades:

Why Am I Really in College?

3

"Learn as if you will live forever; live as if you will die tomorrow."
— Mahatma Gandhi[1]

While grading an essay, an English professor noticed that the student author had obviously not taken the time to proofread before submitting the paper. With a quiet sigh of disappointment, the professor marked the freshman paper with a C (average) and then inserted a small note in the margin which read, "Is this your best work?" Years later, at the retirement dinner for the English professor, the president of the college stood to make a few remarks and read from a letter that he had recently received from one of the professor's former students. The letter of gratitude recounted that moment when the professor had written "Is this your best work?" on a poorly written essay. In the letter, the former student explained, "Those words changed my life." Inspired by those words, the student decided never to take a mediocre approach to learning again. The student began to apply an above-average effort and to produce above-average work. The student eventually graduated with honors.

In this chapter you will learn about the attitudes and approaches to learning that help make students successful. The proper attitude and approach to college learning can convert the average student into an exceptional student. You will learn to develop a focus on learning instead of a focus on grades, to be a responsible learner, to use learning goals as a guide to studying, to engage in deep learning instead of surface learning, and to distribute your study workload over the entire semester instead of cramming the night before for exams. These principles will help you to do your best work.

In the pages that follow, this chapter examines the student's approach to learning with regard to focus, goals, pace, depth, and responsibility.

3.1 Focus

Most students have been socialized to view the acquisition of a credential as the main purpose for college, and therefore they focus on grades rather than on learning. However, the focus-on-grades approach is not as effective in reaching the desired educational outcomes as is the focus-on-learning approach when it comes to reaching the desired educational outcomes. Figure 3.1 illustrates this point.

Students who employ a focus-on-grades approach will naturally learn less than they could because they are likely to think of the grade as something separate from learning. Given this focus, students attempt to achieve the desired grades with the least investment possible—such that the driving question becomes, "What is the least (time, learning, effort, etc.) I can invest and still pass?" Such students may be satisfied if the result is a passing grade because that grade will not prevent them from acquiring a credential. However, this model may prevent them from acquiring the level of true learning of which they are capable. In fact, a focus on grades may result in very little true learning. True learning is distinguished from the type of short-term learning that is produced by cramming for exams.

In contrast, students who focus on learning as the goal will seek to learn as much as they can. They are more likely to embrace, "What is the most I can learn?" as their driving question. In this case, higher grades will be an automatic result (a side effect) of greater learning. These students will earn a credential, and they will also experience a greater degree of true learning with long-term benefits. They may also achieve a higher grade point average since true learning naturally equips them to earn higher grades.

Figure 3.1

Two Approaches: Comparison of a Focus on Grades with a Focus on Learning

Consider the questions listed in Table 3.1. Which focus describes your approach to learning in college? You will be more successful if you focus on learning because higher grades are automatically a result of better learning. The best way to score highly on exams is simply to learn the lesson. Don't settle for a focus-on-grades approach because that approach results in less learning and, as a consequence, lower grades. After all, if you are going to invest years of your life in going to college, don't you want to get more than just grades for your investment of time? You deserve more. You deserve an education, rather than just a credential, because once you truly learn something, no one can ever take that away from you.

Table 3.1

Contrasting Questions Associated with Academic Focus	
Focus on Grades	**Focus on Learning**
What is the least I can do to pass this course?	What is the most that I can learn in this class?
What will be on the test?	What are the lesson objectives?
What do I have to memorize?	What am I supposed to learn?
What shortcuts can I use to prepare for the exam?	What can I do to best learn the important material in this lesson?

3.2 Goals

As T. A. Angelo noted, "When learners know what their educational goals are and figure out how they can best achieve them [and when they] know how and how well their goals fit the instructor's, they tend to learn more and get better grades."[2] Researchers and educational experts have found that goal alignment between teacher and student is key to learning success. Therefore, students will be more successful when they identify the learning goals or objectives for each course, lesson, or exam and incorporate them into their study routine.

Even if you adopt a focus-on-learning approach, you can't learn everything in one semester or course. Therefore, in order to be successful in each course, you will need to identify the goals for that course. The course goals are usually listed in the syllabus. They are usually somewhat broad because they apply to the entire course. Some professors also publish learning objectives (objectives are more specific than goals and are measurable) for chapters, lessons, or exams within a course. Sometimes chapter objectives are listed in the textbook. Lesson objectives make an excellent guide for you to use when you design your study plan. Your focus should remain on learning as much as you can; however, with the addition of specific measurable lesson objectives, *you will know what you are supposed to learn*—and you will have a way to assess what you have learned.

Lesson objectives simply state the desired outcome of the lesson. In other words, they state what the student should be able to do after the lesson. Instead of the term "objectives," we could call them the "intended learning outcomes"[3] because they state what you should be able to do after learning that you could not do before. A typical lesson objective may begin, "Upon completion of this lesson, the student will be able to ..." followed by a specific type of knowledge, analysis, skill, or behavior. Following are some examples of different types of learning goals based on Bloom's Taxonomy:[4]

- Knowledge Goal: Upon completion of this lesson, the student will be able to list and describe the characteristics of a mammal.

- Application/Analysis Goal: Upon completion of this lesson, the student will be able to compare and contrast a democratic society and a communist society.

- Application/Skill Goal: Upon completion of this lesson, the student will be able to perform CPR on an infant and demonstrate this skill using the first aid dummies.

- Behavior Goal: Upon completion of this lesson, the student will design and implement a three-week personal weight-training program to strengthen gross motor muscles.

Since the objectives are usually presented as statements of outcome rather than as questions, it may be useful for you (the student) to convert the objectives into one or more questions that can be used as a study guide. For example, the first learning goal for this chapter can be converted into at least five questions (see Table 3.2). Once you have created your own questions based on the professor's objectives, you should identify information relating to those questions as you read the chapter and attempt to answer them afterward. If you have difficulty answering any of the questions on your own, you can bring them up during class discussion or ask for help outside of class. Professors set aside office hours specifically for the purpose of helping their students with such questions.

You may recall from Chapter 1 that one of the differences between high school and college is that in college, professors schedule regular office hours in order to meet with students individually. Scheduled office hours are usually posted in the syllabus, on the professor's website, and on the office door. As Chapter 1 already noted, you are not interrupting or bothering professors when you meet with them during their office hours. That time has been set aside especially for you. In fact, professors are often impressed by students who take the initiative to write down a question about the reading or lesson and to ask about that question during an office hour visit. So when you have questions about the lesson that are not answered by the reading, lecture, or class discussion, make an appointment to see the professor during office hours. *It is important that you close any gaps between what you have learned so far and what you are supposed to learn.*

Table 3.2	
Example of Study Guide Questions Based on a Lesson Objective	
Objective:	After completing this chapter, you should be able to compare and contrast the focus-on-grades approach with the focus-on-learning approach.
Questions:	1. What is the focus-on-grades approach?
	2. What is the focus-on-learning approach?
	3. In what ways are the two approaches, focus on grades and focus on learning, similar?
	4. In what ways are the two approaches different?
	5. Which approach is more effective?

If neither your professor nor the textbook provides lesson objectives or exam objectives, then you may wish to inquire about them. In the absence of having objectives provided, you will need to create your own list of objectives in order to organize your study regimen.

Reading Comprehension Question 3.1 (Knowledge)

Researchers and educational experts have found which of the following?

a. That goal alignment between the teacher and the student is key to learning success

b. That goals are not a significant part of the educational process

c. That goals cause students to focus on grades and not on learning

d. That students who have goals tend to get bogged down and not learn as much as those who do not have goals

3.3 Pace

Many students wait, incorrectly, until the night before an exam (or a day or two before) to begin studying the material that will be covered. This is famously known as "cramming" for the exam. It is a strategy that may have worked in high school, when less material was covered on a single exam, but it is much less effective in college. Many college courses have only two exams—a midterm and a final. Often the final is cumulative (meaning it covers everything taught in the course, rather than just what was covered after the midterm). Therefore, the student must master a large amount of information in order to perform well on each exam.

Researchers have discovered that *how you study* is more important than *how long you study*.[5] Students who spread out their study time over days and weeks score higher grades than students who study the same number of hours all in one night.

Michaels and Miethe examined more than fifteen variables including study habits and performance for 676 undergraduate college students. They explained the difference that they found between crammers and non-crammers:

> The return of study time and class attendance on grades varies by type of study habits. Among students who study throughout the week (non-crammers), both study time and class attendance have significant positive effects on grades. For crammers, the amounts of study and class attendance have no appreciable effect on college grades. In other words, students who study throughout the week benefit from increased study time and class attendance, whereas students who concentrate their studying before exams do not reap rewards from increases in effort.[5]

One problem with cramming is that it relies on short-term memory. It is difficult, if not impossible, to hold as much information in your short-term memory as is often required on college-level exams (especially comprehensive final exams). The key is to study on a regular basis and *learn* the material a little bit at a time. This method will allow you to encode the course material in your long-term memory, which will serve you well when you take the exam. In fact, some researchers have found that students who reported that they used cramming "for most of their courses" tended to have lower GPAs.[6]

One key to success in learning is to pace yourself. Design a study plan for each course in which you anticipate what you need to learn for each exam, and then divide that huge block of learning into a number of study sessions. Learning the information in smaller sessions spread out over time will enable you to engage in deeper learning.

3.4 Depth

Do you have high expectations for yourself? Are you doing your best work? One way to do your best work is to employ deep learning instead of surface learning.

Learning has been defined as "an active, interactive, self-aware process that results in meaningful, long-lasting changes in knowledge, skills, behaviors, beliefs, and attitudes … that cannot be attributed primarily to maturation."[2] But not all learning is of the same quality. It is useful to distinguish between deep learning and surface learning.

Surface learning is often employed by those who cram for an exam. It involves very limited thinking, analysis, or critical evaluation. Surface learners often separate new material from the context in which they find it, and as a result they have little ability to apply what they have learned to a real-world context. For example, a student who uses surface-learning techniques to study for an exam might simply try to memorize the definitions of all the words printed in **bold** in the textbook. Memorization is not always a bad technique—but when words are memorized out of context, the student is often unable to apply the terms that he or she has memorized because the terms are not fully understood.

Deep learning involves critical thinking and the analysis of new information with the goal of understanding the concepts and acquiring the ability to apply them in different contexts. In deep learning, the student intends to move beyond simple memorization to understanding and application.

You may use the information in Table 3.3 to compare the deep-learning approach with the surface-learning approach. These characteristics have been described by Entwistle[7] and presented by Norton.[8]

Want to learn more? Try these resources.

The following YouTube™ videos explore the differences between surface learning and deep learning. (The videos summarize concepts developed by John Biggs in his book, *Teaching for Quality Learning at University*[9]):

Part 1: http://bvtlab.com/4n8m8

Part 2: http://bvtlab.com/9E77W

Part 3: http://bvtlab.com/67n79

Table 3.3

Comparison of Deep Learning and Surface Learning		
Characteristic	**Deep Approach**	**Surface Approach**
Intent of student	Intends to understand	Intends to complete task requirements
Mode of study	Interacts vigorously with content	Memorizes information needed for assessments
Level of understanding	Relates new ideas to previous knowledge	Fails to distinguish principles from examples
Application of concepts	Relates concepts to everyday experience	Treats task as an external imposition
Integration of concepts	Relates evidence to conclusions	Focuses on discrete elements without integration
Level of critical thinking	Examines the logic of the argument	Neglects to reflect on purpose or strategies

It is important to note that "these approaches [are] not personality traits or intellectual abilities of any kind; *they are simply a reflection of the student's intention* when s/he engages in a given academic task."[8] It may be the case that some students are unaware of the difference between deep and surface learning. Such students may wrongly assume that surface learning is the normal approach taken by everyone. Therefore, now that you are aware of this dynamic, you can adjust your intent and embrace the more effective deep-learning approach. The surface approach nearly always leads to poorer quality outcomes[10] while the deep approach can lead to clear understanding, long-term recall, and higher grades.

Reading Comprehension Question 3.2 (Literal Comprehension)

Which of the following is the main difference between deep learning and surface learning?

a. Surface learning is often used by students who study over several weeks for exams.

b. Deep learning involves critical thinking and analysis of new information.

c. Deep learning tends to distract students from the main goal of the course.

d. Surface learning can help the student learn a lot of information in a very short time.

Think About This

What would be different about the way you read a typical textbook (such as history or sociology) if you used a deep approach rather than a surface approach?

_____

_____

_____

_____

_____

_____

_____

_____

_____

_____

_____

_____

_____

_____

_____

_____

_____

_____

_____

_____

_____

_____

_____

_____

_____

_____

_____

_____

_____

3.5 **Responsibility**

College is an environment where adult students—who already have a foundation of basic academic skills—come together under the guidance of the professor to learn and engage in higher level **critical thinking** about a wide range of subjects that will prepare them for leadership roles in society. As a college student you must take adult responsibility for your own learning. Taking adult responsibility means that you do not wait for the teacher to tell you what to do or what to think, or to ask you questions. Instead you ask questions, design a study plan for your classes, and reach out to the professor and your classmates for assistance in the learning process. Learning is not something that someone else does for you or makes you do. Learning is something you do for yourself with the assistance of your mentors and peers.

"Learning takes place through the active behavior of the student: it is what he does that he learns, not what the teacher does."

— Ralph W. Tyler[11]

Responsible adult learners do not need to be told to read the syllabus, acquire a textbook, read the textbook, develop a study regimen, prepare questions in advance to use in class participation, attend class and other academic functions on campus, participate, keep up their grades, evaluate their own progress on a regular basis, plan for early registration in advance, consult their advisor, or seek help when they need it (long before an exam). Responsible students take the initiative to do all of these things and more, not because they wish to please the professor, but because they wish to gain as much from the educational experience as they can.

Georgia Tech professor and physicist Dr. Kurt Wiesenfeld authored an article in *Newsweek* called "Making the Grade: Many Students Wheedle for a Degree as If It Were a Freebie T Shirt," in which he underscored how important it is for students to take responsibility for learning in order to become competent leaders in society.[12] Professor Wiesenfeld tells the story of how twelve students called him after the semester was completely over in order to beg him to change their failing grades. One student cried, "I will lose my scholarship if you don't change my grade to a D," while another whined, "If you don't give me a C, I'll flunk out." One student dramatically pleaded, "If I don't pass, my life is over." The professor was alarmed that these students were so indifferent toward grades as an indication of personal effort and performance. As he explained,

> Many, when pressed about why they think they deserve a better grade, admit they don't. Having been raised on gold stars for effort and smiley faces for self-esteem, they've learned that they can get by without hard work and real talent if they can talk the professor into giving them a break. … Their arguments for wheedling better grades often ignore academic performance. … Perhaps these students see me as a commodities broker with something they want—a grade. Though intrinsically worthless, grades, if properly manipulated, can be traded for what has value: a degree, which means a job, which means money. The one thing college actually offers—a chance to learn—is considered irrelevant, even less than worthless, because of the long hours and hard work required.[12]

Think About This

What was Professor Wiesenfeld's main message in this article?

Why is Professor Wiesenfeld opposed to grade inflation?

How could Professor Wiesenfeld's students have avoided this situation?

_____

_____

_____

_____

_____

_____

_____

_____

_____

_____

_____

_____

_____

_____

_____

_____

_____

_____

_____

_____

_____

_____

_____

_____

_____

_____

_____

_____

It appears that focusing on grades and shortcuts, instead of on learning, had very serious negative consequences for these physics students. Perhaps some of them lost their scholarships, perhaps some failed and had to change majors, and perhaps some allowed their GPA to drop so low that they were never able to graduate.

However, Professor Wiesenfeld explains that there would also be dire consequences for our entire society if he were to award these students passing grades that they did not deserve:

> These guys had better take themselves seriously now, because our country will be forced to take them seriously later, when the stakes are much higher. They must recognize that their attitude is not only self-destructive, but socially destructive. The erosion of quality control—giving appropriate grades for actual accomplishments—is a major concern. … That's when the misfortunes of eroding academic standards multiply. We lament that school children get "kicked upstairs" until they graduate from high school despite being illiterate and mathematically inept, but we seem unconcerned with college graduates whose less blatant deficiencies are far more harmful if their accreditation exceeds their qualifications. Most of my students are science and engineering majors. If they're good at getting partial credit but not at getting the answer right, then the new bridge breaks or the new drug doesn't work. One finds examples here in Atlanta. … A light tower in the Olympic Stadium collapsed killing a worker, … showing real-world consequences of errors and lack of expertise.[12]

Want to learn more? Try these resources.

You can read Professor Wiesenfeld's entire article online at any one of the following URLs:

http://bvtlab.com/p6g7q

http://bvtlab.com/8gbbp

http://bvtlab.com/a78ec

Reading Comprehension Question 3.3 (Inferential Comprehension)

What was Professor Wiesenfeld's *main* point in the article?

a. That some of his students would be in trouble in the real world because they had an attitude about learning that was not appropriate for a college education

b. That some of his students asked for grades they did not deserve

c. That all students are trying to get away with the least amount of work possible in college

d. None of the above

3.6 Summary

In this chapter you learned how the proper attitude and approach to college learning can help you be successful. Successful students focus on learning and ask, "What is the most that I can learn in this class?" Successful students identify the learning goals or objectives for each course, lesson, or exam and incorporate them into their study routine. For each course, successful students design a study plan in which they divide the learning activities into a number of study sessions spread out over time. Successful students practice a deep-learning approach instead of a surface-learning approach. Successful students take adult responsibility for their learning.

In this book you will learn how to take responsibility for your own learning. This starts with identifying and practicing successful learning approaches. Specific academic skills and habits will be covered in the coming chapters.

Reading Comprehension Question 3.4 (Analysis)

Why did the authors write this chapter on "Learning and Grades"?

a. To enlighten the student on how to approach the topic of learning in a college atmosphere

b. To chide the student on his/her behavior in college

c. To show that students are always trying to get away with the least amount of work

d. To demonstrate that learning is almost impossible in a college setting

Name: _____

Study Guide | Goal 1

The student will be able to compare and contrast the focus-on-grades approach with the focus-on-learning approach.

Questions	Answers & Notes

Name: _____

Study Guide | Goal 2

The student will be able to explain why the focus-on-learning approach is most effective.

Questions	Answers & Notes

Study Guide | *Goal 3*

The student will be able to explain why long-term learning is more productive than cramming for an exam.

Questions	Answers & Notes

Name: _____

Study Guide | Goal 4

The student will be able to describe the characteristics of a responsible learner.

Questions	Answers & Notes

Name: _____

Study Guide | Goal 5

The student will be able to explain how failure to take responsibility for learning—both on the part of students and on the part of professors—can be detrimental to both individuals and society.

Questions	Answers & Notes

Name: _____

Study Guide | Goal 6

The student will be able to explain the difference between deep learning and surface learning.

Questions	Answers & Notes

Study Guide | Preparing for Class

Use this page to record questions or insights to discuss in class.

Name: _____

Review Questions 3.1

Instructions

Following are five true-false statements taken from the information in this chapter. First, try to answer them without looking back at the chapter. Then review the chapter to see how well you did.

Question & Answer	Rationale
Circle true or false for each of the following statements.	Write an explanation stating why each statement is true or false.
1. Cramming for exams is a normal part of college life for most students because it is the best way to learn the large volume of material covered in most college courses. True or False	Your Rationale:
2. A successful approach to studying and learning demands a focus on grades because college students must maintain a certain grade point average (GPA) in order to graduate. True or False	Your Rationale:
3. The surface approach to learning nearly always leads to poorer outcomes and/or lower grades. True or False	Your Rationale:
4. The focus-on-grades model is a failure model. True or False	Your Rationale:
5. "Wheedle" is the nickname or label that Professor Wiesenfeld has applied to students who try to pass the course by cheating. True or False	Your Rationale:

Name: _____

Assignment 3.1

Study Group (2–4 people for 4 meetings)

Goal

The purpose of this activity is to enable the student to use study groups to learn more effectively.

Objective

The student will form or join a study group for one of his or her classes and will keep a record of his or her study group involvement and activities.

Instructions

It is smart to study with other students who are taking the same course and who are serious about learning.

Follow These Steps

Step 1: Consult the following URLs to learn about the value of study groups and how to use them effectively:

- *Study Groups and College Success* from the University of LaVerne, Learning Center (http://bvtlab.com/3wFr6)

- BookRags Article: *How to Form a Study Group in College* (http://bvtlab.com/h5dPe)

Step 2: Form a group and hold at least four study sessions together. Record the following for each group study session:

1. The date, time, and place of the group meeting

2. The signatures of all who attended

3. A brief description of what the group did during that session

Step 3: You can use the Study Group Report form on the next page to keep a record of your group meetings.

Notes

_____
_____
_____
_____
_____
_____
_____
_____
_____
_____
_____
_____
_____
_____
_____
_____
_____
_____
_____
_____
_____
_____
_____
_____
_____
_____
_____
_____
_____
_____
_____

Study Group Report Form

Course:	Your Name:
First Meeting What did the group do at this meeting?	Date: Attendees' Signatures:
Second Meeting What did the group do at this meeting?	Date: Attendees' Signatures:
Third Meeting What did the group do at this meeting?	Date: Attendees' Signatures:
Fourth Meeting What did the group do at this meeting?	Date: Attendees' Signatures:

Chapter Roadmap

Introduction

In this chapter you will examine two major perspectives for understanding learning. You will explore how these perspectives can be useful to you as a student. Then you can apply these perspectives to your understanding of learning preferences and make use of study strategies associated with each preference. The goal of this chapter is to help you become more aware of how people learn, to help you determine your personal learning preferences, and to provide some tips for how you, individually, can learn best.

This chapter roadmap page presents the formal learning goals for this chapter and a checklist that you should follow as you read and study the chapter.

Student Learning Goals

After completing this chapter you should be able to do the following:

1. Discuss two major perspectives of learning: behavioral and cognitive.

2. Describe at least two additional factors that affect the way we learn.

3. Describe eight types of learners and learning preferences.

4. Analyze your own personal learning preferences using the *Index of Learning Styles* (ILS).

5. List at least two study strategies that will help you learn more effectively based on your learning preferences.

Chapter Checklist

You will benefit most if you complete the activities in the order that they are listed.

❑ **Target Date/Deadline:** _____
Complete Critical Thinking Activity 4.1.

❑ **Target Date/Deadline:** _____
Convert the student learning goals to questions that you can answer as you read the chapter. Write your questions on the study guide pages near the end of this chapter.

❑ **Target Date/Deadline:** _____
Read the chapter.

❑ **Target Date/Deadline:** _____
Try to answer the reading comprehension questions as you come to them in the chapter. Check each answer by comparing it to the list of correct answers in the back of the book. If any answer was not correct, then review the passages preceding the question to see why you missed the question.

❑ **Target Date/Deadline:** _____
Answer the student learning goal questions you created. These answered questions will be your study guide.

❑ **Target Date/Deadline:** _____
Write down any questions, insights, or comments that you have as you read so that you can bring them up in class.

❑ **Target Date/Deadline:** _____
Complete Review Questions 4.1.

❑ **Target Date/Deadline:** _____
Complete Assignment 4.1 (Learning Preference Assessment).

❑ **Target Date/Deadline:** _____
Review what you have learned from this chapter.

Critical Thinking Activity 4.1

As a way to begin thinking about the topic of this chapter, please consider the following questions and write your answers in the space provided.

1. For a moment, think about how you learn. Consider a time when you felt that you were learning, and also consider a time when you wanted to learn but found it very difficult. In either of those cases, was there something specific you did to try to make learning easier or more pleasant? If so, did it work? What was the outcome?

2. Have there been times when you were really excited about learning something new?

3. When was that? What was the topic? Was it an active (you actually had to do something physically for the project) or passive (you sat at a computer or in some other quiet place) project?

Learning Preferences:

How Do I Learn Best?

4

"What is important is to keep learning, to enjoy challenge, and to tolerate ambiguity. In the end, there are no certain answers."
— Martina Horner, President of Radcliffe College[1]

In college, learning is the overarching goal—but not everyone learns the same way. This chapter will explore how and why we learn as well as different types of learners and learning preferences. Then you will have a chance to analyze your own learning preferences and to learn about how they can be used to shape your study techniques.

4.1 How Do We Learn?

Historically, there have been many ways to think about learning, and two of them have taken the forefront. Once you have an understanding of these two perspectives, you will be able to think more clearly about how we learn. The first is known as the *behavioral perspective* and, as the name implies, it deals with behaviors or *things we do*. The second perspective is known as the *cognitive perspective*. Cognitive is just another way of saying "related to thinking." As you would expect, the cognitive perspective deals with *how and what we think*. These are not the only perspectives used to explore and study learning,[2] but they are two of the most well known and the only two we will discuss here.

Learning Involves Doing

The **behavioral perspective** is all about how we interact with and respond to the world around us. In particular, the behavioral perspective points out the simple fact that we are more likely to do something again if we are rewarded for doing it; on the other hand, if we are punished for doing something, we are less likely to do it again. This idea applies to more than just your study habits—it's something you may notice in many aspects of your life.

Applied to learning, the behavioral perspective tells us that the best way to encourage good study habits is to set up a system of rewards for doing productive things (like studying for a test, reading from a textbook, or doing extra practice problems for a class) and punishments for doing unproductive things (like failing to study or skipping a class without a good reason). A reward can be something small, like a tasty snack as a reward for finishing the day's study tasks, or something larger, like a special outing as a reward for getting a good grade on a test. By setting up a series of goals and rewards, you are making it more likely that you will do the things you need to do to succeed—even when the tasks themselves aren't something you enjoy.

Learning Involves Thinking

According to the **cognitive perspective,** learning is more than just a series of repeated and rewarded behaviors. In this perspective, learning is about what goes on in our minds. Just like in the behavioral perspective, the cognitive perspective begins with what we encounter in the world around us. But while the behavioral perspective focuses on how we react to the world (and how it, in turn, reacts to us), the cognitive perspective examines how we *think* about the world.

The cognitive perspective tells us that learning is about encountering new information and then processing it in our brains. There are many ways to do this. One example is memorization— where we repeat the new information over and over in the hopes that we'll remember it. While this is sometimes a part of learning, a more effective kind of processing involves connecting the new information to things that you already know. Yet another way to process information is to use a mnemonic. A mnemonic is like a trick to help you remember particular information. Piano students are often taught the phrase "Every Good Boy Deserves Fudge" to help them remember the sequence of notes (E, G, B, D, F) represented by the lines in the treble clef. Similarly, on the TV show *NCIS,* the character Abby sang the entire periodic table of elements to the tune of a well-known song. Setting the elements to music helped her remember them all.

However we process new information, the next step is to store it in our memories. Then, at a later time, when we need that information again, we remember it—or retrieve it from memory. Understanding the cognitive perspective can allow you to find more effective ways to process information than just repeating it in the hopes that you will memorize it. By using a mnemonic or connecting a new concept to one you already know, you can become a more effective learner.

Reading Comprehension Question 4.1 (Knowledge)

What's the biggest difference between the behavioral and cognitive perspectives?

a. The behavioral perspective deals with what we do; the cognitive perspective deals with what we think.

b. The behavioral perspective deals with how we learn; the cognitive perspective deals with why we learn.

c. The behavioral perspective deals with why we learn; the cognitive perspective deals with what we learn.

d. The behavioral perspective deals with what we know; the cognitive perspective deals with what we do.

4.2 Why Do We Learn?

Sometimes learning happens without much thought or effort. Things like walking and talking happen as a child develops; and although parents can help encourage these behaviors, it often seems like children are hardwired to learn them. This is not the case in college. In college, learning is something you must *choose* to do, and it won't happen without conscious effort on your part. So, regardless of how you learn, it is important to consider *why you learn*. What is your **motivation** for learning?

Motivation is a reason for doing something. Not every student has the same reason for going to college. Some may think it's the best way to get a good job. Some may want to enter into a specialized field that requires a particular degree. Some may have no motivation other than an interest in a certain subject, and still others may be doing it because they believe it's what's expected of them. Before you can succeed in college, it is important to understand what brought you there in the first place. What are your personal reasons for wanting to learn?

Even if you are highly motivated, it can be difficult to maintain your motivation over an academic program that lasts for years. That's why it's important to think ahead about how you will maintain your motivation throughout your college career. **Self-regulation**[2] is the way in which people attend to their own thoughts, feelings, and behaviors as they seek to accomplish a particular goal.

The first step in self-regulation is developing your own learning goals. Following the behavioral perspective, you should then figure out a way to reward yourself as you pursue these goals. This will help you stay motivated moving forward. The cognitive perspective has something to offer, as well: It's important to set aside time to think about how you are doing every so often as you move through college. You should consider whether you still feel motivated, whether you are getting closer to your goals, and whether your behavior is still helping you succeed. If you don't feel motivated, if you aren't reaching your goals, or if your behavior is no longer helpful, it's time to make a change.

It's also important to remember that **motivation** and **ability** are two very different things. One student may be very motivated to learn but, for some reason, finds it very difficult—his or her ability to learn is limited in some way. Another student may learn very easily—or have a high ability to learn—but because he or she is not motivated, that student might still wind up with a failing grade.

It's likely that you will encounter a situation in which you need to learn even when you aren't motivated to do so. In such a situation, you could turn again to the two perspectives we discussed above. Using the behavioral perspective, you might offer yourself a reward for learning, and thus create your own motivation. Alternatively, you may find that you truly are motivated and want to learn, but are having trouble anyway. In that case, you may turn to the cognitive perspective. Consider how you are approaching the information you've been asked to learn. Is there some way to make it easier to remember or understand? How does it relate to things you already know?

When it comes to learning, your behaviors, thoughts, and motivations must all align in order for you to be truly successful.

4.3 I've Learned Something—Now What?

In the past, you may have found that it was enough to simply remember what you've been taught. If you recently graduated from high school, you are probably used to learning facts and then recognizing them later (such as on a test), or perhaps practicing with flashcards or other study aides, and then repeating the information later (such as in a presentation). In college, you will likely find that this is no longer enough. You also need to be able to apply what you have learned. As a college student, you need to be able to take your skills and knowledge and apply them in new ways or to different situations.

For example, before nursing students ever touch a patient, they work in a nursing lab where they practice the skills they will need in the hospital. They learn how to give injections by practicing on a grapefruit or an orange. While this is good practice, giving an injection to a piece of fruit is very different from giving one to a living person! When it comes time to give an injection to an actual patient, they will be expected to **transfer** their skills from the lab (injecting fruit) to a new situation (the hospital) where they will need to use those skills in a new way (injecting a person).

Transfer involves prior learning and its effect on new learning. Without transfer, you would have to learn each new piece of information separately and it would have to be specific to a particular situation. Certainly, there are many differences between giving an injection to a piece of citrus and giving one to a living person; but, thanks to transfer, practicing on the former can teach you how to do the latter.

Now that we've given you a brief overview of how people learn, generally, it's time to turn to you as an individual. The following sections will cover learning preferences—the unique ways we each learn best.

4.4 Individual Learning Preferences

You might have already noticed that you tend to learn in certain ways no matter what class you are taking. In high school, you may have noticed that some of your teachers delivered material in a way that made it easy for you to learn and to remember, while in other classes the material seemed difficult to learn and to remember. This is because we each have our own unique way of receiving and organizing information, and faculty members also have their own unique ways of imparting their knowledge.

If your **learning preference** happens to match your professor's teaching style, you may find it easy to remember information from lectures and classes. If your learning preference doesn't match his or her teaching style, however, you may find yourself saying, "I just can't learn in this class; I must be bad at this subject," or "I just can't seem to understand what this professor is trying to teach me." Most students have had the uncomfortable experience of feeling that they "just can't learn" something that is important to them.

To maximize your success in college, it will help if you can identify your own personal learning preferences; then *you* can take specific actions that might help you to learn even when your preference and your professor's style do not match. Helping you to do this is the goal of this part of the chapter.

4.5 **Orientation to Learning**

The goal of this part of the chapter is to help you to become more aware of your personal learning preferences and to provide some tips for how you can learn best. Since college is a place where your primary activity will be learning, it is important for you to discover that you have unique preferences for how you learn. Up to this point, you may not have given this much thought. Consider the following: when you are presented with new information, what are the ways in which you are most comfortable taking it in, making sense of it, and understanding how it relates to the larger topic at hand?

There has been a great deal of research on the topic of learning. How people learn is of interest to educators of all levels, from kindergarten all the way to college at the postgraduate level. Richard Felder teaches engineering and has studied extensively the learning and teaching styles in engineering education.[3] His research provides great ideas for how students and teachers can work toward creating a better learning environment. In addition, he has developed a well-used measurement tool: the *Index of Learning Styles* (ILS).[3] We'll use this tool later in the chapter for determining your personal learning preference.

Earlier in this chapter we discussed learning perspectives. As you now learn about the preferences that you have for learning material, remember the perspectives that were discussed and think about how different learning preferences and techniques for studying might reflect different perspectives of learning.

If we could discover how each person learns best and then tailor information to meet that person's individual learning needs, school would be a much more user-friendly place. But that is a tall order. In fact, it would be impossible to identify just one specific learning preference that a person uses all of the time because we often change our learning preferences to fit a particular situation. You have probably done this throughout your school career even if you weren't aware of doing so. However, there are patterns that can be measured in people's learning preferences, and your preferences will help to guide you in your study habits throughout college and life.

As illustrated in Figure 4.1, a person's **orientation to learning** (or the overall way that a person approaches learning) includes three parts: 1) level of intellectual development, 2) approach to learning, and 3) personal learning preferences. We will explore learning preferences in this chapter, and you will probably recognize yourself in some of them. You will learn how to measure your own personal learning preferences and to think about study strategies that work best with your preferences.

Want to learn more? Try these resources.

If you want to know more about the research and studies regarding learning preferences, about how students learn, and about how faculty try to teach to accommodate student learning, you can access the following websites of interest:

Richard Felder's website:
http://bvtlab.com/qU9Yc

Felder and Silverman (1988):
http://bvtlab.com/6Ngk7

Felder and Brent (2005):
http://bvtlab.com/fTuW9

Figure 4.1

Each Person Has Their Own Individual Orientation to Learning

Reading Comprehension Question 4.2 (Literal Comprehension)

Which of the following groups make up an individual's orientation to learning?

a. Each student's approach to studying, intellectual development, and learning preferences

b. Each student's time spent studying, goals, and courses and outlines for each course

c. Each student's knowledge of a subject, past experience in class, and professors' attitudes

d. None of the above

Reading Comprehension Question 4.3 (Inferential Comprehension)

What is the main idea of the paragraphs discussing approaches to learning and Figure 4.1?

a. Each student has an individual approach to learning.

b. Each professor can teach his or her students how to learn.

c. Each student basically uses a surface approach to learning.

d. Each student has an in-depth approach to learning.

4.6 **Learning Preferences and Strategies**

Students preferentially take in and process information in different ways: by seeing and hearing, by reflecting and acting, by reasoning logically and intuitively, by analyzing and visualizing, and by progressing steadily and in fits and starts. Teaching methods also vary. Some professors lecture, while others demonstrate or lead students to self-discovery; some focus on principles and others, on applications; some emphasize memory and others, understanding.[4] Each of your professors has developed course materials and teaching strategies based on various perspectives of learning that are familiar to them and that they are comfortable with. You are now familiar with two major learning perspectives: cognitive and behavioral. Try to determine whether or not your professors are using one of these two major perspectives to develop their course materials.

Your success in college will depend on your awareness of your own learning approaches, your knowledge of which approaches you tend to use most often, and your ability to identify when your approach does not match the demands of a course. Exercising flexibility in your approach to match the demands of different courses will help you be more successful.

You probably recognize that there are certain things you do when you study that help you to learn. Have you ever noticed that you study differently when you are trying to learn math compared to English or perhaps psychology? Felder has published a lot of research in the area of learning preferences.[3–5] Although there are other theories and ideas about how people learn, for this chapter, we'll focus on the Felder-Silverman model.

The **Felder-Silverman model**[3] suggests that there are eight types of learners (or eight learning preferences). They are **1) active learners, 2) reflective learners, 3) sensing learners, 4) intuitive learners, 5) visual learners, 6) verbal learners, 7) global learners, and 8) sequential learners.** Table 4.1 describes the different types of learners and offers some tips for studying based on learning preference. As you read the table, keep in mind that each person does not have only one learning preference. In fact most of us carry the potential for learning in all the ways that are described in Table 4.1. We tend to use certain types of learning preferences based on the situation in which we find ourselves. You are not locked into a certain learning preference; rather, you can learn to exercise different preferences in different circumstances. Learning preferences are not traits that we cannot change (such as our age or genetic sex); instead, they are fluid characteristics that we can alter if we so desire.

Table 4.1

Learning Preference Descriptions and Tips for Studying*

Learning Style Preference	Description of Learners	Tips for Studying
Active Learners	• Learn by doing something active with the information—role-playing situations, moving, doing, touching, manipulating, using tools—mostly hands-on techniques • Enjoy working in groups • Are able to master skills through practice and imitation	• Study in a group and take turns with explaining concepts to each other, guessing what will be on the next test, and asking each other questions. • Engage in a hands-on activity and try to find ways to do something active with the information you are learning. • Sit near the front of the classroom in order to avoid becoming distracted during lectures.
Reflective Learners	• Learn by thinking about the information—pondering it • Enjoy working alone • Are typically intrapersonal, logical, mathematical learners	• Stop to review what you've read and think of possible questions while reading. • Write short summaries of readings in your own words.
Sensing Learners	• Like to learn facts • Are good with details • Are good at memorization	• Ask your professor for examples of concepts and procedures in class. • Try to find specific examples of concepts in your course textbook or other references.
Intuitive Learners	• Like to independently discover ideas • Like innovation and surprise • Are good at grasping new concepts • Learn quickly and are innovative	• Be aware that you may be bored in a class that uses detailed materials that need to be memorized. • Ask the instructor for interpretations or theories that link these materials together.
Verbal Learners	• Do better with words (i.e., verbal—spoken or discussed—directions or information) and audio books • Tend to memorize well, including names • Enjoy speaking with others • Benefit from study groups	• Write the outline of your course material and transcribe notes from class in your own words. • Work with another person who is in the class and explain material to each other verbally. • Participate in a study group or study with a study partner. • Use rhymes to recall dates, names, facts, etc.

Learning Style Preference	Description of Learners	Tips for Studying
Visual Learners	• Relate best to information that is written, such as graphs, maps, diagrams, charts, highlighted notes, flashcards, etc. • Have difficulty following lectures that are long • Are often good writers, scoring high on written assignments • Can remember precisely where information is located on a page	• Try to find visual materials that represent course material. • Ask your instructor if there are any videotapes or DVDs of course material. • Develop a map of the concepts that you are learning—including boxes, circles, lines, arrows, and flow charts between concepts to show connections
Global Learners	• Might have trouble with content details until the "bigger picture" is understood • Tend to learn material in large jumps—taking in material almost randomly without seeing connections—and then suddenly "getting it"	• Skim through a chapter in the textbook to get the overall view before beginning to study details. • Try to relate the subject to things you already know. • Don't skip the introduction or summary. You will benefit from reading these before you read the actual book.
Sequential Learners	• Might not completely understand the entire topic, but can do something with it (like pass a test or solve a problem) • Tend to plan ahead • Tend to respond to problems with logic first instead of emotions	• Take time to make an outline of the course concepts in logical order when you study. • Ask for clear rules; without them you feel lost. • Group your information into categories. • Sit at the front of class to avoid distractions.

*Table adapted from Felder, R. M., and Soloman, B. A. *Learning Styles and Strategies*. A four-page handout briefly explaining the learning preferences obtained using the *Index of Learning Styles*. Used with permission, and available at: **http://bvtlab.com/B6J99**

_____. *Understanding Your Learning Styles*. Available at: http://bvtlab.com/5Gg5g; Copyright 2008

Website: http://www.pssc.ttu.edu/techhort/lasrvy/a_r.htm (http://bvtlab.com/6Qb76)

Website: http://homeworktips.about.com/od/homeworkhelp/a/global.htm (http://bvtlab.com/74K5f)

Think About This

Try to recall two classes in which you used totally different study strategies. Think about the topic that you were learning in each class (for example, a science class versus a history class). Think about why you chose one particular study strategy for one of the courses but a different study strategy for the other course.

Do you think the type of study activities that helped you most varied depending on the type of course? Why or why not?

_____

_____

_____

_____

_____

_____

_____

_____

_____

_____

_____

_____

_____

_____

_____

_____

_____

_____

_____

_____

_____

_____

_____

_____

_____

4.7 Discovering Your Own Learning Preferences

Richard M. Felder and Barbara A. Soloman of North Carolina State University have developed an *Index of Learning Styles*[4] that can be used to assess preferences on four dimensions (**active/ reflective, sensing/intuitive, visual/verbal, and sequential/global**) of the Felder-Silverman model.[3-5] The index consists of forty-four simple questions that you can answer for yourself online. Then, when you submit your answers, the computer will display a results page that shows to what degree you prefer each dimension. In Assignment 4.1, you will be instructed to browse the ILS webpage, to complete the index, and to print your results. The following pages in this section will explain how to interpret your results page. Before taking the ILS, you should take into account two important points:

1. The ILS results are only one measure of your learning preferences and thus should never be over-interpreted. There are times when you may not agree with the ILS interpretation of your preferences. In those cases, you should always trust your own judgment over the results you get with the ILS.

2. Your learning preference profile gives you a measure of potential strengths as well as habits that might cause you problems in academic settings. The profile does not reflect your ability or inability to be successful in a particular subject, discipline, or profession. Labeling students in this way is misleading—and to do so could be destructive if the label is used as justification for a major shift in your career goals or if faculty were to use the label to change curriculum.

Additional information about learning preferences and the Felder-Silverman model may be found at the *Index of Learning Styles* (ILS) webpage: http://bvtlab.com/56c3w. Much of the information in this chapter has been adapted from resources on that webpage.

Think About This

Using Table 4.1, choose at least six tips for studying and discuss which of the major learning perspectives (behavioral or cognitive) is best reflected in each. Explain why you believe the study tip reflects the perspectives you chose.

_____

_____

_____

_____

_____

_____

_____

_____

_____

_____

_____

_____

_____

_____

_____

_____

_____

_____

_____

_____

_____

_____

_____

_____

_____

_____

_____

_____

_____

_____

4.8 Practice What You Have Learned

Now that you have read about various learning styles and how they compare to each other, you should complete Assignment 4.1: Learning Preference Assessment. Step-by-step instructions for the assignment are given at the end of this chapter. As a part of the assignment, you will complete your own ILS survey.

In order to help you understand how to interpret your own ILS, let's look at the example provided in Figure 4.2. The scores for the example student are indicated by an "X" over the number.

Figure 4.2

Index of Learning Styles Results (NC State University)

Index of Learning Styles												
Results for: Example Student												
ACT								X				REF
11	9	7	5	3	1	1	3	5	7	9	11	
SEN										X		INT
11	9	7	5	3	1	1	3	5	7	9	11	
VIS			X									VRB
11	9	7	5	3	1	1	3	5	7	9	11	
SEQ								X				GLO
11	9	7	5	3	1	1	3	5	7	9	11	

- If your score on a scale is 1–3, you are fairly well balanced on the two dimensions of that scale.
- If your score on a scale is 5–7, you have a moderate preference for one dimension of the scale and will learn more easily in a teaching environment that favors that dimension.
- If your score on a scale is 9–11, you have a very strong preference for one dimension of the scale. You may have real difficulty learning in an environment that does not support that preference.

Analyzing Your ILS Results

Let's look at the results for the "example student" in Figure 4.2. How would he or she interpret the results? What are this student's learning preferences? Well, if we look at the first scale, "ACT" versus "REF," we see that the scale goes from 1 in the center to 11 at each of the end-points, "Active" and "Reflective." The student scored a 5 on the reflective side of this scale, which translates to a moderate preference for reflective learning. This means that such a student typically learns more easily in a teaching environment that favors reflective learning.

Following that example, we can see that the student scored an 11 on the "INT" side of "SEN" versus "INT" (Sensing … Intuitive), meaning he or she has a very strong preference for intuitive learning compared to sensory learning. Because the preference is so strong here, the student might have real problems learning in an environment that doesn't support intuitive learning. (Hmm … Maybe this helps explain my own difficulty in learning chemistry?) Remember that sensing learners tend to focus on sights and physical sensations—and that they tend to be concrete, practical, methodical, and oriented toward facts and hands-on procedures.[5] Intuitive learners learn better in courses that are abstract and include theories and models. (In fact, I do love—and learn much more easily in—courses that deal with theory and thinking compared to hands-on lab courses.)

The sample student scored a 5 on the visual end of the "VIS" versus "VRB" (Visual … Verbal) scale. He or she has a moderate preference for visual learning and would learn better when looking at charts, graphs, pictures, and diagrams—and not so well with spoken explanations.

On the "SEQ" (Sequential) versus "GLO" (Global) scale, the example student's score of 7 on the "GLO" end would indicate a moderate preference for global learning. He or she would tend to learn better when learning in a systems-oriented manner and would tend to look at the big picture before settling down to understanding the details of a situation or topic.

Sometimes your ILS results will mirror your own understanding of how you learn. But if you think you are a sensory learner, and the ILS scores you as a 9 on the "INT" side of the scale, not to worry. Don't discount your own judgment of your learning preferences—that is, trust your gut over the test. You may want to consider retaking the test, as well, to see if your scores change at a later date (because learning preferences can change over time).

Also remember that the ability to shift your learning preferences to match the style in which the new information is presented is a mark of intelligence and is something that you want to work on throughout your college career. You'll be more successful if you can switch between learning preferences in order to match each professor's teaching style.

Finally, remember that learning preferences are not written in stone—and should never be used to determine whether or not you can accomplish something. Even if you are not sensory, visual, or active in your learning, for example, you can still be an engineer, scientist, or nurse. And unfortunately, if your preferred learning style does not match the professor's teaching style (or the subject matter's particular presentation), that still does not excuse getting a D on the exam!

Want to learn more? Try these resources.

For more information about the learning styles model and implications of learning styles for instructors and students, visit:
http://bvtlab.com/Fr6mM

The *Index of Learning Styles* is a self-scoring questionnaire for assessing preferences on four dimensions of the Felder-Silverman model.
http://bvtlab.com/66467

Descriptions of Learning Styles is a four-page handout that briefly explains the learning style preferences obtained using the *Index of Learning Styles*.
http://bvtlab.com/6q6a9

The *Index of Learning Styles* (ILS) is not meant for use as a guide for curriculum change or in determining career choices, and neither of these would be appropriate uses of the tool to do so.[3–5] Instead, it is meant as a guide to understanding how *you* learn best—or within which types of learning environments you learn more easily and which are more difficult for you. Knowing your own personal learning preferences helps you to understand when and where you might need to do extra work or spend extra time in order to take in and understand new materials. Use the ILS throughout your college career to check in with your own understanding of how you learn best; your results will probably change as you grow both intellectually and conceptually.

Reading Comprehension Question 4.4 (Analysis)

What is the main purpose for this chapter on learning?

a. To provide students with a way to change how they learn and their learning preference

b. To make students aware of different theories on learning and their own individual learning preferences so they can use that knowledge for maximum success

c. To make the professor use specific techniques to help students learn in a deeper way

d. To provide students with information about college classes

4.9 Summary

In this chapter you learned about two major perspectives for understanding learning (behavioral and cognitive), and other factors that affect learning (memory, motivation, transfer, and self-regulation). Then you studied different learning preferences, as well as strategies for being successful with different learning preferences. In addition you took a test (the *Index of Learning Styles*) to determine your own individual learning preferences and interpreted the results. You also thought about some strategies for being successful in your coursework. The more you know about your own learning preferences and how to adapt in various situations, the more successful you will be in college. It may be interesting for you to keep track of your learning preference, study strategies, and intellectual development as you go through college to see how much you are changing and growing.

Name: _____

Study Guide | Goal 1

The student will be able to discuss two major perspectives of learning: behavioral and cognitive.

Questions	Answers & Notes

Name: _____

Study Guide | Goal 2

The student will be able to describe at least two additional factors that affect the way we learn.

Questions	Answers & Notes

Name: _____

Study Guide | Goal 3

The student will be able to describe eight types of learners and learning preferences.

Questions	Answers & Notes

Name: _____

Study Guide | Goal 4

The student will be able to analyze his or her own personal learning preferences using the *Index of Learning Styles* (ILS).

Questions	Answers & Notes

Name: _____

Study Guide | Goal 5

The student will be able to list at least two study strategies that will help him or her learn more effectively based on his or her learning preferences.

Questions	Answers & Notes

Study Guide | Preparing for Class

Use this page to record questions or insights to discuss in class.

Name: _____

Review Questions 4.1

Instructions

Following are five true-false statements taken from the information in this chapter. First, try to answer them without looking back at the chapter. Then review the chapter to see how well you did.

Question & Answer	Rationale
Circle true or false for each of the following statements.	Write an explanation stating why each statement is true or false.
1. An individual's orientation to learning can be summed up by two components: learning preferences and chronological age. True or False	Your Rationale:
2. Study techniques that come from the behavioral perspective lead to higher grades than study techniques that come from the cognitive perspective. True or False	Your Rationale:
3. The more you know about your own learning preferences and how to adapt in various situations, the more successful you will be in college. True or False	Your Rationale:
4. The ILS measures a person's learning preferences and can tell you for which profession you are best suited. True or False	Your Rationale:
5. Each person uses one or two learning preferences throughout life and does not change these preferences. True or False	Your Rationale:

Name: _____

Assignment 4.1

Learning Preference Assessment

Goal

This assessment will help you to figure out which learning preferences work best for you. Then you can use the information in this chapter to plan some study strategies that will improve the effectiveness of your studying.

Follow These Steps

Step 1:   Complete the *Index of Learning Styles* (ILS) survey at the following website: http://bvtlab.com/8W873

After you finish the survey, the website will show you your results. They will look similar to the ones depicted in Figure 4.2.

Step 2:   Print your results and save them.

Step 3:   Look at your results page to determine which learning preferences best fit you. Use your results to answer the questions on the form on the following page.

The results page presents a numbered line with a code for a different learning preference on each end. For example, "ACT" is the code for the active learning preference and "REF" is the code for the reflective learning preference. There will be an X over one of the numbers on the number line. The X will be closer to one of the learning preference codes than it is to the other. It will be closer to the preference that you are most comfortable using based on the answers you gave for the ILS survey questions. The number score indicates how strongly you prefer that particular preference compared to the preference on the opposite side of the number line.

Step 3 *(cont.)*:   We can use Figure 4.2 in this chapter as an example. In the figure, the X is placed over the number 5 that is closer to "REF" (Reflective). This means that the person who completed the survey has a stronger preference for the reflective learning preference ("REF") than for the active learning preference ("ACT"). Since the score is 5, we infer that this person has a moderate preference for the reflective preference of learning. A lower score (such as 1 or 3) would suggest a mild preference. A score of 9–11 would indicate a strong preference.

Step 4:   A very important question on the form is "Given your preferences, what are some specific study strategies that you can use?" Review the information in this chapter, and think of some specific study strategies that you could use that match your particular learning preferences. Write these strategies down, and consider adding them to your study regimen.

Notes

Index of Learning Styles: My Results and Analysis

1. Do you consider yourself to be more of an active learner or a reflective learner?

   A. Based on your results' page, which learning preference do you prefer: active ("ACT") or reflective ("REF")? _____

   B. What was your numeric score? _____

   C. Based on your score, how strongly do you prefer this particular learning preference? _____

   D. Given that you are more (circle one → active / reflective), what are some specific study strategies that you could use? _____ _____

2. Do you consider yourself to be more of a sensory learner or an intuitive learner?

   A. Based on your results page, which learning preference do you prefer: sensory ("SEN") or intuitive ("INT")? _____

   B. What was your numeric score? _____

   C. Based on your score, how strongly do you prefer this particular learning preference? _____

   D. Given that you are more (circle one → sensory / intuitive), what are some specific study strategies that you could use? _____ _____

3. Do you consider yourself to be more of a visual learner or a verbal learner?

   A. Based on your results' page, which learning preference do you prefer: visual ("VIS") or verbal ("VRB")? _____

   B. What was your numeric score? _____

   C. Based on your score, how strongly do you prefer this particular learning preference? _____

   D. Given that you are more (circle one → visual / verbal), what are some specific study strategies that you could use? _____ _____

4. Do you consider yourself to be more of a sequential learner or a global learner?

   A. Based on your results' page, which learning preference do you prefer: sequential ("SEQ") or global ("GLO")? _____

   B. What was your numeric score? _____

   C. Based on your score, how strongly do you prefer this particular learning preference? _____

   D. Given that you are more (circle one → sequential / global), what are some specific study strategies that you could use? _____ _____

Chapter Roadmap

Introduction

In this chapter you will learn how to create a study plan for each course that you are taking this semester. In order to create a written study plan, you will need to use a copy of the syllabus for each class you are taking along with the calendar and planning tools found in this chapter.

This chapter roadmap page presents the formal learning goals for this chapter and a check list that you should follow as you read and study the chapter.

Student Learning Goals

After completing this chapter you should be able to do the following:

1. List six behaviors that rob you of time for effective study and explain how each behavior could prevent the student from having a successful study regimen.

2. Describe and create an effective study plan using a semester (or other academic term) calendar, a weekly schedule, and a checklist for individual study sessions.

3. List and describe the components of the Alphabet Approach to time management.

Chapter Checklist

You will benefit most if you complete the activities in the order that they are listed.

❑ **Target Date/Deadline:** _____
Complete Critical Thinking Activity 5.1.

❑ **Target Date/Deadline:** _____
Convert the student learning goals to questions that you can answer as you read the chapter. Write your questions on the study guide pages near the end of this chapter.

❑ **Target Date/Deadline:** _____
Read the chapter.

❑ **Target Date/Deadline:** _____
Try to answer the reading comprehension questions as you come to them in the chapter. Check each answer by comparing it to the list of correct answers in the back of the book. If any answer was not correct, then review the passages preceding the question to see why you missed the question.

❑ **Target Date/Deadline:** _____
Answer the student learning goal questions you created. These answered questions will be your study guide.

❑ **Target Date/Deadline:** _____
Write down any questions, insights, or comments that you have as you read so that you can bring them up in class (if applicable).

❑ **Target Date/Deadline:** _____
Complete Review Questions 5.1.

❑ **Target Date/Deadline:** _____
Complete Assignment 5.1 (Mark Your Monthly Calendar).

❑ **Target Date/Deadline:** _____
Complete Assignment 5.2 (Develop Study Plans for Courses).

❑ **Target Date/Deadline:** _____
Complete Assignment 5.3 (Weekly Appointment Sheet).

❑ **Target Date/Deadline:** _____
Complete Assignment 5.4 (Study Session Tickets).

❑ **Target Date/Deadline:** _____
Review what you have learned from this chapter.

Critical Thinking Activity 5.1

"Failures don't plan to fail; they fail to plan."

—Harvey MacKay[1]

Use the space provided on this page to write your thoughts about this Harvey MacKay quote. What does the quote mean? Give an example to explain the quote. How does the quote apply to success in college?

_____

_____

_____

_____

_____

_____

_____

_____

_____

_____

_____

_____

_____

_____

_____

_____

_____

_____

_____

_____

_____

_____

_____

_____

_____

_____

_____

_____

Getting Organized:

Plan Your Work and Then Work Your Plan

5

"Time is free, but it's priceless. You can't own it, but you can use it. You can't keep it, but you can spend it. Once you've lost it, you can never get it back."
— Harvey MacKay[1]

"I gotta work out. I keep saying it all the time. I keep saying I gotta start working out. It's been about two months since I've worked out. And I just don't have the time. Which uh ... is odd. Because I have the time to go out to dinner. And uh ... and watch TV. And get a bone density test. And uh ... try to figure out what my phone number spells in words ..."
— Ellen DeGeneres[2]

Getting organized when you enter college is one of the most important things you can do to ensure your success. In college, you will quickly find that time is a valuable commodity—and you need to use it wisely. It is often the case that college professors use the first class to discuss their expectations for the course. They also provide a written document, the syllabus, that details these expectations. Sometimes, if the first day of class is taken up by introductions and a discussion of expectations alone, new students get the incorrect idea that they don't have to do anything until the next class. Nothing is further from the truth, however. What you need to do is take the information that the professor has given you and use it to plan how you will approach the course for the entire semester. Your plan should include basic information, such as the dates of exams, and detailed information, like descriptions of the expected content on exams and the nature of other assignments (e.g., papers or presentations). In this chapter, you will learn how to deal with time constraints and how to create an effective study plan for a college course.

One of the differences between high school and college (Chapter 1) was time management. In high school, it's likely that your teachers and parents constantly reminded you of timelines and due dates on assignments. In contrast, as a college student it is your responsibility to set your own schedule and manage your time. The successful student has a plan for how he or she will fit studying into a daily schedule that is already full of responsibilities. To be successful as a student, you will need to purposefully plan time for studying, rather than thinking you can just "fit it in" as you go along. The challenges of gaining an education demand that you value your time highly—and the same goes for those whom you love. Going to college is a major life decision; one that should be made with an understanding that you must make space in your life for school. It is not an "add-on" that you can just plunk into your schedule for a few hours a week, hoping you will "get through it." To be successful, you will need to treat school as the serious obligation that it is; one that requires time, money, and other important resources. Having said that, college is also an exciting and challenging time during which you will grow and learn in amazing ways.

This chapter is about time management specifically as it relates to the needs of college students. First, you will learn about time management in general, including some tips on balancing your time. Then you will learn, step-by-step, how to develop your own successful study plan. Also in this chapter, you will learn how to use your syllabus and a calendar to design a study regimen that will enable you to learn what you need by the deadlines that you have been given.

5.1 Time Management: A Myth

In reality, there is no such thing as time management. Time itself cannot be manipulated or controlled (outside of science fiction). No matter how hard you try, you cannot add a single second to the day. *It is not time that can be managed, but rather how one uses time that can be controlled.* How efficiently do you use time? Knowing how to use your time well is vital when it comes to success in college. In college, you will probably spend around fifteen hours a week in classes; but much more time will be needed to read, study, think, and learn everything that you need to be successful in those classes. It takes time to be successful in college. There simply is no shortcut.

Reading Comprehension Question 5.1 (Knowledge)

Which of the following is true of time management?
a. You can manipulate the time you have for studying.
b. You can't manage your time, but you can control how you use it.
c. You will find that time management is usually not helpful in college.
d. You will discover that time itself can actually be controlled.

Time Pirates

Pirates are thieves who roam the seas to rob unsuspecting mariners of their treasures. When you were in high school, you might have noticed that you were—and perhaps still are—susceptible to certain behaviors and other factors that robbed you of time. You may be unaware of other factors or behaviors that nevertheless have the same effect. The roll call of these time pirates includes procrastination, distractions, use of cell phones, use of excessive alcohol or drugs, use of shortcuts when studying, and feeling that you must be nice to all at the expense of your own top priorities. Some of these pirates even come disguised as time savers. In truth, these pirates are an even bigger problem in college because they are compounded by the stress of being a first-time college student. So it is more important than ever to recognize them, get the jump on them, and take measures to prevent them.

Procrastination is when you put off doing something until a later date or time. Usually people use procrastination because they really just don't want to do that particular task—maybe because it's hard or boring. They let themselves off the hook mentally by thinking, "I can do it later." One problem with this behavior is that sometimes "later" never comes and the task never gets done. Another problem is that sometimes the task gets done, but it gets done poorly because it was put off until the last minute. For example, if you wait until the last few days before a paper is due to begin writing the paper, you will forfeit the opportunity for revision; thus, the quality of your work will suffer. The end result is a lower grade. Finally, procrastination sometimes has the negative effect of making you more stressed and making you feel guilty. Therefore, procrastination is a time pirate because it steals the time that you needed to produce quality work and feel good about it. Most of us have been robbed by procrastination at one time or another—just don't let it steal your college success.

Distractions can take the form of environmental factors that keep you from doing what you need to do, such as a roommate's loud music or the neighbor's barking dog. In such cases, you may need to change your environment or find a better place or time to study. Other lower priority tasks, such as doing laundry, can also be a distraction from studying. This is why it is important to include the basics of daily living in your time management plan. If you know that you have a special time set aside for laundry and a different time set aside for studying, then you don't have to deal with the psychological stress of worrying that perhaps you should be studying while you are doing laundry and vice versa.

In recent decades, a new kind of distraction has become common: technology, including social networking sites. The Internet can suck your time up quickly and you may not even realize it. Be sure to keep an eye on the time you spend online doing frivolous activities that will not further your college goals. It may be helpful for you to plan a specific time to use the Internet to check email and Twitter®, Instagram®, or Facebook®, plan the amount of time you will spend, and stick to that schedule. The **cell phone** is another potential technological distraction. For some students, the phone becomes a proverbial "ball and chain" because anticipating the next text message prevents them from paying attention in class or fully concentrating when they study. The cell phone does not steal your study time—it kills your study time (by rendering it ineffective) and in so doing kills your grades, making it the worst type of time pirate.

Many students incorrectly assume that their multitasking skills will enable them to keep up with text messages on their phone while listening to a college lecture. That is a myth. In reality, if you are texting (or reading a text) during a class session, you will not gain the full benefit of that lecture or discussion—and if you are called on, you will likely appear dumbfounded and out of it because you haven't really kept up with what was going on in class. You also distract other classmates from paying attention to the lecture if you are playing with your phone during class. If you can't resist playing with your phone, then it would be better for you to turn it off and put it away during class or study sessions. Don't let the cell phone steal your success.

I often recommend that my students take a few minutes before each of their classes to use their cell phones (perhaps to check email, Facebook, Twitter, or some other social account, and to send any urgent messages). Then put the phone away for the entire duration of class and check the phone again as soon as class is over. Even if you have classes back to back, you usually have time to check your phone if it's truly important. Since most college classes last only about an hour, the check-before-and-after system works pretty well for most students.

Another time pirate that kills your grades is a **belief in shortcuts for studying**. You will not perform well on college-level exams if you employ a shallow learning approach (e.g., trying to memorize all of the bolded words in the textbook rather than building an understanding of the concepts that are presented) because you think that is a way to study faster. Such so-called shortcuts may save you time, but they will kill your grades because a meaningful percentage of a college-level exams will extend beyond merely defining terms—instead requiring you to understand and apply concepts.

One of the most common misconceptions, which many students perceive as a shortcut, is the idea that you can cram for an exam the night before. "Cramming" is the practice of not reading or studying anything for weeks and then trying to do it all the night before the exam. If it is the night before an exam and you haven't studied for a while, then cramming may be your one and only option. But if, long before the exam date, you think to yourself: "I don't need to study every night because I will just cram before the test instead (as a shortcut)," then you have incorrectly assumed that cramming will be enough to make you successful. The truth is that you will earn higher grades and find college much more pleasant (and less stressful) if you study a little each day rather than counting on cramming to save the day. So plan out your study time at the beginning of the semester and commit to your plan, and you will have much greater success.

Aside from the health dangers associated with **excessive drinking and drug use**, any time you spend in a compromised mental state due to the abuse of any substance is definitely not time that can be used to study effectively. Therefore, when your drinking or drug use extends into the time that you have reserved for studying—or if its aftereffects (i.e., a hangover) compromise your study time—you have been robbed by a time pirate. Later in the book you will find information on what to do if you feel your drinking or drug use is getting out of control. Help is available to you on your campus, and you should make use of it if you ever begin to think you might need it.

Finally, **trying to be nice at the expense of your top priorities** can cause you to use your time poorly. Being successful means that you will have to say "no" on occasion to invitations, opportunities, or pleas that take you away from your study schedule. The desires of others, when put above your own needs, can steal your study time. Just say "no" if you know that saying "yes" will prevent you from necessary studying.

How Much Time Do I Have, Anyway?

In order to "manage" your time, you must have an idea of how much time you have available to manage. The first step in time management is to assess your own, unique, personal schedule. You can do this by estimating the time you spend on certain activities; or if you are unsure, you can write down when, and for how long, you do various things over the course of a week to see where your time goes. It may be helpful for you to keep a log for your first few weeks of college. Keeping a log is much more accurate than trying to "guesstimate" the time you spend. Although keeping a log requires some effort, you will find that time spent analyzing your schedule can be worth its weight in gold.

Reading Comprehension Question 5.2 (Literal Comprehension)

Which of the following are time pirates in college?

a. Procrastination
b. Social media
c. Use of cell phones
d. Drinking excessively
e. All of the above

How Much Time Do I Have for Studying?

With regard to success in college, the pertinent question will be "How much time do I have for studying?" As part of the study plan described in this chapter, you will use a weekly planner to map out when you will be in classes, at work, and fulfilling other obligations. Then you can look at the remaining blank time slots to decide when you will study for each of your classes. This simple procedure will give you an idea of how many hours you have left for studying and when those hours are during the day or week. So how do you become more efficient? How can you use the time that you have to maximize your success? This is where a well-designed study plan helps you succeed.

Plan Your Work, Then Work Your Plan!

Effective time management involves getting organized, setting goals, understanding what is required to achieve your goals, establishing priorities, planning activities, avoiding distractions, staying on track, maintaining balance, and following through with your plan. It is as simple as this: you must plan your work and then work your plan.

Many students know how to get organized but never make the effort to do it. Just do it. There are many books, tapes, videos, and websites that detail various organizational approaches. You might like one type of plan more than another. However, for the purpose of this book, a simple, specific, and detailed plan that targets your needs as a college student will be outlined.

5.2 The Study Plan

Every student needs to have some sort of planner—whether it is a paper-and-pencil planner, an online planner, or some other sort of electronic planner. A planner should include a calendar and should allow you to keep track of meetings, events, and commitments; to schedule tasks and activities that support your goals; and to flag items for priority. This chapter will discuss how to use a planner, how to develop a plan for studying, and how to break down your study plan into manageable parts.

If you don't use a planner already, it would be a good idea to get one that you like. Paper-and-pencil planners are usually for a one-year period and are divided into either months or weeks. You can even get planners specifically for the academic year, which are sometimes helpful in college; these are most readily available at your college bookstore. It would be preferable to get a planner that has each week outlined with hours for each day. That way you can write out a detailed schedule including specific times for each activity.

This chapter will describe the steps you can follow to create your study plan using a paper calendar or planner to illustrate the process. Even if you prefer to use an electronic planner instead of a paper calendar, you should still find it easy to apply ideas from this chapter. However, you will probably need to use paper worksheets or paper calendar pages to figure out the details of your own schedule before you record it electronically.

Paper calendar booklets are available at very low cost. A worksheet and some blank calendar template pages are provided at the end of this chapter along with the assignment pages. Make copies for yourself as needed. Always save one blank version of each template in this book for making future copies if the need arises.

You will need to design a study plan that is consistent with the academic term used at your college. An academic term is the period of time between the first day of classes and either the last day of classes or the end of final exams (which usually occur the week after the last day of classes). Many colleges operate on a semester system in which the college year includes two 15–16 week semesters (usually called fall semester and spring semester). There may also be opportunities to take classes during one or more shorter summer semesters. Other colleges use a quarter system in which there are four 10–11 week terms, called quarters, with short breaks in between. Still other colleges have scheduling arrangements different from the semester or the quarter systems. You should simply tailor your study plan to match whichever scheduling arrangement your college uses. For the sake of simplicity, throughout this book we will use the term *semester* to refer generically to the academic term. Keep in mind, however, that your study plans should be built around whatever system is used at your particular college.

Components of the Study Plan

It is a good idea to design a study plan with three levels using three tools:

1. A plan for the semester (using a monthly calendar)

2. A plan for each week (using a week-at-a-glance appointment page)

3. A plan for each study session (using a study session ticket, discussed below)

Once you have figured out an overall plan of action (which will be described in the next few pages), you should reserve a few minutes every week to review your progress within your plan and to make adjustments.

Your plan needs to be *written* (not just remembered in your head), *specific,* and *detailed.* Then you can look at it, think about it, follow it, make adjustments to it (by rescheduling tasks anytime you see that you have failed to follow it), and use it as a guide to help you keep your priorities straight. Remember, a good study plan must include not only *when* and *how long* you plan to study but also *exactly what study activities you will do* during the scheduled study time. Table 5.1 details each part of the study plan.

Table 5.1

Study Tools		
The Tool	**What to Organize**	**What to Write Down**
Semester Calendar (Use the appropriate weeks on a monthly calendar.)	**Due Dates** Make a note of when things are due and any college-related deadlines that affect you.	Due dates for all assignments Dates of exams College deadlines Relevant college events
Weekly Appointment Page	**When Class Meets, When You Will Study,** and **For How Long**	**Separately** for each course you will write the following: • When class meets • Exactly what times during the week you will study for the class
Study Session Ticket	**What You Will Do** (when you study) and **How You Will Do It**	For each study session, write down things like the following: • What will you read? (include page numbers) • What will you write? • What other learning strategies will you use? • What learning activities will you do during that study session?

Creating Your Study Plan Tools

Now, let's go through each of the components of the study plan outlined in Table 5.1. The following text, together with Assignments 5.1, 5.2, and 5.3 (found at the end of this chapter), will guide you as you create your own personal study plan tools.

Tool 1: The Monthly Calendar

Start with the big picture. For this you will need a monthly calendar or a semester-at-a-glance calendar. These two options are illustrated in Figure 5.1.

Some students like to use a calendar that has all of the dates for the entire semester on a single page. A semester-at-a-glance calendar page can help you to get a good feel for how the deadlines and exams are spaced out over the term. Some colleges provide copies through a student resources center or on the college website, but if you prefer the semester-at-a-glance format and your college does not provide one, then you can always create your own. Otherwise, you can simply use any monthly calendar. The advantage of the monthly calendar is that you can record more information for any single date. A few blank calendar template pages are provided for you at the end of this chapter. You can make copies of those and use them to create your own calendars, if you wish.

Some students already keep all of their appointments and deadlines on a computer, an electronic tablet, or a cell phone. That is fine if it meets your academic needs. However, you may find that for your very first year of college, a paper-and-pencil calendar will be more helpful to you. Whichever type of calendar you choose, just be sure it is the one you are most comfortable with and that you will be able to use it to keep up with your studies.

Assignment 5.1 guides you through the steps of marking your monthly or semester calendar. Before you start, you will need to obtain a copy of the official college calendar (usually found on the college website) and a syllabus for each of your classes. Then you will be ready to copy all of the important events from each of these documents onto your semester or monthly calendar (see Figure 5.1). Some students find it helpful to use a different color to highlight the items associated with different classes. When you mark your calendar, remember to include the following items (when applicable):

- The dates for all of your quizzes or exams

- The due dates for all of your assignments (e.g., papers or projects)

- The dates for administrative deadlines (e.g., the last day to withdraw without academic penalty, the fee deadlines, the graduation application deadlines, and the date midterm grades will be posted)

- The dates and times of your final exams (some college finals may be given on a different day and time than your normal class session)

- The dates of campus events that you may wish to attend

Figure 5.1

Record Assignments and Deadlines on the Monthly Calendar

MONTH: *January*

	Monday	Tuesday	
	20	21	
		Sociology Exam 1	
		English paper due	

Week	Monday	Tuesday	
1	Jan 13 Classes Begin	Jan 14 Schedule Adjustment	
2	Jan 20 *MLK Holiday, College Closed*	Jan 21 *Sociology Exam 1* *English paper due*	
3	Jan 27	Jan 28	
	Feb 3	Feb 4	

Tool 2: The Weekly Appointment Calendar

The second tool you will need for your personal study plan is a weekly appointment calendar page. This is simply a page that allows you to block off appointments for different times during each day and to see the appointments for one entire week on a single page.

In order to create this tool, you will need some of the same materials that you used to mark your monthly calendar. These include a copy of the syllabus for each of your courses, a copy of each course schedule (usually found in the syllabus), and the dates of events that you wish to attend (such as club meetings).

You can use the weekly appointment page as part of your study plan by blocking off and labeling the times that you have classes and the times that you plan to study for each course. Class attendance and study time are the top priorities of successful college students. The idea is that you are making an appointment with yourself to attend class and to study because you expect to do those things at the same time every week during the semester. You should also follow this procedure for other aspects of your weekly routine that repeat. Assignment 5.2 provides a worksheet that will help you plan when you will study for each course. Assignment 5.3 will guide you in the actual process of creating a weekly appointment page. A blank weekly appointment page is included for you to copy and use. Since step-by-step instructions are given with the assignment pages, there is no need to repeat them here.

Take a look at your schedule, and decide when the best times would be to study for each class. When you block out a period of time on your appointment calendar for studying, don't just give it a generic label, such as "Study." Instead, label it very specifically, such as "Study Calculus" or "Study English Lit." You want to make sure that you plan enough study appointments to meet each course's study demands.

When planning how much study time to devote to a particular course, take into consideration what study activities are associated with that course and estimate how much time it will take you to complete those activities. (Some courses may require reading a book while others may require attempting to solve example problems.) *Remember: About two-thirds of the time you spend on studying and learning will be outside of class.* If you find that you need less time or more time for a particular course as the semester progresses, you can adjust your schedule for subsequent weeks. You should reserve a few minutes every week to review your progress regarding your plan and to make adjustments.

Once you have created one weekly appointment sheet that shows all of your regular commitments (including classes and study times), you can use it as a template that can be copied and filled in with the obligations particular to a given week. You should make enough copies of your template so that you have one for each of the weeks in the semester. Then, week by week, you can schedule other events for any of the times that are not already committed to class or studying.

Once you are finished with your weekly appointment calendar (Figure 5.2), your firm obligations will already be blocked off for each week and day; the remaining blank spaces now represent time slots that you have open for leisure activities or appointments that come up each week. If a major change occurs that alters your normal weekly schedule (such as getting a job in the middle of the semester), you will need to revise your master weekly schedule to reflect those changes.

Figure 5.2

Weekly Appointment Calendar

What if something important comes up that you need to do during a time slot that you had reserved for studying? You may need to cancel your study appointment to attend to something urgent or important. However, you should never cancel study time unless you reschedule it. Why? Because if you have done a good job of estimating the study demands of a particular course, reducing the time that you had planned may keep you from earning a good grade.

For example, suppose Penny had scheduled ten hours of reading and studying (on ten different days) for her history course before the next exam. However, she had to cancel two of those study hours because of her job, and she did not reschedule the study time. When she took the next history exam, she found that she was only able to answer about 75 percent of the exam questions correctly. She could have earned an A+, but she was only able to earn a C because of the loss of those two hours of reading and studying. Canceling two study sessions because of her job was not the problem—the problem was that she did not reschedule her planned and necessary study time.

You may find it useful to block out time for the basics of daily living in your weekly appointment calendar—but as a matter of priority, try to schedule them around your study commitments and not the other way around. As stated elsewhere in this chapter, if you know that you have a special time set aside for laundry and a different time set aside for studying, then you don't have to deal with the stress of worrying that perhaps you should be studying while you are doing laundry and vice versa.

Remember that the time you spend mapping out your detailed schedule for the entire semester is time well spent. This is how you create an environment for yourself in which you can be successful! It is similar to creating a financial budget—sometimes it feels tedious, but in the end it's worth it.

Tool 3: The Study Session Ticket

The information needed to complete the next assignment, the creation of a task list for each study session (or your "ticket" to study), can be found in the forms you completed for Assignment 5.2.

In order to be successful in college, *you need to plan each study session.* It is not good enough to simply mark the date and time that you plan to study on the calendar; you *must also make a checklist of exactly what you plan to do during the study session.* We call this your "study session ticket" because it will provide the information you need to complete a particular study session and because you can cut them out and use these tickets as bookmarks or markers in your calendar to keep up with exactly how and what you need to study for that week. This keeps your schedule and your study plan in the forefront of your mind, which is what you want in college.

You may need to create different types of study session tickets for different types of classes. For example, the study activities that you would do to prepare for a history class may be very different from the study activities that you would do to prepare for a math class. A blank study session ticket template is provided with Assignment 5.4. You can make copies of the template and adapt it for each course. Then make as many of the adapted copies as you need. You will need one for each study session. Examples of things that you may wish to include on the study session ticket are: "Read pages 324–425," "Review notes," "Define new vocabulary," and "Record questions to ask in class." (See Figure 5.3 for an example of a completed study session ticket.)

The appropriate study activities will be different for each course. *Just make sure that you include enough detail to assess your own progress and to determine whether you are studying enough.* As you can see, Sharon Cooper (Figure 5.4) has set aside six hours of studying for approximately three hours of class per week. She is following the "two hours outside of class for every one hour inside class" formula. She will need to monitor her progress to determine whether or not this formula works for her. She might need to either reduce her study time or increase it, depending on her success in the course. The important thing is that she makes time to *evaluate* how she is doing with her study plan overall. You will need some time to reflect on your studying, classes, activities, and choices—perhaps after you have spent two or three weeks on campus. The ability to evaluate your progress is an important skill for success in college.

Once you have some experience putting study plans into action, you might find that it is more efficient to complete two to four weeks of study plans at a time. In other words, you may not want to map out the entire semester of study session tickets for all your courses in one sitting. That's fine. Just be sure to plan time to complete your tickets for each course in the remaining weeks of the semester, and don't procrastinate!

Figure 5.3

Example of a Completed Study Session Ticket

Study Session Ticket

Name: Sharon Cooper

Course: Theoretical Physics

Date: M   9/12   **Time:**   10–11 a.m.

☑ 1.	Check online for announcements
☑ 2.	Review updated class notes
☑ 3.	Review Ch 2 Learning Goals
☑ 4.	Read Ch 2, pp. 64–78
☑ 5.	Check course online for professor's blog & mail
☑ 6.	Make flashcards for Ch. 2
☐ 7.	
☐ 8.	
☐ 9.	
☐ 10.	

Questions to ask in class:

Ask professor to explain the difference between protons and electrons when they are in zero gravity.

Note: Had to quit early and didn't finish goals, so I need to add an extra thirty minutes and six more pages to the next session to catch up.

Figure 5.4

Example of a Completed Worksheet

Student Name: *Sharon Cooper*	Course: *Theoretical Physics 231*
Date: *August 19, 2015*	Credit Hours: *3*

Meeting Days and Times for the Course: *M, W, F; 8:30–9:45*

Details of the Study Plan:

When will you study?

What Days?	What Times?		How Long?	
	Start	Finish		
Monday	*10:00 a.m.*	*11:00 a.m.*	*1 hour*	*00 minutes*
Tuesday	*10:00 a.m.*	*11:00 a.m.*	*1 hour*	*00 minutes*
Wednesday	*10:00 a.m.*	*11:00 a.m.*	*1 hour*	*00 minutes*
Thursday	*10:00 a.m.*	*11:00 a.m.*	*1 hour*	*00 minutes*
Friday	*10:00 a.m.*	*11:00 a.m.*	*1 hour*	*00 minutes*
Saturday	*10:00 a.m.*	*11:00 a.m.*	*1 hour*	*00 minutes*
Sunday				
Weekly Total (Study Hours):			*6 hours*	*00 minutes*

What study strategies will you use? (List what you will do.)

1. *Make flashcards.*

2. *Recopy notes in my own words.*

3. *Do the exercises at the end of each chapter.*

4. *Check to see if a study group is meeting.*

5. *Highlight important parts of the textbook and take notes when reading.*

6.

Other notes or information about this course:

Teaching Assistants (TAs) are available M, W, F 10–11 a.m.

Hollis Hall, Room 203; 555-123-1234; teachphysics@mycollege.edu

5.3 **The Alphabet Approach**

Now that you have developed a serious study plan, you will be required to make a lot of time management decisions. Following is a simple technique that you may find helpful.

Nist and Holschuh discuss time management using what they call the "Alphabet Approach."[3] Specifically, they recommend the following four practices:

A = Anticipate and Plan

Once you have your class schedule for the term set, you can begin to map out your study time using the procedures already described in this chapter. The basic idea of having a concrete plan is that you will be able to anticipate your study needs and address them more effectively.

B = Break Tasks Down

Some learning activities or assignments must be done in stages over time, rather than all in one day. An example of such an assignment would be writing a research paper. You cannot write it all in one study session. Instead, you must break the large task of the research paper into smaller parts (such as selecting a topic, finding information about the topic in the library, taking notes on the information, outlining the paper, writing a rough draft, revising and improving the draft, and finally printing the final draft). Plan times for each of the parts (usually on different days), and schedule the entire project in such a way that you will meet the deadline.

Creating tickets for each study session is another way to "break tasks down." The large task may be "study for history class," but that directive alone is too vague. So you make a list of the things you plan to actually *do* when you study for history class (for example, plan to read the chapter, outline the chapter, read your notes from class, make flashcards, answer questions assigned by the professor, and so on). You may also break down the study demands for a particular course by selecting a certain number of pages to read each day, rather than trying to tackle a lengthy reading assignment all at once. To determine how many pages to read each day, simply divide the total number of pages you have to read by the number of study sessions that you have planned before the date of the exam or the date on which the reading assignment is due. For example, if you have an exam coming up in two weeks covering one hundred pages of material and you have scheduled ten study sessions between now and the exam date, you will need to read and study ten pages during each study session.

C = Cross Things Off

As you work your way through your week, you will find that there is a certain sense of accomplishment gained from crossing things off your list. For some students, lists are also a great way to mitigate stress. Be sure to cross out any activities that you have completed. If you find that lists help you, you may want to eventually have short-term as well as long-term goals in list form. That way you can keep track of the small steps you are taking in order to reach a larger goal.

D = Don't Procrastinate

There are many reasons people procrastinate, including a fear of being wrong, a need to be perfect, a fear of limitations, or a feeling that you are facing an overwhelming task.[4] If you find that you really struggle with putting things off until the last minute, you may want to explore this topic in more depth than we have time for here. Many books have been written on procrastination. Consider the following techniques in your efforts to avoid it:

- Set reasonable goals

- Plan regularly

- Break tasks down into smaller parts

- Make and use "To Do" lists

- Post monthly and yearly calendars at home

- Force yourself to get started on a task even if you do not feel like it

- Ask for help

- Give yourself permission to be less than perfect

- Remember to schedule relaxation time ("down time") for yourself

- Reward yourself for tasks completed

Reading Comprehension Question 5.3 (Inferential Comprehension)

Nist and Holschuh discuss time management using what they call the "Alphabet Approach." Specifically, they recommend which of the following practices?

a. Anticipate and plan, break tasks down, cross things off, and don't procrastinate.

b. Ask for help, reward yourself, don't be a perfectionist, and space out your work.

c. Set goals, plan regularly, use "to do" lists, and post a calendar.

d. All of the above

Want to learn more? Try these resources.

Are you a procrastinator?

These websites provide some definitions and some helpful hints:

http://bvtlab.com/77Y98

http://bvtlab.com/7qGJ8

These academic websites are devoted to helping students analyze and address procrastination:

http://bvtlab.com/3rg88

http://bvtlab.com/P88m7

Reading Comprehension Question 5.4 (Analysis)

Why is time management so important for student success?

a. Time is something many students have never learned to manage appropriately.

b. Time can be controlled and manipulated.

c. Time: the more you have, the more studying you can do.

d. Time is elusive, and there is never enough time to do what you need to do.

5.4 Summary

This chapter has addressed some basic principles that will help you manage your time effectively. You learned how important it is to design a personal study plan. Individual plans may vary somewhat for different personalities and different courses; however, a good plan is one that is 1) written, 2) detailed, and 3) specific.

In order to apply what you have learned in this chapter, you will need to organize your schedule using three tools: 1) the semester-at-a-glance or the monthly calendar, 2) the weekly appointment calendar, and 3) the individual study session ticket. Your plan should identify your goals; make provisions for the activities that are required to achieve your goals; support your top priorities; and allow you to maintain a healthy balance between work, study, and recreation. No plan can be successful unless you follow it, so *plan your work and then work your plan!*

Name: _____

Study Guide | Goal 1

The student will be able to list six behaviors that rob the student of time for effective study and explain how each behavior could prevent the student from having a successful study regimen.

Questions	Answers & Notes

Name: _____

Study Guide | Goal 2

The student will be able to describe and create an effective study plan using a semester (or other academic term) calendar, a weekly schedule, and a checklist for individual study sessions.

Questions	Answers & Notes

Name: _____

Study Guide | Goal 3

The student will be able to list and describe the components of the Alphabet Approach to time management.

Questions	Answers & Notes

Study Guide | Preparing for Class

Use this page to record questions or insights to discuss in class.

Name: _____

Review Questions 5.1

Instructions

Following are five true-false statements taken from the information in this chapter. First, try to answer them without looking back at the chapter. Then review the chapter to see how well you did.

Question & Answer	Rationale
Circle true or false for each of the following statements.	Write an explanation stating why each statement is true or false.
1. Using the Alphabet Approach to scheduling involves techniques that begin with each letter of the alphabet, A to Z. True or False	Your Rationale:
2. Procrastination is a classic time pirate because it eats away at your time while you do nothing toward accomplishing the goal at hand. True or False	Your Rationale:
3. A good study plan must include not only when and how long you plan to study but also exactly what study activities you will do during the scheduled study time. True or False	Your Rationale:
4. The chapter explains how you can create your own academic planner. True or False	Your Rationale:
5. Research shows that, in recent years college students have developed multitasking skills that enable them to keep up with text messages on their cell phones while effectively listening to a college lecture. True or False	Your Rationale:

Name: _____

Assignment 5.1

Mark Your Monthly Calendar

Goal

The purpose of this activity is to enable the student to create an organized record of deadlines and other responsibilities in a monthly planner.

Objective

The student will record deadlines, due dates, and other academic responsibilities on an appropriate monthly calendar, as described in Chapter 5.

Instructions

A calendar planner is a very important tool for any student who wishes to be successful in college. You should use one to remind yourself of important deadlines and events and to keep yourself on track with a regular study regimen for each of the courses that you are taking. For this assignment you will simply record all of the important information about your courses on calendar pages.

Follow These Steps

Step 1: Gather the materials that you will need to complete this assignment. These include the following:

- A monthly calendar

- A copy of the syllabus for each of your courses

- A copy of your course schedule (usually found in the syllabus)

- A copy of the official college calendar (usually available online)

- A list of dates and times for events that you wish to attend (such as club meetings)

Step 2: Review the materials you gathered for Step 1 to find all of the deadlines and other important dates you will need to remember. Record each of these deadlines or meeting dates in your monthly calendar.

Notes

_____
_____
_____
_____
_____
_____
_____
_____
_____
_____
_____
_____
_____
_____
_____
_____
_____
_____
_____
_____
_____
_____
_____

Example Semester-at-a-Glance Calendar

Week	Monday	Tuesday	Wednesday	Thursday	Friday
1	Jan 13 Classes Begin	Jan 14 Schedule Adjustment	Jan 15 Schedule Adjustment	Jan 16	Jan 17
2	Jan 20 MLK Holiday, College Closed	Jan 21	Jan 22	Jan 23 Fee Deadline	Jan 24
3	Jan 27	Jan 28	Jan 29	Jan 30	Jan 31
4	Feb 3	Feb 4	Feb 5	Feb 6	Feb 7
5	Feb 10	Feb 11	Feb 12	Feb 13	Feb 14 End of 5th week of classes
6	Feb 17 Midterm grades reported: Registrar	Feb 18	Feb 19	Feb 20	Feb 21
7	Feb 24	Feb 25	Feb 26	Feb 27	Feb 28
8	Mar 3	Mar 4	Mar 5 Last day to withdraw w/o penalty	Mar 6	Mar 7
9	Mar 10	Mar 11	Mar 12	Mar 13	Mar 14
10	Mar 17 Spring Break	Mar 18 Spring Break	Mar 19 Spring Break	Mar 20 Spring Break	Mar 21 Spring Break
11	Mar 24	Mar 25	Mar 26	Mar 27	Mar 28
12	Mar 31	Apr 1	Apr 2	Apr 3	Apr 4
13	Apr 7	Apr 8	Apr 9	Apr 10	Apr 11
14	Apr 14	Apr 15	Apr 16	Apr 17	Apr 18
15	Apr 21	Apr 22	Apr 23	Apr 24 7–8 pm Honors Program	Apr 25
16	Apr 28	Apr 29	Apr 30	May 1	May 2 Classes End
17	May 5 Finals Week May 5–8	May 6	May 7	May 8	May 9 Graduation

Note: A blank semester-at-a-glance calendar, a blank two-page-per-month calendar, and a blank one-page-per-month calendar appear on the following pages.

Week	Monday	Tuesday	Wednesday	Thursday	Friday
1					
2					
3					
4					
5					
6					
7					
8					
9					
10					
11					
12					
13					
14					
15					
16					
17					

Month: _____

Monday	Tuesday	Wednesday	Thursday

Friday	Saturday	Sunday	Notes

Plan Your Work and Then Work Your Plan

Month:

Monday	Tuesday	Wednesday	Thursday	Friday	Saturday	Sunday

Name: _____

Assignment 5.2

Develop Study Plans for Courses

Goal

The purpose of this activity is to help the student to create a written study plan for each course.

Objective

The student will create a specific, detailed study plan for each course.

Instructions

For this assignment you must write a brief description of your study plan for each of the courses you are taking this semester. Use the form called **Study Time Management Worksheet for a Single Course.**

Follow These Steps

Step 1: Prepare the proper number of forms.

Earlier in the chapter (Figure 5.4) is an example of a completed **Study Time Management Worksheet for a Single Course.** Following is a blank copy of the form. You will need one for each of your courses. Therefore, please make copies of the form as needed and always keep one blank copy on hand. If you find that this exercise really helps you, then you may wish to use it again in future semesters. Keeping an extra blank form will come in handy then.

Step 2: Complete a form for each of your courses.

Use the form to plan and write down the following information:

- On what days or dates do you plan to study for this course?

- For how long do you plan to study for this course during each study session?

- At what time of day (from x time to y time) do you plan to study for this course? (Time must not overlap with other courses or responsibilities.)

- In what types of study activities will you engage during the study sessions? Be specific. (For example, don't simply report that you will read the textbook; instead, note how many pages you will read during each session).

The forms you complete for this assignment will provide you with the information needed to complete the next assignment (Assignment 5.3), which is related to the creation of a weekly study appointment sheet. Also the information you include in the strategy section of these forms will provide you with ideas for the study session tickets (task lists) that you will create in Assignment 5.4.

Notes

Study Time Management Worksheet for a Single Course

Student Name:	Course:
Date:	Credit Hours:

Meeting Days and Times for the Course:

Details of the Study Plan:

When will you study?

What Days?	What Times?		How Long?	
	Start	Finish		
Monday			hour(s)	minutes
Tuesday			hour(s)	minutes
Wednesday			hour(s)	minutes
Thursday			hour(s)	minutes
Friday			hour(s)	minutes
Saturday			hour(s)	minutes
Sunday			hour(s)	minutes
Weekly Total (Study Hours):			hour(s)	minutes

What study strategies will you use? (List what you will do.)

Other notes or information about this course:

Name: _____

Assignment 5.3

Weekly Appointment Page

Goal

The purpose of this activity is to guide the student in the process of using information from the worksheets in Assignment 5.2 to create a single weekly appointment sheet. The product will be a page that represents study appointments that the student can repeat each week during the semester.

Objective

Based on information from Assignment 5.2, the student will create a weekly appointment sheet (calendar page) that designates, at a minimum, when he or she will study for each course and when he or she will attend each class.

Instructions

Transfer the information from your **Study Time Management Worksheet for a Single Course** forms (provided with Assignment 5.2) onto the **Weekly Study Appointment Sheet** (provided on the following pages). The process for how to do this was described in Chapter 5. The basic idea is that you make an appointment with yourself to study for each course.

Follow These Steps

Step 1: Draw and label boxes as necessary to indicate when you will be in class for the various courses that you are taking this semester. You can't change the times of your classes and, by enrolling, you have already made a commitment to attend at the times specified; class time is a fixed commitment.

Step 2: Draw and label boxes to represent other commitments that you cannot change (such as your work schedule). (Wait until after you complete Step 3 to indicate when you will handle commitments that are flexible with regard to time.)

Step 3: Realize that this is a very important step. Draw and label boxes on the weekly schedule that indicate when you plan to study for each class. Do not simply indicate a generic study time; instead, specify exactly when you will study for each of your different classes.

Step 4: Make enough photocopies of the completed weekly schedule for you to have one for each week of the semester.

Step 5: Notice that the remaining blank spaces on your completed weekly appointment sheet (those not earmarked for studying or class meetings) represent your free time. Week by week you can use the free time slots to pencil in appointments or commitments that are flexible without letting those other commitments interfere with your study appointments.

Note: The study appointments that you created in Step 3 are appointments like any other, except that they are appointments that you have made with yourself. If you have to break a study appointment with yourself, remember to reschedule it for another time during that week so that you do not get behind in your studies.

Notes

Weekly Study Appointment Sheet

DATE →							
TIME ↓	Monday	Tuesday	Wednesday	Thursday	Friday	Saturday	Sunday
8 a.m.							
9 a.m.							
10 a.m.							
11 a.m.							
12 p.m.							
1 p.m.							
2 p.m.							
3 p.m.							
4 p.m.							
5 p.m.							
6 p.m.							
7 p.m.							

Weekly Study Appointment Sheet

DATE →							
TIME ↓	Monday	Tuesday	Wednesday	Thursday	Friday	Saturday	Sunday
8 a.m.							
9 a.m.							
10 a.m.							
11 a.m.							
12 p.m.							
1 p.m.							
2 p.m.							
3 p.m.							
4 p.m.							
5 p.m.							
6 p.m.							
7 p.m.							

Name: _____

Assignment 5.4

Study Session Tickets

Goal

The purpose of this activity is to guide the student in the process of creating individual tickets for each study session he or she plans to have throughout the semester.

Objective

Based on the description given in Chapter 5, the student will create a collection of study session tickets that can be used during the study sessions that he or she has planned.

Instructions

Create as many tickets as necessary to use when you study for each class. This process was described earlier in Chapter 5.

Follow These Steps

Step 1: Look at your calendar to see when the next exam or assignment is due. Count how many study appointments you have made for yourself between now and the exam or other due date. You will need to make one ticket for each study session appointment.

Step 2: Decide what activities you will actually do during each study session. For example, for a history class you may do things like read the chapter, write outlines or draw tables to distinguish what information from the reading was most important, make flashcards to use when memorizing new vocabulary from this study session, and so on. For a math class you might do things such as read the chapter in the math textbook, work practice problems, create flashcards of theorems or formulas that you wish to memorize, and so on. If you are preparing to submit a research paper, then your task list for your first study session may simply read "select a topic," for the next session "find articles in the library," for the third session "read articles and make notes," and so on until you finish the paper.

Step 3: Write your tasks on the ticket. Before you write anything, you will need to make enough copies of the blank ticket template so that you will have one for each study session. For example, if you have made appointments with yourself to study for your psychology class on ten separate dates leading up to the next psychology exam, then you would need to make ten copies of the template so that you can make a ticket for each study appointment.

The next few pages in this book provide you with blank ticket forms. Several pages of tickets are provided in this book to get you started, but they will not be nearly enough to cover the entire semester. Therefore, you should make enough photocopies of these tickets so that you will be able to complete a separate ticket for each time you study for each course. It is important that you take a deliberate and active approach to studying and that you follow a plan that will result in getting the job done. These tools will help you.

If you develop a written study plan for each of your courses using the calendars and tickets as described in Chapter 5—and follow the plan—then you are likely to greatly improve your grades.

Notes

Study Session Ticket

Name:	
Course:	
Date:	Time:

- ❏ 1.
- ❏ 2.
- ❏ 3.
- ❏ 4.
- ❏ 5.
- ❏ 6.
- ❏ 7.
- ❏ 8.
- ❏ 9.
- ❏ 10.

Questions to ask in class:

Study Session Ticket

Name:	
Course:	
Date:	Time:

- ❏ 1.
- ❏ 2.
- ❏ 3.
- ❏ 4.
- ❏ 5.
- ❏ 6.
- ❏ 7.
- ❏ 8.
- ❏ 9.
- ❏ 10.

Questions to ask in class:

Figure 5.5

Example of a Ticket Before and After a Study Session

Example Before Study Session

Study Session Ticket

Name: Jeefus Strickland

Course: Sociology

Date: M   9/17   **Time:** 2–4 pm

☐ 1.	Check online for announcements
☐ 2.	Review & update notes from class
☐ 3.	Review notes made about Ch 1
☐ 4.	Review Ch 2 learning goals (pg. 64)
☐ 5.	Read Ch 2 (pp. 64–76)
☐ 6.	Make notes (find answers) about learning goals from reading

Questions to ask in class:

Example After Study Session

Study Session Ticket

Name: Jeefus Strickland

Course: Sociology

Date: M   9/17   **Time:** 2–4 pm

☑ 1.	Check online for announcements
☑ 2.	Review & update notes from class
☑ 3.	Review notes made about Ch 1
☑ 4.	Review Ch 2 learning goals (pg. 64)
☑ 5.	Read Ch 2 (pp. 64–76)
☑ 6.	Make notes (find answers) about learning goals from reading

Questions to ask in class:

Ask professor to explain the difference between validity and reliability.

Note: Had to quit early and didn't finish goals so I need to add extra 30 minutes and 6 more pages to next session to catch up.

Chapter Roadmap

Introduction

In this chapter you will learn techniques for effective listening and note taking. This chapter addresses these skills as a complete cycle—beginning with preparation for class, followed by listening and note-taking skills, and ending with strategies for review.

This chapter roadmap page presents the formal learning goals for this chapter and a checklist that you should follow as you read and study the chapter.

Student Learning Goals

After completing this chapter you should be able to do the following:

1. Describe the nature of the cycle of learning, including the characteristics of each stage (before class, during class, after class).

2. Compare and contrast half listening, sound listening, and active listening and describe the characteristics of active listening.

3. Explain the ways in which effective listening involves behaviors from all three stages of the cycle of learning.

4. Describe the Cornell Method of Note Taking, including the page layout, the Five R's, and how each component can be applied to a lecture class.

5. Demonstrate the ability to practice active listening and effective note taking in college.

Chapter Checklist

You will benefit most if you complete the activities in the order that they are listed.

❑ **Target Date/Deadline:** _____
Complete Critical Thinking Activity 6.1.

❑ **Target Date/Deadline:** _____
Convert the student learning goals to questions that you can answer as you read the chapter. Write your questions on the study guide pages near the end of this chapter.

❑ **Target Date/Deadline:** _____
Read the chapter.

❑ **Target Date/Deadline:** _____
Try to answer the reading comprehension questions as you come to them in the chapter. Check each answer by comparing it to the list of correct answers in the back of the book. If any answer was not correct, then review the passages preceding the question to see why you missed the question.

❑ **Target Date/Deadline:** _____
Answer the student learning goal questions you created. These answered questions will be your study guide.

❑ **Target Date/Deadline:** _____
Write down any questions, insights, or comments that you have as you read so that you can bring them up in class.

❑ **Target Date/Deadline:** _____
Complete Review Questions 6.1.

❑ **Target Date/Deadline:** _____
Complete Assignment 6.1 (Practice Taking Notes).

❑ **Target Date/Deadline:** _____
Review what you have learned from this chapter.

Critical Thinking Activity 6.1

Please answer the following true-false questions as a way to begin thinking about the topic of this chapter.

1. I am in class almost every day.   True or False

2. I participate in class.   True or False

3. I take notes in class.   True or False

4. I review my notes every day.   True or False

After you have answered, consider the analysis below.

Did you answer true to question 1?

> Being "in class" means that you are really present during the class period. This involves staying focused during class time, staying alert and awake, completing assigned readings in advance of class, and trying to understand and relate to the topic being discussed.

Did you answer true to question 2?

> Participating in class is an active process that includes asking questions about course content in class. Active participation is a very important component in effective listening because it helps you get more out of the class than you might otherwise. We will explore this further later in the chapter.

Question 3 asks about taking notes during class.

> Have you ever felt like you did not know what to write down when you took notes in class? Have you ever had difficulty understanding your notes when it was time to study for a test? Would you say that it is sometimes difficult for you to read your own handwriting when you try to study your notes? If your answer is "yes" for any of these questions, then this chapter is designed with you in mind.

Question 4 asks about reviewing the notes you take in class.

> Do you review your notes on a regular basis, or do you wait until the night before an exam to review them? Writing notes during class is a skill that you can work on, and it is important to develop effective strategies for actually using the notes that you take during class.

Listening and Taking Notes:

Do You Hear What I Hear?

"Do you understand the words that are comin' out of my mouth?"
— Chris Tucker (as Detective Carter in the movie *Rush Hour*)[1]

"He listens well who takes notes."
— Dante Alighieri, *The Divine Comedy*[2]

Effective listening involves behaviors from all three stages of the cycle of learning. Effective listening begins with preparation before class and ends with review after class.

6.1 Listening for Success

As previously explained, at the college level approximately two-thirds of learning occurs outside of class and about one-third of learning occurs during class. Figure 6.1 illustrates the cycle of learning.

Preparing to Listen

Preparing to listen involves completing out-of-class assignments, removing distractions, and doing everything that you can to position yourself in the classroom for the most effective listening experience. This advance preparation is critical if you wish to listen effectively and gain the maximum benefit from the lecture or class discussion.

Complete Required Reading and Other Assignments in Advance

Effective listening starts long before the class begins. Completing the assigned reading prior to class is one way to prepare for effective listening. Most college courses require students to complete reading assignments and/or other learning activities before each class session. The syllabus for the course almost always contains a table or list identifying which readings are associated with each class session. Students are expected to complete the required reading or other learning activity (such as solving math problems) prior to the class session in which the reading is discussed. Students who complete the reading assignment before class are better able to understand and retain information presented in the lecture or discussion because the reading gives them a foundation from which to approach the topic. In contrast, students who do not read in advance often feel "lost" during the lecture. The unprepared student may perceive the lecture as being "too fast" and may experience difficulty keeping up with the speaker.

Figure 6.1

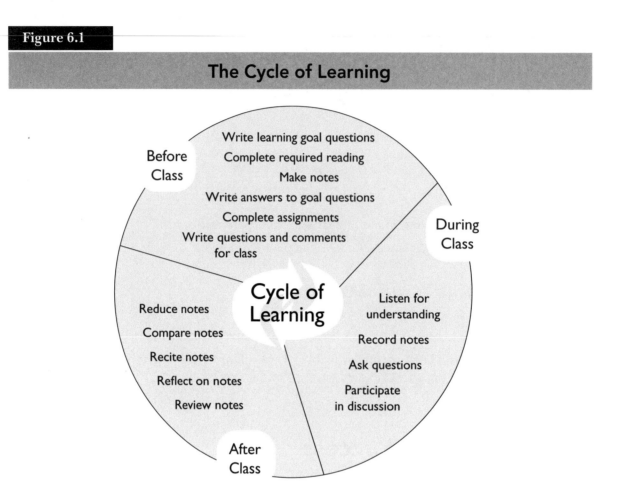

The Cycle of Learning

Before Class
- Write learning goal questions
- Complete required reading
- Make notes
- Write answers to goal questions
- Complete assignments
- Write questions and comments for class

During Class
- Listen for understanding
- Record notes
- Ask questions
- Participate in discussion

After Class
- Reduce notes
- Compare notes
- Recite notes
- Reflect on notes
- Review notes

Cycle of Learning

Prepare Questions in Advance

As you complete the required reading or solve practice math problems, you are likely to discover that you have questions about the material. It is wise to write these questions down and take them to class with you. If your question is not automatically answered in the lecture, you can pose the question to the professor during or at the conclusion of the class. Writing your questions down when they occur to you will help you to remember them during class, and getting answers to all of your questions will improve your performance on exams.

Prepare Your Physical Environment in Advance

Arrive early so that you can get a good seat. It is often the case in college classes that students are allowed to sit anywhere they choose in the class. An important way to prepare to listen is to choose a seat that allows you to see and to hear clearly. Position yourself in such a way that you can more easily tune out any distractions. This usually means selecting a seat near the front and middle of the class, close to the speaker and to any audiovisual presentations that the professor may offer.

You may have limited control over some aspects of the physical environment, such as the seating arrangements; however, you can control the part of the environment that you bring with you: your notebook, planner, textbook, pen, highlighter, cell phone, PDA, iPod®, computer, and appropriate attire. *Remember: Bring to class all the supplies that you will need to listen, take notes, and participate in class discussion.* Make sure that your pens and highlighters are in good working order before class. Consider turning off, disabling, or leaving at home anything that might distract from your academic listening experience. Always bring your planner so that you are ready to immediately record information about exam dates, lab assignments, or other announcements that are made in class.

If you arrive early, you may wish to use the time before class to compare your notes from previous lessons with a classmate. It is a good idea to use this time before class to get to know some of your classmates because it sets the stage for a team approach to the listening and discussion that will take place during class. However, once class begins, all personal chatting (as well as text messaging, listening to music, playing computer games, surfing the web, talking on the cell phone, and eating snacks) should stop—and you should focus all of your attention on the lesson at hand. Some students pop a sugar-free lifesaver or breath mint into their mouths when class starts as a silent signal to themselves that it is time to stop chatting and start listening.

Many colleges have an emergency alert system for faculty, staff, and students that allows the college to send messages via cell phones, text messaging, and email to notify the campus community about severe weather, campus closing, or other emergencies. Cell phones are usually permitted in class because they are used by the college for emergency notifications. However, before class starts, you should set your cell phone to silent or vibrate mode so that it does not distract you or others during the lecture or discussion. If there is a campus emergency, then everyone's phone (including the professor's phone) will ring at the same time. You must respond to emergencies, but you should delay responding to all other communications until after class is over if you wish to be an effective listener.

Reading Comprehension Question 6.1 (Knowledge)

Preparing to listen in a class would include all *except* which of the following activities?

a. Completing the required reading and other assignments before class

b. Preparing questions in advance

c. Preparing your physical environment in advance

d. Having electronic devices, such as an iPod®, prepared ahead for writing emails and notes to classmates

Active Listening During Class

Deb Peterson has suggested that there are three levels of listening: half listening, sound listening, and active listening.[3] If you doodle, chat with others, tune out part of the time, or allow yourself to be distracted during the lecture, then you are only half listening. If you find yourself hearing the words but failing to comprehend the message or the meaning, then you are only listening to the sounds. **Active listening** is characterized by an engaged disposition. The active listener ignores distractions, makes eye contact with the speaker, keeps an open mind, focuses on the message rather than the speaker, seeks to understand the message, asks questions when appropriate, and remains engaged while taking notes.

Numerous writers have identified habits that detract from effective listening.[4] Some of these poor listening habits include defining the topic as boring, tolerating internal and external distractions, half listening, sound listening, trying to write down everything verbatim, focusing on points of disagreement, criticizing the speaker, listening only for facts rather than meaning, failing to ask questions, failing to participate in discussion, and failing to take notes. If you are aware of these problem behaviors, you can avoid them and instead practice active listening.

Avoid Defining the Topic as Dull

Some professors and some topics may seem lackluster, especially when compared to current advancements in the entertainment industry. However, whether or not the subject or speaker is dull isn't relevant to the successful student. The successful student takes personal responsibility to learn regardless of the quality or appeal of the presentation.

Avoid Distractions

Distractions abound in the classroom. Internal distractions are personal issues that you may have been dwelling on during the day, such as financial problems, dating or marriage relationship problems, and grade anxiety. Internal distractions are sometimes difficult to dismiss. Try to compartmentalize your thinking. When you enter a class, try to mentally put yourself in a frame of mind that will allow you to focus on learning. Tell yourself, "Right now, I am going to clear my mind and focus on the lesson until this class is over—and then I will deal with these problems."

External distractions are things in the physical environment that draw your attention away from the lesson, such as the temperature of the room, the noise in the room, the fact that someone you find extremely attractive just sat down next to you, and the professor's goofy hair or tie. You may not be able to do much about the professor's hair unless you are a cosmetologist, but you can often take simple steps to reduce other distractions. Select a seat that places your love interest out of your immediate view (at least for the duration of the class). If the class is always cold, bring a sweater. If people are making unnecessary noise chatting, you could respond by politely asking them to keep it down, moving away from them and closer to the professor, or asking the professor to address the problem.

Don't Let Points of Disagreement Stop You from Listening

It is almost certain that you will hear things in college lectures with which you disagree—sometimes strongly. That is okay. Being a college student does not mean that you have to agree with everything that the professor says. Professors often disagree with one another. Professors sometimes present many alternative views in a lesson or course, even if they do not personally embrace some of those views. Learning about a variety of views and theories and learning to think about them critically are part of what a college-level education is all about. F. Scott Fitzgerald said, "The test of first rate intelligence is the ability to hold two opposing ideas at the same time and still retain the ability to function."[5] Don't allow your reaction to one point in the lecture distract you from actively listening to the rest of the lecture and learning what you need to know. The Elmhurst College Learning Center (http://www.elmhurst.edu/academics/1265687.html) recommends, "Hear the speaker out … Don't jump to conclusions … Don't stop listening because of an emotional response to a word or topic," and "Don't give up because the subject is difficult."

Engage the Professor and Others in the Class

An important part of active listening is asking and answering questions. Since the goal of active listening is to ensure that you understand the message, it is often necessary to ask questions for clarification. There may be portions of the class period when it would be inappropriate to interrupt the speaker with a question, but effective teaching and learning cannot take place unless some portion of the class is set aside for questions and discussion. In most cases, the professor's lecture is organized into a number of sections (covering several different points). Most professors are prepared to entertain questions following each of these sections during their lecture. Unfortunately, students often remain silent at these times. Many students also appear reluctant to answer questions that are posed to the class by the professor. Researchers have documented this nationwide trend of timidity among students when it comes to discussion in class and have labeled the phenomenon "the silent college classroom."[6] Recent research has found that typically only about 25 percent of students participate in classroom discussion while the rest of the students remain silent.[7]

One way that you, as an individual, can overcome this handicap is to write questions in your notes. If any questions come to your mind during the lecture, or if anything about the lecture is unclear to you, write it down in your notes. Then you will be ready to introduce your question when the class discussion starts. You should also jot down any questions you think of during your preparatory reading before class. Then if they are not answered by the lecture, you can introduce them during the class discussion.

Taking notes is also part of active listening. Taking notes is one way to improve your listening and retain more information from class. It could be said that note taking is an extension of listening.

Reading Comprehension Question 6.2 (Literal Comprehension)

How is active listening different from half listening?

a. Active listeners keep an open mind, focus on the message, and keep an engaged disposition.

b. Active listeners sometimes write notes to their classmates during class.

c. Half listening requires engagement and attention.

d. Active listening results in a better understanding of what is being said during the lecture.

e. a and d

Want to learn more? Try these resources.

Read more about listening techniques at the following URLs:
How to Listen and Retain: Active Listening Tips, by Grace Fleming:
http://bvtlab.com/8h8qj

Listening, L.I.S.T.E.N. (California Polytechnic State University):
http://bvtlab.com/a78g6

6.2 Taking Notes for Success

Has anyone ever formally taught you how to take notes in class? One professor has posed that question to classes of freshmen students on the first day of class for more than ten years—always with the same results. Very few, and often none, of the freshmen in his classes recalled ever being taught how to take notes. Perhaps this reflects a general, widely held misconception that note taking is so simple that it requires no instruction. The truth is that effective note taking is a skill that must be learned and can be improved upon. This section of the chapter will suggest some methods and principles of effective note taking that will help you improve this skill.

We will describe the Cornell Method of Note Taking and offer some general guidelines. There are many "formulas" for how to take notes. Ultimately, however, the best method is the method that works best for you as an individual and best fits your own learning style.

The Cornell Method of Note Taking

One tried-and-true method for taking notes is known as the Cornell Method.[8] It was developed decades ago by professor Walter Pauk, who served as director of the Reading-Study Center at Cornell University. The Cornell Method involves dividing the note page into three sections. One of the sections is used for taking notes in class, and the other sections are used to record questions and update the notes during the review and study process.

Figure 6.2

Diagram of the Cornell Method of Note Taking

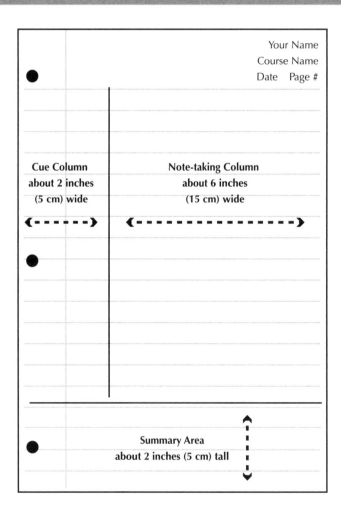

As is illustrated in Figure 6.2, when using the Cornell Method you must draw one vertical line and one horizontal line on your note page so that it is divided into three sections: a cue section, a note-taking section, and a summary section. The horizontal line should be drawn about 2 inches (5 cm) above the bottom of the page. The space below the horizontal line is the **summary area.** The vertical line should divide the space above the summary section into two columns. The vertical line should be drawn about 2 inches (5 cm) from the left side of the page. It should extend from the top of the page to the horizontal line. The space to the left of the vertical line is called the **cue column,** and the space to the right of the vertical line is called the **note-taking column.** Since a standard piece of notebook paper is 8.5 inches wide, you should have a cue column that is approximately 2 inches (5 cm) wide and a note-taking column that is approximately 6 inches (15 cm) wide. Always label each page with your name, the title of the course, the date, and the page number. This **identification label** will be especially helpful if you use looseleaf pages because it will make it easier to keep the pages organized and in order. Pauk described note taking as a five-step process. The Five R's of note taking include (1) Record, (2) Reduce, (3) Recite, (4) Reflect, and (5) Review.

Figure 6.3

Example of a Note Page During Class

Reading Comprehension Question 6.3 (Inferential Comprehension)

Why is the Cornell Method of Note Taking a good method?

a. It helps the student write down the instructor's words, verbatim.

b. It has been used for many years.

c. It allows the student to accomplish homework while taking notes during class.

d. It provides a way for the student to take notes, review the notes, and study after class.

Step 1: Record (During Class)

Use the note-taking column to record your notes during class. Leave the cue column and the summary area blank until after class. This is illustrated in Figure 6.3. Following are a few tips that will help you record your notes effectively during class:

- Arrive early. If you are late, you may miss important information.

- Sit in the front and middle of the class so that you can hear better, see better, and block out distractions more easily.

- Avoid carrying on conversations, sending or reading text messages, surfing the web, daydreaming, sleeping, or letting anything distract you during class when you should be listening and taking notes.

- Listen carefully with understanding as your goal. If you obsessively copy down every word but do not understand what you are writing, then your notes will not serve you well as a study tool. Do not try to write down everything that the professor says but instead identify the important concepts that you will need to help you study later. Your goal when taking notes should be to create an outline or paraphrase of what the professor has said.

- Look for cues as to what points the professor thinks are most important. These include structural cues (such as transition words), nonverbal cues (body language), visual cues (such as when the professor provides a handout or writes on the board), and phonological cues (such as when the professor changes volume or repeats information).

- Write legibly. Some students prefer to write in cursive because it is faster, while others prefer to print in block letters because it is easier to read later. Experiment and see what works better for you, but make sure that you will be able to read and understand what you have written when you study.

- Skip one line between ideas and several lines between topics so that you will have some space to add a note or two later if needed.

- Use symbols and abbreviations to save time, but be sure that you write in such a way that you can read and understand it with ease later.

- Ask questions. Most professors allow time for questions, and many encourage students to ask questions. Take advantage of this opportunity to ask for clarification of difficult points or simply to fill in information you missed. The chances are high that other students in the class also need to hear the answer. Therefore, asking your questions will help the professor teach better, and it will help everyone learn better. In answer to your questions, the professor may discuss the material in different words or add illustrations that will simplify the material. Take notes on his or her answers.

- Make sure to get the information that you need to learn the material and to prepare for exams. If you missed something that the professor said, ask him or her to repeat it or go to the professor after class and ask for clarification. If you are in a rush after class, you can ask the professor at the beginning of the next class or try to find the answer from a friend or from the textbook. If that does not work, make an appointment and visit the professor during office hours.

The University of Washington website (http://www.washington.edu/doit/college-survival-skills) provides the following advice for students who may have trouble taking notes:

> If you have trouble taking notes, find someone in the class who takes good notes and ask if they would be willing to give you a copy of them. Continue to take your own notes because listening to the lecture and writing notes at the same time helps you remember the information better. Then check your notes against the other set of notes after class. Look at the information your classmate is recording, and use this example to improve your note-taking skills. You may also want to consider tape recording lectures and then listening to the tapes while reviewing both sets of notes. Be sure to obtain the lecturer's permission before taping a lecture.

Step 2: Reduce (Immediately After Class)

As soon as possible after class, use the cue column to write down questions based on your notes. Pauk explains that writing questions will help you to "clarify meanings, reveal relationships, establish continuity, and strengthen memory."[9] Also at this time, you should tidy up your notes by adding any information that you did not have time to write down in class. You may need to add definitions to words that you don't know, spell out the meaning of unusual abbreviations, or clarify any other ambiguous information. In addition, you should write a short summary of the notes in the summary area at the bottom of the page. The Reduce process is illustrated in Figure 6.4.

You need to perform this step as soon as possible after class. Try to do it immediately after class while it is fresh in your mind because if you wait until after dinner that night you are likely to have forgotten some of it already. The remaining three steps (Recite, Reflect, and Review) should be done at a later time—the time you have scheduled to study for this class.

It is also a good idea to compare your notes to those of a classmate on a regular basis. It may be that your classmate included something in his or her notes that you inadvertently overlooked. When you compare notes, you can add that information to your own notes.

Figure 6.4

Example of a Note Page After Class

Step 3:   Recite (During a Routine Study Session Prior to the Next Class)

Recite means to read aloud. When you sit down to study your notes, you can use the questions that you have written in the cue column as a way to begin learning the material. Cover the note-taking column with a piece of paper so that you cannot see it. Then as you read down the cue column, say the answers to the questions aloud. Lift the cover to confirm the accuracy of your answers.

Step 4:   Reflect (During a Routine Study Session)

Reflect means to think. It is important that you take time during your study session to think about the information that you have learned. In order to master a college-level course, the student must do more than simply memorize definitions or facts. The student must strive to understand the concepts. Pauk suggested that students ask themselves questions such as the following: "What is the significance of these facts? What principle are they based on? How can I apply them? How do they fit in with what I already know?"[9]

Step 5: Review (During Every Routine Study Session)

Finally, it is very important that you schedule time every night or week to review all your previous notes. Each time you review, start at the beginning (i.e., the first page of notes that you wrote for that class or unit) and review the notes for each day until the current date. This process does not take as much time as you might assume because the more times you read the same material, the faster you can read it. This day-to-day review process will enable you to develop greater understanding of the important concepts and actually learn rather than simply memorizing. Then the knowledge will be recorded not just in your short-term memory but in your long-term memory as well.

Reading Comprehension Question 6.4 (Analysis)

Which of the following is true of note taking in college?

a. Students who take notes every class will have a record of attending all their classes.

b. Good notes provide material for in-depth studying of the course content.

c. Good notes are not as important as reading the textbook.

d. All of the above

Want to learn more? Try these resources.

You can download Microsoft® Word® templates to create Cornell note-taking pages at the following URL:
http://bvtlab.com/N6e72

Graph paper version:
http://bvtlab.com/88287

6.3 Summary

In this chapter you learned about two valuable skills in the cycle of learning: active listening and note taking. Students who practice half listening or sound listening will not be as well equipped to succeed in college as students who practice active listening. Effective listening actually begins before class with preparation. During class, the active listener ignores distractions, makes eye contact with the speaker, keeps an open mind, focuses on the message rather than the speaker, seeks to understand the message, asks questions when appropriate, and remains engaged while taking notes.

Note-taking skills can be learned, practiced, and improved upon. The Cornell Method of Note Taking is recommended. It involves a five-step process for note taking: Record, Reduce, Recite, Reflect, and Review. The cycle of learning is completed as the student reviews and studies his or her notes. Reviewing and studying your notes should be part of your routine study plan for each course that you take. The particulars of how to develop a study plan were discussed in Chapter 5.

The assignment for this chapter will be to use the blank note-taking page provided to take notes for one of your classes or at a public event with a speaker.

Study Guide | Goal 1

The student will be able to describe the nature of the cycle of learning, including the characteristics of each stage (before class, during class, after class).

Questions	Answers & Notes

Name: _____

Study Guide | Goal 2

The student will be able to compare and contrast half listening, sound listening, and active listening and describe the characteristics of active listening.

Questions	Answers & Notes

Name: _____

Study Guide | Goal 3

The student will be able to explain the ways in which effective listening involves behaviors from all three stages of the cycle of learning.

Questions	Answers & Notes

Name: _____

Study Guide | Goal 4

The student will be able to describe the Cornell Method of Note Taking, including the page layout, the Five R's, and how each component can be applied to a lecture class.

Questions	Answers & Notes

Name: _____

Study Guide | Goal 5

The student will be able to demonstrate the ability to practice active listening and effective note taking in college.

Questions	Answers & Notes

Study Guide | Preparing for Class

Use this page to record questions or insights to discuss in class.

Name: _____

Review Questions 6.1

Instructions

Following are five true-false statements taken from the information in this chapter. First, try to answer them without looking back at the chapter. Then review the chapter to see how well you did.

Question & Answer	Rationale
Circle true or false for each of the following statements.	Write an explanation stating why each statement is true or false.
1. Effective listening starts as soon as you enter the classroom. True or False	Your Rationale:
2. The goal of active listening is to ensure that you will be able to write down everything the professor says. True or False	Your Rationale:
3. Part of the Cornell Method of Note Taking is reading your notes aloud. True or False	Your Rationale:
4. Reviewing your class notes once before an exam is enough to encode them in your long-term memory. True or False	Your Rationale:
5. This chapter explains that the best method for note taking is the Cornell Method of Note Taking. True or False	Your Rationale:

Name: _____

Assignment 6.1

Practice Taking Notes

Goal

The purpose of this activity is for the student to master using the Cornell Method of Note Taking.

Objective

The student will demonstrate understanding of the Cornell Method of Note Taking by using the technique to take notes for a class lecture, a workshop, or a public meeting.

Instructions

Chapter 6 of this textbook explains a note-taking technique called the Cornell Method. Use information from Chapter 6 to practice taking notes.

Follow These Steps

Step 1: Review the Cornell Method of Note Taking in Chapter 6.

Step 2: Attend a class lecture, a workshop, or another meeting where a speaker is making a presentation, and use the Cornell Method of Note Taking to take notes at the meeting. Use the following page for this purpose.

Step 3: After the meeting, review your notes and compare them with the content in Chapter 6 to see if you understand how to take notes according to the Cornell Method of Note Taking.

Notes

_____
_____
_____
_____
_____
_____
_____
_____
_____
_____
_____
_____
_____
_____
_____
_____
_____
_____
_____
_____
_____
_____
_____
_____
_____
_____
_____
_____
_____

Name: _____ _____ _____ / _____ _____

Event Title   Date   Page

College Success: A Concise Practical Guide

Chapter Roadmap

Introduction

In this chapter you will learn how to improve one of the most important academic skills that you will use in college and in life—reading. Topics include how to effectively read textbooks and how to respond to new vocabulary. You will learn strategies for reading that have been proven by research to be most effective, such as the SOAR and SQ3R methods. You will be asked to practice these methods in the assignments associated with this chapter.

This chapter roadmap page presents the formal learning goals for this chapter and a checklist that you should follow as you read and study the chapter.

Student Learning Goals

After completing this chapter you should be able to do the following:

1. Explain why reading textbooks in college is so important.

2. Demonstrate how to use a textbook effectively and describe strategies that can improve reading comprehension.

3. Describe and use the SOAR method.

4. Describe and use the SQ3R method.

5. Use concept mapping as a way to move beyond definitions to associations when learning new vocabulary.

Chapter Checklist

You will benefit most if you complete the activities in the order that they are listed.

❑ **Target Date/Deadline:** _____
Complete Critical Thinking Activity 7.1.

❑ **Target Date/Deadline:** _____
Convert the student learning goals to questions that you can answer as you read the chapter. Write your questions on the study guide pages near the end of this chapter.

❑ **Target Date/Deadline:** _____
Read the chapter.

❑ **Target Date/Deadline:** _____
Try to answer the reading comprehension questions as you come to them in the chapter. Check each answer by comparing it to the list of correct answers in the back of the book. If any answer was not correct, then review the passages preceding the question to see why you missed the question.

❑ **Target Date/Deadline:** _____
Answer the student learning goal questions you created. These answered questions will be your study guide.

❑ **Target Date/Deadline:** _____
Write down any questions, insights, or comments that you have as you read so that you can bring them up in class.

❑ **Target Date/Deadline:** _____
Complete Review Questions 7.1.

❑ **Target Date/Deadline:** _____
Complete Assignment 7.1 (Practice Identifying New Vocabulary).

❑ **Target Date/Deadline:** _____
Review what you have learned from this chapter.

Critical Thinking Activity 7.1

Following is a problem-solving question similar to those that students often face. Your responses to such problems involve critical thinking and problem solving and could mean the difference between success and failure as a student—between graduating with a college degree and not graduating at all.

Suppose you can't afford to buy a textbook in time for the first day of classes. Going without a textbook is not an option. Use critical-thinking and problem-solving skills to make a list of solutions (permanent or temporary) that will allow you to complete the assigned reading on schedule.

Write your list in the space provided on this page. Be prepared to share your ideas in class if asked to do so.

Reading Textbooks:

What They Never Taught You in Kindergarten!

Which is more difficult to read, fiction or non-fiction?

While it is noteworthy that fiction and non-fiction are usually written in different styles, with different features, and in a different structure, the answer to this question may be partly dependent on the purpose behind your reading. If you encounter a difficult book when reading for pleasure, you may simply discontinue reading and switch to something easier. You will not have that option when it comes to the required reading assignments you have in college. While some of your assigned reading in college will include works of fiction, a substantial portion of the required reading will be a special type of book: the textbook. Even when reading fiction works in college, you will be required to think more deeply about those fiction books than you might if you were reading them for pleasure. In many cases the required reading in college will constitute both a challenge and a pleasure. One of the most important activities that will occupy your time in college is reading. Reading is, in effect, the key to success in college.

In this chapter you will learn why reading textbooks is so important in college and how to use a textbook effectively. We will explore some reading and studying strategies, such as the research-proven SOAR method and the widely accepted SQ3R method. These principles will help you to read more effectively.

Try This!

In the left column below are a series of quotes about reading with the author identified. Use the space provided in the right column to write what message you think the author wanted to convey. Consider the author in your analysis.

Quote	Intended Message
"The more you read, the more things you will know. The more that you learn, the more places you'll go." – Dr. Seuss	
"Some people will lie, cheat, steal and back-stab to get ahead ... and to think, all they have to do is READ." – Fortune	
"Once you learn to read, you will be forever free." – Frederick Douglass	
"Not all readers are leaders, but all leaders are readers." – Harry S. Truman	
"The man who does not read good books has no advantage over the man who can't read." – Mark Twain	
"You don't have to burn books to destroy a culture. Just get people to stop reading them." – Ray Bradbury	
"Think before you speak. Read before you think." – Fran Lebowitz	
"Reading is to the mind what exercise is to the body." – Richard Steele	
"My alma mater was books, a good library ... I could spend the rest of my life reading, just satisfying my curiosity." – Malcolm X	

Source: Quotes from The Literacy Company.

7.1 What Is Reading?

Nagaraju offers the following definition of reading:

> Reading is not a simple, passive process of linear reading of words and internalizing their meaning one at a time. Reading is a complex interaction between the text and the reader shaped by the readers' prior knowledge and attitude, a process of language acquisition, communication and sharing information and ideas.[2]

Much can be written about reading in general, but our primary focus in this chapter is to briefly identify principles and techniques that college students can apply to the reading of their textbooks.

7.2 Why Textbooks?

Many introductory-level textbooks are quite impressive in terms of the volume of information they contain. Textbooks don't just present the core concepts of the discipline; they are also loaded with vignettes—boxed essays related to, but separate from, the body of the text—pictures, charts, tables, maps, and so on. These are all desirable components; taken together, however, they sometimes result in a book measuring over two inches thick and costing more than $200. It is easy to understand how a first-year college student taking five classes could be overwhelmed by the massive content (and cost)!

Nevertheless, making good use of your textbooks is without a doubt one of the most important skills you must learn. The textbook is absolutely essential for the vast majority of college courses. Failing to acquire and read a textbook is one of the biggest mistakes that a student can make in a course. If you are enrolled in a course for which you think the textbook is optional, ask the professor if he or she thinks that you will be able to perform well in the course without the textbook. If the professor agrees, then it will be fine. Otherwise, assume that the textbook is critical and not optional.

As the Austin Phelps's quote that began this chapter suggested, obtaining a textbook must be a budget priority for any student who wishes to be successful in college. Critical Thinking Activity 7.1 asked you to think of ways to complete the required reading assignment for a college course if you could not afford a textbook. Can you think of additional ways to obtain a textbook if you cannot afford to buy one? This is a problem that you might need to solve in order to be successful in college.

In the next section of this chapter, we will explore how to read a college textbook effectively. Your attitude about reading will make a big difference in your likelihood of success. Table 7.1 presents statements associated with succeeding and failing attitudes about reading. How many of the failing ideas have you agreed with in the past? How many of the succeeding ideas have you agreed with in the past? If you want to be successful in college, you will need to abandon the failing ideas and adopt successful ideas and behaviors regarding reading.

Table 7.1

Failing and Succeeding Dispositions Toward Reading a Textbook	
Failing Ideas	**Succeeding Ideas**
I don't plan to buy (or otherwise acquire) a textbook.	I will make owning the textbook a top budget priority.
I will not buy a textbook on the first day of class, but I might buy one at some time later in the semester.	If I can't afford the book, then I will look for another way to acquire one so that I can complete the reading and adequately prepare for class.
I don't plan to read the textbook.	I will prepare to read by planning specific times in my schedule for that purpose.
Instead of reading, I will just skim the textbook to look for items that I think will be on the exam.	I will adopt a reading strategy such as SOAR or SQ3R to ensure that my reading is effective.
I will wait until after the professor lectures on a chapter before I read the chapter so that I can use the lecture for clues about what parts of the book will be on the exam.	I will read the assignment before the class where it will be discussed, so that I will be prepared for each class and will not fall behind.
I expect the professor to go through the book during the class, before an exam, and to tell the students which pages are important. I will wait until then to read.	When we do discuss a chapter in class, I will ask questions about anything that I did not understand from my reading.
I'll let the professor teach me what I need to know; after all, that's what he gets paid for, so it is his responsibility.	I will take adult responsibility for my learning, and I will not expect the professor to spoon feed the information to me as if I were an elementary school child.

Reading Comprehension Question 7.1 (Knowledge)

Why are textbooks important in college?

a. Because introductory textbooks have all the information you need to pass that course

b. Because these books replace the professor's lecture materials for most classes

c. Because in most college courses, textbooks provide essential information for understanding and learning the course material

d. None of the above

7.3 How to Read a Textbook

The first step for success in reading is to actually read the textbook. Too many students try to get through a course without actually reading. They may not buy a book and therefore don't read at all, or they may acquire a book but never open it. Activities such as skimming, highlighting sentences when the professor reads them in class, or staring blankly at the page while in study hall do not constitute effective reading.

In his blog, D'Agostino, a former mathematics and physics professor and textbook writer and editor, addressed the question of why students do not read textbooks.

> In the frenzy of deadline after deadline (assignments due, quizzes, tests, labs, lab reports, etc.), it's all they can do to put out the next fire. As a result, they are very inefficient; they can't take the time to do a good job of learning the material, which would involve reading the textbook, working through the examples, and doing many practice exercises. Instead, they devote far more time to completing the assignments than would be necessary if they had done many practice exercises, because they attempt the assignments before they really understand the material. But they don't see an alternative, because the assignments are worth marks, and so they are (unfortunately) a higher priority than actually learning the material. By the end of the course, they understand very little, even if they have managed to score a decent grade.[3]

Does D'Agostino's explanation fit your situation? Do you have trouble reading effectively? If so, can you identify any barriers that prevent you from reading success? In order to become a better reader, you should devote time to reading, treat reading as a top priority, seek a reading environment without distractions, and employ proven strategies such as the SOAR and SQ3R methods.

Expect to Devote Time to Reading

Effective reading and studying take time. The number of hours that students spend studying has gradually decreased since the 1960s, from twenty-four hours per week in 1961 to fourteen hours per week in recent years.[4] We could hypothesize that students need less time to study today due to technological advances (after all, a calculator is faster than a slide rule); however, if so, then we would expect them to learn more and earn higher grades. They don't. Researchers have observed that, unaided, students make the same types of study errors using electronic media as they do using other media. Bottom line: If you want to be successful in college, you are going to have to devote a lot of time to reading and studying.

Don't Try to Multitask

Any adult can understand why texting while driving is a serious mistake. The dangers of texting on your phone or another electronic device while reading your textbook may not be immediately apparent to some students, but it is also a big mistake. If you want to learn and be successful in college, then you are going to have to be so committed to studying that you are willing to turn off your phone, TV, music, or any other distraction while you study.

Read in an Environment That Supports Studying

Are you planning to read and study in the dorms? No way! There are too many distractions and interruptions. Go to a place that will enable you to concentrate on your reading and studying. The library is usually a great place to study. Tutoring labs are also good. But it does not have to be a place labeled "study hall," as long as it is a place free from distractions, where you can read, think, take notes, and concentrate.

Want to learn more? Try these resources.

The Virginia Tech website has a Study Environment Analysis tool that lets you type in three locations and then evaluate them as reading locations by answering twelve simple questions. Try it yourself by browsing to the following URL:

http://bvtlab.com/GPe8Z

Employ Proven Strategies for Reading

There are many good strategies that you could adopt to improve your reading. In this chapter we will review two of them: the SOAR method and the SQ3R method. These methods are very useful when reading the typical textbook.

SOAR

Would you like to score twenty-nine to sixty-three points higher on your next exam? Through research, Kenneth Kiewra discovered four techniques that, when practiced by students while studying, significantly improve learning. They are known by the acronym SOAR, which stands for Selecting, Organizing, Associating, and Regulating. **Selecting** refers to distinguishing what information is important.[5] **Organizing** involves converting information from its initial form to comparative charts and illustrations.[6] **Associating** involves creating meaningful connections between ideas.[7] **Regulating** includes learning through practice and self-evaluation.[8] Kiewra found that "undergraduates in the study scored 29 to 63 percentage points higher on tests when they used study techniques like recording complete notes, creating comparative charts, building associations, and crafting practice questions."[9]

As Kiewra noted, "Learning occurs best when important information is selected from less important ideas, when selected information is organized graphically, when associations are built among ideas, and when understanding is regulated through self-testing."[9] The elements of SOAR can be incorporated into a popular method called SQ3R.[7]

Table 7.2		
Description of the SOAR Method		
S	Select	Distinguish important information from the information that is less important.
O	Organize	Convert the important information into another format such as a table, list, chart, timeline, etc., that reflects your understanding of the main points.
A	Associate	Recognize the connections between the different important facts, ideas, or concepts.
R	Regulate	Assess yourself at regular intervals to determine how much of the important material you have adequately learned. When you discover a gap in your knowledge or a deficiency in the quality of your understanding, engage in additional learning to correct the problem.

Sources: Jairam & Kiewra 2009; Jairam & Kiewra 2010; Kiewra 2002; Kiewra 2005; and University of Nebraska-Lincoln 2010.

SQ3R

Effectively reading a college textbook or journal article involves a lot more than simply moving your eyes across the page and decoding the words. This is illustrated by a summary of the SQ3R method.[10] SQ3R stands for Survey, Question, Read, Review, and Recite.[11] The principles of the SOAR method can be incorporated into the SQ3R strategy.

Table 7.3		
Description of the SQ3R Method		
S	Survey	Using this method, you should begin your reading assignment by **surveying** what you are expected to read to get a general overview of it. Observe how the document is organized or divided. Textbooks often include reading tools embedded into the chapter to help you read more effectively. Look to see what reading tools are included in the document, such as a list of learning goals for the chapter, a list of key terms, definitions set out in the margins, the important terms or phrases printed in bold, an outline, or a summary. Surveying the document before reading will help you to distinguish the most relevant information from any less relevant parts (this is referred to as **selecting** in the SOAR model).
Q	Question	**Question** means to actively engage with the text by asking yourself questions before and while you read. Examples of questions you might ask include the following: What is this chapter about? What is the main idea? What facts support the main idea? What examples are given? What information in this chapter is relevant and important? What information will help me address the **learning goals** for the course, chapter, or lesson? Clearly stated goals for each chapter can help students with the very important study task of determining what facts or concepts presented in the reading or lecture are most important. If the goals are not already provided for you in the textbook, the syllabus, or a handout from the professor, then ask the professor what his or her goals are for the chapter or lesson in question.

Description of the SQ3R Method *(Cont.)*

R	Read	Once your survey of the document is complete, you are ready to begin **reading** sections of it. Especially in the case of reading a textbook, you should write notes about what you are reading. Do not write everything, but instead isolate the most important points and organize them in a way that makes sense to you. Yep, effective reading involves writing! The point of this note taking is to shrink the important content of the chapter down to a few brief summary pages that will help you learn the information. You should try to convert the information from its initial form to comparative charts and illustrations—this is called **organizing** in the SOAR model. Note taking will help you concentrate on your reading. Sometimes this reading will move along quickly, especially when you are covering familiar material. At other times you will need to slow down and concentrate to make sure that you understand what you are reading. Understanding is paramount. While it is true that some things—such as special vocabulary—should be memorized, the main objective of your reading should be to learn and understand the content.
R	Review	At the college level, reading something one time usually isn't enough to master it. This is where the notes you take while reading come in handy. You should plan time to **review** them on a regular basis. Difficult material may need to be reviewed more often than less challenging material. When you **review,** try to make connections between the information in your notes, information in other reading assignments, information from lectures, and information from class discussions (this is called **association** in the SOAR model). This is a very important part of the process because it will help you to elevate your studying from the level of memorization to the level of critical thinking and understanding.
R	Recite	**Recite** means to say the information out loud or to write it out on paper. In order to get the full benefit from your reading, you should set aside time each week to recite your notes. This is an activity that can be done with a partner who is learning the same material. Hearing another person's notes may help you to improve your understanding and memory of the information—even more so than if you used just your own notes. Use your notes to test yourself. The act of learning through practice and self-evaluation is called **regulating** in the SOAR model.

Reading Comprehension Question 7.2 (Literal Comprehension)

Why is it important that students use the SOAR method of reading and studying?

a. Students should use it because any method is better than no method.

b. Students should use it because it is the most recent method developed by reading experts.

c. Research has proven that students score much higher on tests when they use the SOAR method.

d. It is not recommended that students use the SOAR method; they are urged to use the more popular SQ3R method, instead.

Want to learn more? Try these resources.

The Dartmouth site has a number of additional videos and written (downloadable) resources that address student success. View resources at Dartmouth College at the following URL:

http://bvtlab.com/CZ697

Download the list of Active Reading Strategies from the McGraw Center for Teaching and Learning at Princeton University at the following URL:

http://bvtlab.com/4cNb7

7.4 Road Signs for Reading

Effective reading is a stop-and-go process. Efficient readers vary their reading according to the material being read and their purpose for reading it. Some reading material is intended to be read faster, such as magazines or newspapers. Textbooks are generally read more slowly, but even within textbooks there are passages that can be read quickly. Following are some general tips to help you read more efficiently:

1. **Merge—read phrases instead of individual words.** Normally, when you read, you can read faster and comprehend better if you focus your eyes on groups of words that make up phrases instead of focusing on each word individually.

2. **Slow down for difficult passages.** Avoid reading the same phrase over and over without understanding it. Instead, if you are dealing with a difficult passage in a book, slow down, concentrate, and read the passage more carefully. In the long run, it may take less time to read a difficult passage slowly with understanding than it would to read it many times quickly without understanding.

3. **Stop to think about what you have read.** Periodically, as you read, you should stop and think about what you have read. What was the point of the passage? What part of it is most important? What did you learn by reading it? Was there any part of it that did not make sense to you? Was there any vocabulary that is new to you (that you need to look up)? Do you need to write notes about anything in the passage?

4. **Speed up for easier material.** You may read faster when dealing with not-so-difficult passages of the text. In other words, you should vary your reading speed and technique so that it matches the difficulty level and writing style of the passage.

Reading Comprehension Question 7.3 (Inferential Comprehension)

Based on the information in Road Signs for Reading, how should you read a textbook?

a. You should use the skim method to get the main idea without reading everything.

b. You should read the textbook slowly, line by line

c. You should read as fast as you can because college students have a large amount of required reading.

d. You should take time to read and to understand what you're reading, knowing that you may need to vary your reading according to the content.

7.5 Responding to New Vocabulary

No matter how much education you acquire, as long as you keep reading, you will continue to encounter new vocabulary. This is positive because it means that you are learning new things. How do you go about learning new words and their meanings?

Identifying New Vocabulary

When you read something strictly for pleasure, such as a novel, you usually don't worry about new vocabulary. If you come to a word you don't know, you simply continue reading and figure out what the author meant from the context. It is not essential that you understand the meaning exactly as long as you understand the passage as a whole. This is often not the case when you read a textbook. Identifying, understanding, and applying new vocabulary is often critical when reading a textbook. Following are some ways that you can identify and understand words that are new to you.

Use Phonics to Sound Out the Word

Using phonics involves determining the sound of a word by making the sounds represented by each letter or letter group in the word. It is a good idea to try to sound out a word phonetically—especially if you were taught to read using phonics when you were a child. Unfortunately, the English language does not provide phonetic rules that can be applied to every word. Some students (and even adults!) have a large vocabulary of words that they simply haven't heard in conversation or elsewhere. Nevertheless, phonics skills can provide an important link between vocabulary acquired by hearing and vocabulary learned through reading. Using phonics may also help you to spell words more easily.

Use Context Clues to Derive Meaning

Many times you can figure out what a word means by observing how it is used in the sentence or paragraph. What part of speech is the unfamiliar word? You may not realize it, but if you can't figure out the meaning of the word, then you may not understand the passage very well. When this happens, you should look up the unknown word in a dictionary in order to make sure that you understand the passage.

Use Resources Such as a Glossary or a Dictionary

Does the textbook have a glossary? A glossary is a listing, sometimes found in the back of a textbook and sometimes found at the end of a chapter in the book, which provides definitions for words or concepts that the author feels are important to the particular discipline the textbook covers. Sometimes information in the glossary can help you better understand the point of a passage where a glossary word has been used. Dictionaries of various types are also a great resource for college students.

Learning New Words and Definitions

While understanding is always your primary goal, you may discover some discipline-specific vocabulary that you will need to memorize. Flashcards are one helpful tool in such cases. Standard three-by-five-inch index cards are ideal for this activity. Write the vocabulary word or concept on one side of the card and the definition on the opposite side. Test yourself by reading the word and then, without looking at the definition, reciting the definition aloud. Then turn the card over to see if you were correct. If you were correct, go to the next card. If you were incorrect, recite the word and read the correct definition aloud to help fix it in your memory.

Figure 7.1

Example of a Flashcard

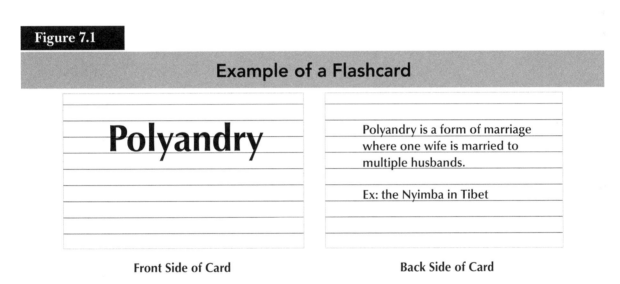

Front Side of Card   **Back Side of Card**

Moving Beyond Definitions to Associations

It is usually not enough to simply memorize the definitions for new words; you need to understand how these terms relate to other terms and to larger concepts. One strategy that may help you do this is called *concept mapping*.[13]

Concept mapping involves drawing a diagram of the terms to show the relationships between them. For example, if you encountered new vocabulary when reading about different types of marriage, you might draw a concept map like the one illustrated in Figure 7.2. The diagram helps you to easily recognize the ways in which the terms are similar and the ways in which they are different. Monogamy and polygamy are different types of marriage. Strict monogamy and serial monogamy are different types of monogamy. Polygyny and polyandry are different types of polygamy.

Other types of visual organizers include tables, charts, graphs, timelines, flowcharts, diagrams, and webs. Examples of these may be found online.

Figure 7.2

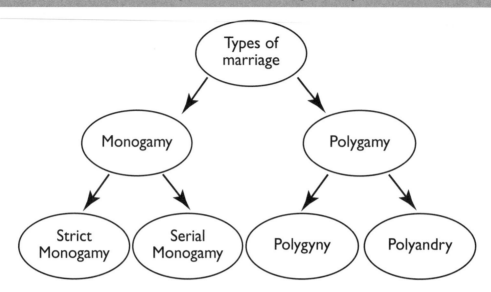

Example of a Concept Map

Reading Comprehension Question 7.4 (Analysis)

Which of the following statements is accurate according to this chapter?

a. Reading involves writing.

b. Reading involves asking questions.

c. Reading involves testing yourself.

d. Reading involves distinguishing what information is important.

e. All of the above

Want to learn more? Try these resources.

A table called Graphing Various Types of Conceptual Relationships is presented online at the following URL:

http://bvtlab.com/nmsXj

Information about concept mapping can be found at the following URL:

http://bvtlab.com/7898R

In addition, examples of five different types of visual organizers are presented at the following URL:

http://bvtlab.com/8srAc

7.6 Summary

In this chapter you learned why obtaining and reading the textbook in college is so important, as well as how to read a textbook effectively. Proven reading and learning strategies were described, including the SOAR (Select, Organize, Associate, and Regulate) method and the SQ3R (Survey, Question, Read, Review, and Recite) method. Good and bad attitudes toward reading in college were compared. The section on reading road signs explained ways to vary your reading rate and technique so that they match the difficulty level and writing style of the passage. Methods for dealing with new vocabulary were identified, including using phonics and using context clues or other resources (a glossary or a dictionary). The chapter also offered techniques for learning new terms and concepts and for making associations between them.

Name: _____

Study Guide | Goal 1

The student will be able to explain why reading textbooks in college is so important.

Questions	Answers & Notes

Name: _____

Study Guide | Goal 2

The student will be able to demonstrate how to use a textbook effectively and describe strategies that can improve reading comprehension.

Questions	Answers & Notes

Name: _____

Study Guide | Goal 3

The student will be able to describe and use the SOAR method.

Questions	Answers & Notes

Name: _____

Study Guide | Goal 4

The student will be able to describe and use the SQ3R method.

Questions	Answers & Notes

Name: _____

Study Guide | Goal 5

The student will be able to use concept mapping as a way to move beyond definitions to associations when learning new vocabulary.

Questions	Answers & Notes

Study Guide | Preparing for Class

Use this page to record questions or insights to discuss in class.

_____

_____

_____

_____

_____

_____

_____

_____

_____

_____

_____

_____

_____

_____

_____

_____

_____

_____

_____

_____

_____

_____

_____

_____

_____

_____

_____

_____

_____

_____

Name: _____

Review Questions 7.1

Instructions

Following are five true-false statements taken from the information in this chapter. First, try to answer them without looking back at the chapter. Then review the chapter to see how well you did.

Question & Answer	Rationale
Circle true or false for each of the following statements.	Write an explanation stating why each statement is true or false.
1. A student can be successful in college without buying textbooks. True or False	Your Rationale:
2. The SOAR method is good for students who don't have a strategy for reading and studying, but students who already have a strategy will perform better if they stick to their own strategy because they are most comfortable with it. True or False	Your Rationale:
3. Memorizing new vocabulary is necessary, but understanding will always be your primary goal. True or False	Your Rationale:
4. Concept maps are a strategy that is designed to help you memorize new vocabulary. True or False	Your Rationale:
5. Not understanding words in the textbook is a sign that the student does not have much education. True or False	Your Rationale:

Name: _____

Assignment 7.1

Practice Identifying New Vocabulary

Goals

The purposes of this activity are to help students use and identify new vocabulary and thus read more effectively and to teach students to value this activity as a means of gaining a greater understanding of what they read.

Objective

The student will analyze a reading passage from a college-level textbook to identify new vocabulary, and then use multiple techniques to understand the vocabulary and gain greater understanding of the passage.

Instructions

Get a highlighter. Then pick a chapter in one of your textbooks and start reading. As you read, each time you come to a word that you don't know, highlight that word but don't stop reading. Keep going until you have read a few pages. Then use the analysis questions that follow to think about the words you have identified. Write notes about each question and what you learned in the space provided.

Notes

_____
_____
_____
_____
_____
_____
_____
_____
_____
_____
_____
_____
_____
_____
_____
_____
_____
_____
_____
_____
_____
_____
_____
_____

Analysis

How many words did you highlight?

Think about each word. Were you able to figure out the meaning for some of the highlighted words just by considering the context of the passages around it? How many of them could you figure out that way?

Look a few of them up to see if the meaning you have assumed, based on the context, is correct. Did you get them all correct, or were there some that you misunderstood?

Now look at the remaining highlighted words. How many of the highlighted words are left for which you were not able to figure out the meaning just from context? Look up the definitions of those words in the glossary (or if no glossary is available, use a dictionary). Do you understand the chapter better now that you know the definitions for those words?

How many of those highlighted words would you consider "important" for this class? Do you think that looking them up will help you score a higher grade on the exams in this class than you would have otherwise?

_____

_____

_____

_____

_____

_____

_____

_____

_____

_____

_____

_____

_____

_____

_____

_____

_____

_____

_____

_____

_____

_____

Chapter Roadmap

Introduction

In this chapter you will examine some guidelines for writing a formal, college-level paper. You will also learn how to plan and organize your writing efforts for maximum success.

This chapter roadmap page presents the formal learning goals for this chapter and a checklist that you should follow as you read and study the chapter.

Student Learning Goals

After completing this chapter you should be able to do the following:

1. Delineate and discuss the steps for creating a formal college-level paper, including designing a reasonable timeline.

2. Distinguish between peer-reviewed journal articles and other types of literature.

3. Apply specified style manual rules (such as MLA or APA) as well as basic formatting to a college-level paper.

Chapter Checklist

You will benefit most if you complete the activities in the order that they are listed.

❑ **Target Date/Deadline:** _____
Complete Critical Thinking Activity 8.1.

❑ **Target Date/Deadline:** _____
Convert the student learning goals to questions that you can answer as you read the chapter. Write your questions on the study guide pages near the end of this chapter.

❑ **Target Date/Deadline:** _____
Read the chapter.

❑ **Target Date/Deadline:** _____
Try to answer the reading comprehension questions as you come to them in the chapter. Check each answer by comparing it to the list of correct answers in the back of the book. If any answer was not correct, then review the passages preceding the question to see why you missed the question.

❑ **Target Date/Deadline:** _____
Answer the student learning goal questions you created. These answered questions will be your study guide.

❑ **Target Date/Deadline:** _____
Write down any questions, insights, or comments that you have as you read so that you can bring them up in class (if applicable).

❑ **Target Date/Deadline:** _____
Complete Review Questions 8.1.

❑ **Target Date/Deadline:** _____
Complete Assignment 8.1 (Practice Finding Resources).

❑ **Target Date/Deadline:** _____
Review what you have learned from this chapter.

Critical Thinking Activity 8.1

As a way to begin thinking about the topic of this chapter, please consider the following question.

Do you think you could eat a whole pizza by yourself?

Your answer is likely, "Sure I can," because you know that pizzas come in many sizes including a small, individual serving size.

Imagine, however, a pizza that is six feet in diameter—a pizza that, if you stood it up in one end, would be taller than most people.

Design a plan that would enable you to eat—all by yourself—an entire pizza that is six feet in diameter. Record the steps of your plan in the space provided below. Be prepared to share your plan in class if asked to do so.

_____

_____

_____

_____

_____

_____

_____

_____

_____

_____

_____

_____

_____

_____

_____

_____

_____

_____

_____

_____

_____

_____

_____

Writing College Papers:

I Have a Paper Due!

"When asked, 'How do you write?' I invariably answer, 'One word at a time,' and the answer is invariably dismissed. But that is all it is. It sounds too simple to be true, but consider the Great Wall of China, if you will: one stone at a time, man. That's all. One stone at a time."
— Stephen King[1]

"The most important thing is to read as much as you can, like I did. It will give you an understanding of what makes good writing and it will enlarge your vocabulary."
— J. K. Rowling[2]

As a college student, you will be asked to do many types of writing. The following four basic categories of writing assignments are typically used in college: personal writing, academic writing, public writing, and creative writing. Personal writing, when used as an assignment, includes things like personal journal responses, in-class essay responses, and shorter opinion paper assignments. Academic writing includes research papers, analysis papers, article reviews or summaries, more formal in-class essays, and essay exams. The purpose of academic writing is to allow the student to demonstrate understanding. Public writing is identified as writing for an outside audience and includes résumés, business letters, and so on. Creative writing, or writing for creative expression, includes poetry and short stories.

In this chapter you will learn some basic tips for writing that will apply to any writing assignment, and you will learn some more specific guidelines that apply to writing a research paper. You will also learn how to plan for writing a research paper or similar writing project, because those types of writing assignments cannot be completed in a single sitting. You will need to plan when you will complete each step in the process of writing a research paper.

8.1 Guidelines for College Writing

It may be helpful to review these tips before beginning a formal writing assignment.

College Success: A Concise Practical Guide

Follow the Professor's Instructions

Different professors may require different formats or other particulars for the paper. Even within the same course, different writing assignments may have different requirements. For example, a research paper has different content and format restrictions than an opinion essay. Make sure to find out what the specific requirements are for each writing assignment, and then make sure that you follow those instructions.

Sometimes students do silly things with the formatting of a written assignment—such as using a very large font or very large margins because they think it will make the paper appear longer. Your professor is not an idiot. He or she will recognize this manipulation immediately. The professor will not be impressed; instead, it sets low expectations for your paper.

Use the Proper Format

How will you format your paper? There are many different styles that are used in college and professional research publications. Four common style guides are the American Psychological Association (APA), the Modern Language Association (MLA), the Chicago Manual of Style (CMS), and the Council of Science Editors (CSE). APA is the style most commonly used within the social and behavioral sciences. MLA is the style most commonly used within the liberal arts and humanities. CMS is the style often used by researchers of history. CSE is often used within science disciplines. These four are not the only styles that are used, but they are the ones that you are most likely to encounter during your undergraduate education.

If your professor requires a particular style guide (such as MLA or APA) for the writing assignment, take the time to look at the guide and make sure that your paper conforms to the proper format. Most of the style guides are available in the library, and college library websites often have links to information about the various formats. Make sure that you are using the most current version of the guide or the version that your professor has specified.

Want to learn more? Try these resources.

The APA website offers a very impressive online tutorial, complete with downloadable examples, where you can learn almost anything you need to know about formatting in APA style. You can access the *Basics of APA Style Tutorial* online at the following URL:

http://bvtlab.com/6866R

The following webpage provides information about MLA, APA, CMS, and CSE—including example papers:

http://bvtlab.com/a6M97

The *Purdue Online Writing Lab (OWL)* has many excellent resources for information about the different style guides. A very useful resource is the "Comparison Chart for MLA, APA, and CMS." It is a table that shows side-by-side examples from each of the three styles for the most common formatting questions. You can download it as a PDF file from the following URL:

http://bvtlab.com/98w2S

Do Not Plagiarize, and Keep a Copy of Your Sources

When you use the actual words or even just the ideas of others in a paper, you must give credit to the original author. This is usually done by including a citation for the quote or idea within the paper and a reference identifying the original source at the end of the paper. Failure to properly cite the use of another's ideas is called plagiarism. The penalty for plagiarism can be very severe. Ask the professor if you are unsure about some part of your paper. Check and correct before you submit the paper.

It is very important that you avoid plagiarism when you write a research paper. Sometimes students are inadvertently guilty of plagiarism. However, it does not matter whether or not the student did it intentionally when the professor sits down to grade the essay. The professor has no choice but to assign a grade of zero to a plagiarized paper because he or she may not be able, by reading, to determine your intent. It is the student's solemn responsibility to avoid plagiarism.

Copying from a book (or other source) without properly identifying the source is plagiarism. It is particularly problematic for a graded assignment because copying does not demonstrate understanding. A first grader could copy from the book but would be unlikely to understand what he or she has written. What you write in your research paper should demonstrate that you understand the concept about which you are writing.

It is important that you understand what plagiarism is and that you take care to do your own thinking and to write in such a way so as to demonstrate your understanding of the topic. The process of thinking about the topic and putting it into your own words, possibly with your own examples, will help you own the information and forge it into your long-term memory.

Quoting from the textbook or other sources is permissible when it is properly cited, but it is not acceptable to submit an essay that is basically just one big quote. Try to convey your thoughts with a combination of quotes and paraphrased concepts in your own words. In many cases, using your own examples of the concept (instead of copying examples from the textbook) is a good way to demonstrate understanding. It is also acceptable to challenge or question ideas presented in a book or an article.

The easiest way to avoid plagiarism is to include citations in your essay so that the original authors are credited for their words or ideas. Citations in a paper may impress the professor during grading because the citations suggest that the student has read and thought about the articles or other resources that were cited. Such a paper may be more impressive than one in which the student presents nothing but his or her opinion—without any evidence of prior reading or study. However, the citations in your paper must conform to a specified format. There are many different styles or formats for citations, so remember to ask your professor what style is required for each assignment.

Keep copies of the articles you use in your paper until after the paper has been graded because the professor may ask to see some of them. If the topic of your paper is one that you are likely to study again in another course, then you may wish to keep those copies of your sources for future reference. You will not be allowed to submit the same exact paper again— that's called *self-plagiarism;* but you may write a new paper on a similar topic for which some of the same references will be useful.

Write with Purpose

Make sure that the paper demonstrates your mastery of the topic or assignment. Provide support for the main points in the paper with details—such as examples, explanations, and references to supporting documents (with citations).

Following are a few general tips for writing any type of paper and also a few tips to use when writing a research paper. Follow these guidelines unless your professor tells you to do something differently.

Tips for General Writing

- Create an outline and use it to write your paper. It may be helpful to write your first draft on top of your outline—filling in the text under each section of the outline. Even if you delete the outline from the paper after you have finished it, an outline is a good tool to help you organize your thinking during the writing process.

- Use introductory sentences. Don't just launch into a main section of your paper without informing the reader of the "big picture."

- Use transitional sentences. These are sentences that bridge the different parts of your paper, connecting them together. Include them at the end of one main part of your paper to prepare the reader for the next main section of your paper.

- Do not quote the dictionary in your paper. As Williams and McEnerney from the University of Chicago Writing Program have explained, "If a concept is so important to your paper that you feel compelled to specify its meaning, its dictionary definition will be too generic for your purposes. A somewhat better strategy here is to cite a definition by a specialist in a particular field or by an otherwise admirable individual."[3]

- Avoid redundancy.

Tips for Writing a Research Paper

- Do not put your personal opinion or anecdotal stories in the paper because these are not appropriate for a formal research paper. A research paper presents the findings and analysis of research projects that were conducted on the topic you are writing about. You can use your own words to summarize the research, but do not include your own unverified opinion.

- Do not use Wikipedia® as a source for a research paper because Wikipedia articles are not original research and are not refereed, so they may not be accurate. However, you may read Wikipedia articles to get ideas about a topic and then look up the original research Wikipedia cites.

- Use current sources that are no more than about five years old. Including an older, famous foundational article or including a series of articles that go far back in history to establish a historical perspective would be exceptions to this rule. Ask your professor to be sure with regard to any specific assignment, but it is generally expected that the sources for a research paper be very current. (This may be more true for the sciences than other fields; even English majors write research papers, but because their field changes more slowly, the age of the source may be less relevant.)

- Use primary research and refereed journal articles describing original research. You should not use opinion pieces or articles that summarize research conducted by someone other than the author. Instead, get the original article written by the author who actually conducted the research.

- Remember that personal pronouns (such as *I*, *we*, and *you*), contractions (such as *don't* and *can't*), and colloquial language or slang are almost always inappropriate for this kind of assignment.

- Consult the appropriate style guide for formatting rules—including rules for citation, punctuation usage, capitalization, and when to use numerals or write out numbers as words.

- Do not use vague terms to describe the findings of research (for example, "A good many of the respondents agreed …"). Instead, be specific and accurate (for example, "Fifty percent of the respondents agreed …").

- Be aware that the term *significant* has a special mathematical meaning in research. Therefore, you should not use the word *significant* unless you are reporting on a test of significance that was performed. In cases where a measure of significance was used, do not describe it in terms of varying degree (for example, it was "a little" or "somewhat" or "the most" significant). There are no degrees of significance; instead you would report that the results either were or were not significant.

Proofread, Do Your Best Work, and Grade Yourself First

The paper you submit for a grade should be a polished product. It should reflect your best effort. Therefore, never submit your first draft. Instead, review your paper, and make corrections or improvements. This is called proofreading. It is kind of like grading yourself. Don't let the professor become your proofreader. You need to find the problems and fix them first so that the professor never sees them.

Make sure that your paper has correct spelling, grammatical construction, and punctuation before you submit it. Your essay must also be written in complete sentences. It must make sense. As part of the proofreading process, you should read the paper aloud to yourself to check for clarity. It is also advisable that you ask a friend or a tutor to look over your paper. A fresh pair of eyes may quickly see errors that you have overlooked. This way you can do one final edit and correct those errors before you submit your paper for a grade.

Reading Comprehension Question 8.1 (Knowledge)

Susan has written a paper on adolescent pregnancy and has copied two paragraphs from a journal article. She has not given a citation for the paragraphs that she used. This would be which of the following?

a. This would be okay, if she types the paragraphs verbatim.

b. This would be a problem if the paragraphs do not support her thesis.

c. This would be plagiarism, for which there may be severe penalties.

d. This would be a way for Susan to show her professor how much she knows.

8.2 Resources for College Writing

In most cases, when you have a formal college writing assignment, you will need to find resources to inform and support your writing. Usually, the best place to find those resources is the college library and its website.

Using Sources from the Internet

The Internet can be a great resource for your writing, but you must take care how you use it. Unlike refereed journals, much of the information on the Internet is not reviewed or validated in any way. If you are not careful, you could wind up putting inaccurate information in your paper because you got the information from an unreliable source. For writing a college-level paper, if you need references, you should use your college's library collections of journals and peer-reviewed sources. Avoid using any online sites such as Wikipedia. Although they might give you some information of interest, and even some references (which you could look up, read, and use in your paper if they are from a legitimate source), articles in Wikipedia should not be used as a source in a college paper. Remember that many things that are written on the Internet are opinions or personal pieces from only that author's point of view. Be safe and use your own college library sources for writing your paper.

Using Scholarly Publications

As already mentioned, unlike the Internet, refereed scholarly journal articles are a reliable source for information. This is especially important when you are writing a research paper.

What is a scholarly journal? Generally, scholarly journals have a sober, serious look. They often contain many graphs and charts with few glossy pages or exciting pictures. In addition, scholarly journals always cite their sources in the form of footnotes or bibliographies. Articles are written by a scholar in the field or by someone who has done research in the field. Furthermore, the language of scholarly journals is that of the discipline covered, and they assume some scholarly background on the part of the reader. The main purpose of a scholarly journal is to report on original research or experimentation in order to make such information available to the rest of the scholarly world. Many scholarly journals—though by no means all—are published by a specific professional organization.

The articles that you will find in a scholarly journal almost always follow the same basic outline. They start with an abstract and end with a list of references. Table 8.1 lists the headings that you almost always see in a research journal article.

In addition, you will see that tables, charts, figures, and statistical data are often found throughout the article. A few examples of scholarly journals include the following:

- *American Economic Review*
- *Archives of Sexual Behavior*
- *JAMA: The Journal of the American Medical Association*
- *Journal of Marriage and the Family*
- *Modern Fiction Studies*
- *Sex Roles: A Journal of Research*

Table 8.1

Research Journal Article Headings	
Title	The title and author(s) name(s) appear at the top, often with information about the author's affiliation(s).
Abstract	This summary helps the reader to determine how relevant this study is to the reader's interests.
Literature review	This is where the author(s) briefly describes previous research on the topic and shows where the current study fits into an overall understanding of the topic.
Purpose of the study	This section often includes the hypothesis and problem statement.
Methodology	This section describes the research design and procedures.
Findings	This section describes the results obtained by the methods previously described. Here is where you see if the hypothesis was supported or not. It presents data only and does not include opinion.
Discussion	This section is where the author(s) discusses what he or she thinks the findings mean.
Conclusion	This section serves as a summary and often discusses implications or ideas for future studies.
References	This section is where you will find the works cited in a research article.

Sources that are not considered scholarly include newspapers (such as the *Atlanta Journal*), popular magazines (such as *Newsweek*), journals of opinion (such as *The New Republic*), and many websites (such as Wikipedia).

If you are looking for scholarly journals, then you should connect to the webpage for the college library. That is your best source for scholarly articles and, best of all—it is free.

Reading Comprehension Question 8.2 (Literal Comprehension)

Which of the following is true about writing a research paper for college?

a. It is usually easy to decide on a topic for a research paper

b. Searching for materials to support your research topic is a quick and easy task

c. A paper should be researched, written, edited, and rewritten before it is submitted to the professor.

d. None of the above

Want to learn more? Try these resources.

The *Purdue Online Writing Lab* offers information and tips on different types of writing.
http://bvtlab.com/P7R97

An excellent resource for students learning to write college-level papers is the book, *Writing in College: A Short Guide to College Writing* by Joseph M. Williams and Lawrence McEnerney. This resource is available at the following URL for the University of Chicago website and is part of the University of Chicago Writing Program:
http://bvtlab.com/cC273

Another outstanding resource, found at the following URL, is the article, "What Is an Academic Paper?" written by Karen Gocsik of Dartmouth College. It is part of the Dartmouth writing program:
http://bvtlab.com/7FF62

Reading Comprehension Question 8.3 (Inferential Comprehension)

You have chosen to do a research paper on techniques for success in college. Which of the following is most likely to be scholarly and refereed?

a. An article on a website selling books and DVDs on how to make straight A's

b. An article in the *Atlanta Journal Constitution* newspaper

c. An article you found in the library, in a journal, that includes an abstract, a literature review section, a methods section, a findings section, and a references list

d. An article from Wikipedia

8.3 Planning the College-Level Paper

Writing a formal paper in college usually involves several steps: (1) selecting a topic, (2) collecting information about the topic, (3) reading and thinking about the information, (4) writing the first draft, (5) proofreading, and (6) producing the final copy. If the formal paper is a research paper or if it involves a project or experiment, then additional steps may be required. It should be clear, then, that most formal college-level writing cannot be done in a single day. It is a task that you will have to divide into smaller parts, or steps, which you will complete over time.

Consider the critical thinking exercise that appears at the beginning of this chapter. On that page, you were asked to devise a plan whereby you could eat a pizza of six feet in diameter all by yourself. At first you might muse that such a task is impossible because it is far too much for any human to eat in one sitting. However, almost anyone could eat the giant pizza if they simply broke it up into many smaller meals and ate them one at a time over many days.

Writing a formal college-level paper is like eating a giant pizza, in that it is not something that you can complete in one sitting on one day. It is nearly impossible for you to do your best work on a paper if you try to write the entire paper in one day or one weekend. You need to *break the large task of writing the paper into the smaller tasks* (or steps) that are involved in writing the paper. Then simply plan a time to complete each smaller task so that everything is complete before the deadline. You can *use the calendars* and *task list templates* provided in this book to plan your college writing project.

So, how do you plan a major college writing project? First, you should estimate how much time each step will require. Second, working backward from the due date, mark each step on your calendar, adding each step to the task list for those dates.

Identify the Tasks Involved and Estimate the Time Required for Each

In the example depicted in Tables 8.2 and 8.3, you can see how a student might plan the date on which to begin a writing project and the various dates on which to complete each step. Please note that the estimates listed in the example may not accurately reflect the amounts of time that you will need for a similar project. It is also true that your personal task list may vary from the items in the example. The estimates for each actual assignment will vary based on the requirements for the assignment and how long it takes you to read your sources and write your draft. Therefore, you will have to make your own time estimates for your writing project. Try to make your estimates as realistic as you can. After you have more experience with writing college papers, you will be better at accurately predicting the time required for various tasks.

Table 8.2

Task List Planning Example	
Step	**Time Estimate**
1. Select a topic.	
A. Look at a few resources in the library and/or online to make sure that enough information on the topic is easily available.	1 hour
B. Get the topic approved by the professor (after class or during the professor's office hours).	5 to 10 minutes
2. Collect information about the topic.	
A. Search for sources in the library and/or online.	2 hours
B. Think about how the sources could be put together to support a topic and about how the topic may be narrowed.	1 hour
C. Read initial sources and make notes.	2 hours

Task List Planning Example *(Cont.)*	
Step	**Time Estimate**
3. Study (think more deeply about) the information that you collected on the topic.	
A. Identify questions about, or aspects of, your topic that were not adequately covered by the initial sources.	30 minutes
B. Survey the initial sources for leads to additional sources.	30 minutes
C. Collect additional sources.	2 hours
D. Read additional sources and make notes.	2 hours
4. Write the first draft.	
A. Create an outline.	30 minutes
B. Write the text that fills in the various sections of the outline, citing sources as appropriate.	2 hours
C. Continue writing the text.	2 hours
D. Create the reference list.	1 hour
E. Write the introduction/abstract.	30 minutes
5. Proofread and revise	
A. Read the paper aloud to make sure that it makes sense.	1 hour
B. Check for grammar and spelling errors.	30 minutes
C. Check each citation to make sure that it matches the reference list.	30 minutes
D. Check the entire paper for format compliance to whichever style guide the professor requires.	30 minutes
E. Proofread aloud, a second time, to make sure that all of the errors were corrected.	30 minutes
F. Print the final copy and prepare it for submission.	30 minutes
6. Submit	

Reading Comprehension Question 8.4 (Analysis)

The main idea of "Planning the College-Level Paper" is which of the following?

a. Planning a paper ahead of time is not necessary in college.

b. Planning the paper can help you to write and revise the paper in time to turn it in.

c. Planning a project takes time that most students do not have in college.

d. Planning a paper ahead of time is not an efficient use of a student's time.

Add the Tasks to a Calendar

Once you have identified the tasks associated with writing the paper and estimated the amount of time each item will require, you should record the tasks as appointments on your monthly calendar and on the task list (to-do checklist) for each day affected.

Even though the total amount of time required to complete the project is less than twenty-four hours (if the time estimates on the task list planning example are accurate), it cannot be done in only one or two days. These tasks have to be done over a period of time with some time to think between tasks. (You may have noticed by now that you are supposed to do a lot of thinking in college.)

Figure 8.1 is an example of a monthly calendar with times allocated to complete each individual project task or step. To figure out when you should do each step, simply start with the last one (Task 6, Submit) and work your way backward through the calendar. Schedule the steps at times that fit within your regular schedule and in reverse order (Task 5, 4, 3, 2, and finally Task 1). Note that, in this example, the student has left a two-day gap between when the *final paper is printed* and the *actual due date*. This gap was planned so that the student would be prepared to deal with any last-minute delays that might arise, such as a broken printer or the discovery that more time is needed to correct errors than was expected. Do not wait until the due date to complete assignments. Plan ahead so that you can do your best work. Once again, as with many other academic endeavors, good planning is a key to success in college-level writing.

Figure 8.1

Example Monthly Calendar with Tasks Planned						
Mon	Tue	Wed	Thu	Fri	Sat	Sun
1 Step 1A START DATE	2 Step 1B	3	4 Step 2A	5	6	7
8 Step 2B	9 Step 2C	10 Step 3A Step 3B	11 Step 3C	12	13 Step 3D	14
15 Step 4A	16 Step 4B	17	18 Step 4C	19	20 Step 4D Step 4E	21
22	23 Step 5A Step 5B Step 5C	24 Step 5D	25	26	27 Step 5E	28
29 Step 5F	30	1	2 Step 6 DUE DATE	3	4	5

8.4 Summary

This chapter addressed some of the challenges that come with a formal, college-level writing assignment or a research paper. Some basic guidelines for how to approach a writing project were offered. You also learned how to use the calendar and task list as tools to plan a writing project in such a way that you have time to read, write, think, proofread, and revise. This will empower you to do your best work and to submit a paper of which you can be proud.

Name: _____

Study Guide | Goal 1

The student will be able to delineate and discuss the steps for creating a formal college-level paper, including designing a reasonable timeline.

Questions	Answers & Notes

Name: _____

Study Guide | Goal 2

The student will be able to distinguish between peer-reviewed journal articles and other types of literature.

Questions	Answers & Notes

Name: _____

Study Guide | Goal 3

The student will be able to apply specified style manual rules (such as MLA or APA) as well as basic formatting to a college-level paper.

Questions	Answers & Notes

Study Guide | Preparing for Class

Use this page to record questions or insights to discuss in class.

Name: _____

Review Questions 8.1

Instructions

Following are five true-false statements taken from the information in this chapter. First, try to answer them without looking back at the chapter. Then review the chapter to see how well you did.

Question & Answer	Rationale
Circle true or false for each of the following statements.	Write an explanation stating why each statement is true or false.
1. Good planning is a key to success in college-level writing. True or False	Your Rationale:
2. If you are writing a paper for a psychology class, you will probably be asked to use the MLA guidelines to format your paper. True or False	Your Rationale:
3. You should record the tasks associated with writing a college-level paper on your calendar in reverse order (e.g., record the last task first and so on). True or False	Your Rationale:
4. The chapter compared writing a formal college-level paper to eating a giant pizza because if you take on too much at one time you will get sick. True or False	Your Rationale:
5. It is a good idea to quote from the dictionary (and cite it because it adds an extra source to your paper and helps support your argument). True or False	Your Rationale:

Name: _____

Assignment 8.1

Practice Finding Resources

Goal

The purpose of this activity is for the student to master using the library to collect sources for a college research paper.

Objective

The student will demonstrate understanding of how to use the library to retrieve a refereed journal article and how to write a citation for the article in both APA and MLA styles.

Instructions

In preparation for this assignment, you should review the information from this chapter about how to distinguish a scholarly article from other types of publications and about the APA and MLA style manuals. You will find a comparison chart for MLA, APA, and CMS styles very helpful when you write the citation information for the article you retrieve. The comparison chart is available at http://bvtlab.com/98w2S.

Follow These Steps

Step 1: Determine the topic of your research quest.

Step 2: Log on to your college library website, and conduct a search for a refereed (also called peer-reviewed) article on the topic you chose. Once you find an article, save it as a PDF file so that you can look it over later. If you don't know how to search for a peer-reviewed article, ask the librarian for help.

Step 3: Answer the questions about your article in the space provided on the next page. Remember that you can use the comparison chart mentioned above to easily figure out how to write the citation.

Notes

_____
_____
_____
_____
_____
_____
_____
_____
_____
_____
_____
_____
_____
_____
_____
_____
_____
_____
_____
_____
_____
_____
_____
_____
_____
_____
_____
_____
_____
_____

Fill in the appropriate information in the space provided on this page.

What topic did you search for?

What is the title of the article that you found?

Write the citation for the article as it would appear in the reference list for an APA paper.

Write the citation for the article as it would appear on the works cited page for an MLA paper.

How did you determine that this was a scholarly article? List *several* ways.

Chapter Roadmap

Introduction

It is often a difficult transition from home to college in that you must now learn how to balance all your responsibilities—academic, psychological, physical, and financial—entirely (or mostly) on your own. So far in this text, we have covered maintaining balance and achieving success from an academic standpoint. However, even academic success is influenced by how well you balance the other areas of your life, such as your finances and your physical and mental health. At times, it may feel as if you are walking a tightrope in college.

This chapter roadmap page presents the formal learning goals for this chapter and a checklist that you should follow as you read and study the chapter.

Student Learning Goals

After completing this chapter you should be able to do the following:

1. Define *balance* and list the important elements of overall balance as well as the characteristics of a balanced student.

2. Discuss four reasons why balance is important in college.

3. List three common psychological problems faced by college students.

4. Discuss one common way in which you can help yourself if you experience psychological problems during your college years.

Chapter Checklist

You will benefit most if you complete the activities in the order that they are listed.

❑ **Target Date/Deadline:** _____
Complete Critical Thinking Activity 9.1.

❑ **Target Date/Deadline:** _____
Convert the student learning goals to questions that you can answer as you read the chapter. Write your questions on the study guide pages near the end of this chapter.

❑ **Target Date/Deadline:** _____
Read the chapter.

❑ **Target Date/Deadline:** _____
Try to answer the reading comprehension questions as you come to them in the chapter. Check each answer by comparing it to the list of correct answers in the back of the book. If any answer was not correct, then review the passages preceding the question to see why you missed the question.

❑ **Target Date/Deadline:** _____
Answer the student learning goal questions you created. These answered questions will be your study guide.

❑ **Target Date/Deadline:** _____
Write down any questions, insights, or comments that you have as you read so that you can bring them up in class.

❑ **Target Date/Deadline:** _____
Complete Review Questions 9.1.

❑ **Target Date/Deadline:** _____
Complete Assignment 9.1 (Maintaining Balance in Life During College).

❑ **Target Date/Deadline:** _____
Review what you have learned from this chapter.

Critical Thinking Activity 9.1

Before you read this chapter and without looking up any information about the topic on the Internet or elsewhere, use the space provided on this page to write your answers to the following questions:

1. When you think of balance, what comes to mind? Write your thoughts below.

2. What do you think the author meant by this quote?

> *"The major work of the world is not done by geniuses. It is done by ordinary people, with balance in their lives, who have learned to work in an extraordinary manner."*

— Gordon B. Hinckley[1]

3. Think of ways in which your life could become out of balance during your first year of college. How might you prevent this? List at least two ways.

Psychological Balance:

Walking the Tightrope

9

"My point is, life is about balance. The good and the bad. The highs and the lows. The pina and the colada."

— Ellen DeGeneres, *Seriously … I'm Kidding*[2]

"Mathematics expresses values that reflect the cosmos, including orderliness, balance, harmony, logic, and abstract beauty."

— Deepak Chopra[3]

"Life is like riding a bicycle. To keep your balance, you must keep moving."

— Albert Einstein[4]

9.1 Balance Defined

Balance could be defined as a state in which you are meeting all of your obligations to yourself and others. Some people might also use the term *equilibrium* to denote a state of balance. Having balance in your life implies that you feel things are under control. In practice, however, balance can be an elusive concept. Each person might define *balance* in life differently. How do you define balance in your life? Think for a moment about a time when you felt that your life was in balance. What did it feel like? Was it a calm period in your life? How did you feel about yourself? Now, take a moment to think of a time when you might have characterized your life as *not* in balance. How did that differ from when you felt you were in balance? What does it feel like to be out of balance? Was it a calm period, or was it chaotic? How did you feel about yourself?

Comparing times in which you have and have not been in balance is a good exercise. It can give you a new perspective on life and how you might be living yours. It is possible to get out of balance through no fault of your own. Sometimes balance is a natural state, and things that happen to us as we live our daily lives can throw us out of balance. At other points in our lives, our own actions can influence whether we are in balance, and we can develop behaviors that lead to imbalance.

As you grow and develop through your college years, perhaps you will become more aware of those behaviors that tend to throw you out of balance; then you can work toward controlling them so that you do not become imbalanced. You can learn which behaviors tend to move you toward a state of balance and health, and which behaviors tend to move you toward a state of imbalance and discomfort. In this part of the book, you will learn about behaviors and attitudes that can move you toward wellness and balance in your life.

At the core, being balanced means that you are doing the things that you need to do to keep yourself as stress-free and healthy as you can. It does *not* mean that you have *no stress*—nor does it mean, necessarily, that you have no illnesses or diseases. As a college student, achieving balance could be described as maintaining some sort of equilibrium in the four main areas: academics, finances, physical health, and psychological health. Let us take a moment to explore each of these four areas briefly.

Reading Comprehension Question 9.1 (Knowledge)

In college, it is important to maintain balance in which of the following areas?

a. Finances

b. Academics

c. Psychological health

d. Physical health

e. All of the above

9.2 Elements of Balance

Academic

Academic balance can be described as a state in which you are meeting the requirements for all of your courses and are learning what you need to learn in order to pass each course. As we have discussed throughout this textbook, passing means that you are actively learning the information that you need to learn in order to progress in college. Achieving balance in your academic life includes understanding the material covered in each course you are taking, planning to fulfill each of the course requirements, and then executing the requirements for each course successfully. Hopefully, this book has given you information that will help you to stay in academic balance. Because you have read and learned about academics throughout this text, that topic will not be covered again in depth here.

Financial

Financial balance is important for the college student because college is expensive. For the college student, financial balance implies being able to pay for college expenses as well as cost-of-living bills. Sometimes, parents, relatives, or friends might help to cover bills. However, many students are alone in their responsibility for paying for educational as well as living expenses. When this is the case, managing your finances can be stressful; it is important to pay attention to whether or not you are in financial balance. Please refer to Chapter 11 for an in-depth treatment of financial balance and the way in which you can maintain yourself financially through college.

Physical

Physical balance is a state in which your physical body is in equilibrium. It does not necessarily mean you have no illness or disease. It does mean, however, that you have your illness *or* disease under control. For example, someone with diabetes could still be physically balanced if he or she is managing the diabetes with proper diet, exercise, and medication. The person would be out of balance if his or her diet, medication, or stress level caused a drastic increase or decrease in blood sugar, however. If it is midterm week and you get the flu, your body is likely to be out of physical balance. So sometimes we cannot control whether or not we are in balance physically; yet there are many things we can do to help ourselves to stay in physical balance—such as incorporating healthy diet and exercise into our routine, to name but two. Physical balance encompasses diet, exercise, sleep, love and romantic relationships, drug and alcohol management, appropriate visits to the doctor, and time management.

Reading Comprehension Question 9.2 (Literal Comprehension)

In college, which of the following best describes physical balance?

a. Thinking and behaving in ways that are helpful to you in maintaining balance
b. Ensuring you have no stress, depression, or eating disorders
c. Being able to pay both college bills and cost-of-living bills
d. Using diet and exercise to ensure that your body is in equilibrium

Psychological

Psychological balance might be described as a state in which you think, feel, and behave in ways that are helpful to you in achieving your goals in life. It means that you are able to complete your daily living activities (such as bathing, dressing, and eating) and that you feel a sense of well-being most days. Everyone has times during which they feel "down," sad, or anxious. However, if you are in psychological balance, these times are fleeting—they do not last, and you can behave in ways or do things that will alleviate those kinds of feelings. Later in the chapter, we will discuss what happens when these feelings overwhelm and color most of your days. Psychological balance in college can be thought to encompass stress reduction, using social supports, behaving and thinking in ways that contribute to a sense of well-being, maintaining daily activities, having friends and relationships that contribute to feelings of well-being, and monitoring behaviors, moods, and feelings so that you do not slip into the more common psychological problems experienced by college students. Such problems can include stress, depression, anxiety, and eating disorders, to name a few.

So far we have discussed the four characteristics that contribute to balance for a college student (see Figure 9.1). A balanced college student is someone who is learning what is needed to pass all his or her college courses, feels and behaves in ways that facilitate his or her life goals, has a body that is in equilibrium, and is able to pay for college and cost-of-living bills. Balance does not necessarily imply perfection. Stress is an inevitable part of life and people feel stressed under many life circumstances, including college. Rather balance implies that, given your life circumstances, you are able to get through your daily activities and have a sense of well-being about your life in general.

Figure 9.1

Four Elements of a Balanced College Student

During certain times in our lives, we have all experienced a lack of balance. It is not a good feeling. Examples of events that can occur in your freshman year that could cause a disruption in your balance include:

- Parents' divorce
- Being diagnosed with a chronic illness, such as diabetes, or a serious mental illness
- Homesickness, feelings of loneliness, or feeling like you are isolated
- Worrying about money
- Unplanned pregnancy
- Recent or past physical or sexual assault
- A loved one's death
- Identity or sexual identity confusion
- Academic or family pressures
- Cultural oppression or being discriminated against
- Failing a course (or courses)
- Overuse of alcohol or drugs

Research shows that college students encounter a host of developmental challenges and stressors, including loneliness, homesickness, conflict, distress in interpersonal relationships, and high stress levels.[5] In an article about coping with freshman year in college, Hollinger, in his interviews with freshmen, found that the major challenges experienced by these students were homesickness, living with roommates, managing money, and dealing with much more difficult academics in college compared to high school.[6] In general many studies have shown that college is a stressful life event that, for many students, requires a relevant social network to successfully navigate.[7]

When we do not have balance or support, we are more susceptible to physical and psychological illnesses, and we may experience extreme levels of stress. During college, you are no exception. Being healthy means that you monitor your own body and mind and that you are aware of the things that contribute to being in or out of balance. Reaching out when you are feeling unbalanced is also a key factor in whether or not you can regain your balance in a timely manner. When you do so, you will be better able to conduct yourself in ways that maintain balance as opposed to ways that cause disruption.

As you can see, maintaining balance is an important skill to have in college. The following are major reasons why balance is so critical in college:

1. Students cannot reach their college goals unless they maintain some semblance of balance in their everyday lives while in college. College is a time of many life changes. Maintaining balance is critical in meeting the physical, academic, psychological, and financial goals of college.

2. Each individual needs to learn exactly what balance means for them. Balance is extremely individualized, and you must determine for yourself how and when you consider yourself to be in balance or out of balance.

3. Imbalance in one area of your life often leads to imbalance in other areas. It is important to learn how to monitor yourself and to monitor those behaviors and attitudes that lead you into a place of balance in all areas of your life.

4. It is difficult, if not impossible, to progress through the developmental stages of growth that you will need to go through while you are in college if you find yourself always in a state of imbalance. Imbalance distracts an individual from critical college goals.

Want to learn more? Try these resources.

This webpage is a self-help guide for students. It contains good information about coping, maintaining balance, patterns of thought, and ways to help yourself. It is a great place to get ideas for how to cope with a situation or stressor.

http://bvtlab.com/37B78

This is an excellent website that provides tips on how to reduce stress levels while in college. Topics include time management, sleep, exercise, energy, and much more.

http://bvtlab.com/n8Gca

9.3 Maintaining Psychological Balance

Let's start by discussing a typical student—let's call her Jessica.

Jessica arrived at college and settled into her dorm room about a month ago. Classes have begun. Even though she was a straight-A student in high school, she is worried and feels very stressed about the challenges of college-level learning. She is also frightened by the fact that she is now free—free to do whatever she wants, whenever she wants. When she was in high school, freedom was something that she craved, and she could hardly wait to get to college and have her very own space and her very own schedule. But now that she has arrived, it seems like a daunting task to keep her grades up, study, take complete care of herself, and generally have a totally independent life separate from her parents and old friends.

Speaking of parents and old friends, she is also having feelings of intense homesickness. Sometimes her stomach begins to hurt and she feels physically ill from missing home. Her feelings seem to be getting worse each week, and she is beginning to feel like she is losing control of her own life.

On top of all the academic stress, Jessica is finding that she probably needs to get part-time job to get her through financially. Her parents have provided ample financial support for her tuition and fees, books, and food. However, she is noticing that there are lots of little expenses that she didn't anticipate (like wanting to go out to dinner with friends).

All in all, Jessica is feeling quite overwhelmed. She's been having small episodes where it's hard to breathe, she gets sweaty palms, everything seems to be crowding in around her, and she feels irritable toward her newfound friends. She is beginning to stay in her dorm room during the day and to avoid phone calls—both of which are very unusual because she is normally a very outgoing, gregarious person. These feelings are not like her at all and she is beginning to get worried that something bad is happening to her.

Think About This

Stop for a moment and make a list of four or five ways that Jessica might work on maintaining psychological balance in these difficult first weeks of college.

1. _____

2. _____

3. _____

4. _____

5. _____

The things Jessica is experiencing are common during the stressful transition from high school to college. But they are also intensifying as the weeks go by, and that is something she should pay attention to. Jessica is beginning to think that something is wrong, and that is a sign that she should seek help now—before her symptoms progress any further.

Jessica talks with a good friend, Carol, whom she met the first week of classes. She is surprised to find that Carol shares many of the same thoughts and fears as Jessica. The two friends sit down together and begin to problem-solve about Jessica's situation. She and Carol come up with a few things they can do to help reduce their stress levels and thus maintain their psychological balance.

They can reduce stress by:

- Engaging in specific behaviors that build strong coping skills (which will be discussed later in this chapter)

- Finding and using social support networks (like family members, campus counseling centers, and classmates) in a directed way to support their goals

- Maintaining daily activities so that things (like laundry and chores) don't pile up

They should monitor the following behaviors, moods, and feelings:

- Anxiety

- Depression

- Eating disorders

- And other signs of imbalance

If any of these issues are present in a serious way, or if they seem to be getting worse in spite of Jessica and Carol's best efforts to deal with them, these students should seek outside help immediately!

It is very important for you to remain psychologically balanced, especially during your first year of college. Freshman year is filled with many new experiences, and your adjustment to them sets the stage for the remainder of your college years. This chapter will provide information about several common psychological problems often experienced by new college students.

Being balanced psychologically is important because your psychological health provides the basis for your behavior, thoughts, and ability to learn. In addition, psychological health allows you to grow and change in positive ways while you are in the new environment that a college campus offers. In the same way that physical health and balance enables your body to maintain health and wellness, psychological health and balance enable your mind to think and feel in healthy ways, to be resilient in the face of stress, and to complete your goals for learning in college. Although psychological and social issues are not always given as much emphasis as physical issues, they are just as (and sometimes even more) important when it comes to meeting your developmental and life goals in college.

The truth is that most students go through college with little or no stress. In fact, several researchers studying college students have found that the most common trend across the four years of college was that of little to no distress.[8] They found that this was particularly true for those who used flexible coping mechanisms. As they say, sometimes you need to "go with the flow." Even though modern college life is stressful—and students face challenges such as environmental changes, loss of social support networks, academic pressures, the need to establish new peer relationships, and increases in personal responsibility in housing and money management—in all likelihood, you will be able to rise to the occasion and grow into your new role. If you find you are struggling, however, keep in mind that too much stress has been found to have negative effects on the mental health of students.[8,9] It's a good idea to get help as soon as you notice something is wrong.

This chapter presents information about several problems that can be experienced in college. Neither this chapter nor any of the websites presented in it takes the place of a physician's assessment. Be sure to use your college counseling center if you feel you might be at risk or that something is seriously wrong. There has been an increase in recent years in the number of college students who make use of college counseling centers.[10] A 2011 survey of counseling center directors found that 10.6 percent of college students sought counseling at their campus counseling center—an increase from 9 percent in 2008.[10,11] When students seek out the counseling center for issues such as depression, anxiety, eating disorders, and alcohol use, they are often experiencing a lack of peer support,[12] a loss of and separation from relationships at home,[13] dissatisfaction with their bodies,[14] or feelings of not being connected with the college campus. Keep in mind that these problems are both common and treatable.

Just the act of talking through the details of college stressors can enhance academic success and can improve overall health. These findings have been replicated across multiple socioeconomic levels, ages, languages, educational levels, and cultures.[10]

Reducing Stress Levels

Maintaining physical health is discussed in Chapter 10, but it is important to note that the same behaviors that enhance physical health can also help reduce stress levels. Stress is the body's reaction to things that have the potential to harm you. When you enter a brand-new environment, such as college, it is natural to feel stressed. Normally, this passes with time. However, if it lasts for a long time, it can become a serious problem and can negatively impact your physical and mental health. In a life-threatening situation, stress can save your life. But when it happens in a situation that is not life threatening—as it did with Jessica and Carol in college—and when the stress response does not turn off, you might begin to experience health problems as a consequence.

Going to college means plunging headfirst into a new world—new classes, new demands and responsibilities, new roles, and new living arrangements, even a new roommate! It is critical that you recognize when you are stressed and that you do things to reduce your stress level. There are many things you can do to keep your stress down to a minimal level. These include but are not limited to:

- *Engaging in directed behaviors that reduce your level of stress*

  Stress-reducing activities might include reading a good book, relaxing by the pool, or going to the gym. What activities make you feel relaxed and happy? These are the things you should do to reduce your stress. Think about what behaviors work best for you in reducing your feelings of stress and use these behaviors in a *directed* way. Participating in behaviors in a directed way means that you actually plan out when, what, how, and where you are going to do these things.

- *Using social support networks to help when you are feeling out of balance*

When you get to college, it is a good idea to try to make friends as soon as possible. For some people, this is easy; for others, not so much. However, when you are new in college, it is very helpful to seek out friends who have the same life goals as you (finishing college, for example). Friends can be a huge source of support while you are adjusting to college life. Such friends can be found in your classes, in student clubs, and by participating in other activities. If you have a hard time joining groups or meeting new friends on your own, your college counseling center is a great place to get support.

- *Behaving in ways that contribute to a sense of daily well-being and goal accomplishment*

Do what makes you feel good on an everyday basis. It is important to maintain your daily living activities, such as bathing, washing, personal care, doing laundry, etc. Be certain to make up a schedule that includes these daily activities. This can greatly reduce stress, can keep you grounded, and can give you a sense that you are in the right place, doing what is needed to get your college degree. Other regularly scheduled behaviors might include making sure you are eating three meals a day, exercising, and socializing. Sometimes you may feel like you don't know what to do to make yourself feel better. At these times, focusing on your life goals (e.g., finishing the difficult course you are taking or finishing the semester) can be helpful. Giving yourself goals to focus on can take your focus off small, everyday annoyances and help you to focus on the future instead.

Want to learn more? Try these resources.

This website is brought to you by the Nemours Center for Children's Health Media, a part of The Nemours Foundation, a nonprofit organization created by philanthropist Alfred I. duPont in 1936 and devoted to improving the health of children. This site offers practical and helpful information about seeking and selecting a roommate, about the importance of communication, about day-to-day issues, and about problem solving with a roommate. You can either read or listen to the article:

http://bvtlab.com/a7khp

This website, also from Nemours, provides an excellent review of stress, causes and signs of stress overload, tips on how to keep your stress under control, and ideas for building your resilience to stress. You can either read or listen to the article:

http://bvtlab.com/K67ku

This website provides ten good tips with practical suggestions about how to deal with stress as a college student. The page is also excellent because it provides many more links to topics that may be of interest to you as you begin your first year of college life:

http://bvtlab.com/a6fZV

Monitoring Your Behaviors, Moods, and Feelings

Anxiety

Anxiety is a natural response to stress. As we discussed above, our bodies have an automatic response to life-threatening stressors. Our bodies are designed so that when we are exposed to stressors, we feel anxious or fearful. With this anxiety and fear come physical changes, such as increases in breathing rate and heart rate, and suppression of digestion, to name but two. These automatic physical changes work in our favor when we truly are facing an immediate threat to our lives. However, over time, if we do not or cannot "turn off" our automatic stress response, our bodies begin to experience negative effects.

Cases of mild or even moderate anxiety—such as when you are taking an exam—can be helpful to you because mild to moderate anxiety can stimulate you to pay attention, to be alert, and to think clearly. This can help you in your studies. When stress and anxiety rise to an extreme level, however, they can be counterproductive to you as a student. Sometimes you can feel overwhelmed. Jessica, in the story above, was beginning to experience a sense of being overwhelmed in her dorm room. This is a red flag telling you that something more than routine or normal anxiety is taking place as a response to stress.

In some severe cases, you might even experience panic attacks. The key difference between a mild to moderate response and an extreme response to stress is *functional ability*—this means your ability to perform the activities of daily living (such as going to class, eating, resting, reading, studying, bathing, etc.). If you feel anxious to the point that you are unable to do your required daily activities, you need to seek help immediately at your college counseling center. Severe anxiety—during which you are unable to complete your daily living activities—can be controlled with therapy and medication. It is important to get help as soon as you can in order to avoid longer-term problems.

Attention-Deficit/Hyperactivity Disorder (ADHD)

Have you ever felt like you cannot pay attention for any length of time? Do you make careless mistakes, find it very difficult to follow through on instructions, or have difficulty organizing your tasks or activities? Have you ever been diagnosed with attention-deficit/hyperactivity disorder (ADHD)? Everyone gets distracted sometimes; and throughout your college career, you may find some classes to be less engaging than others. However, if you have chronic trouble concentrating and it begins to affect your grades, you may be experiencing a more serious problem.

ADHD is not just a problem for young children; it can also be a problem in college and can affect your learning and, therefore, your grades. If you feel you might have ADHD, or if you are having serious difficulty completing your work for classes because of a lack of attention span (or difficulty reading and studying, for example), you should see your college counselor as soon as possible.

The counseling center at your college will be able to assess you for symptoms of ADHD and can refer you to a specialist in this area. It is important to get assessed before your college learning is significantly affected. If you do have ADHD and it affects your ability to take tests, you can make arrangements for special testing circumstances if needed, in accordance with ADA (Americans with Disabilities Act) requirements. So be certain to see a counselor if you suspect you might suffer from ADHD.

Want to learn more? Try these resources.

This website from the National Institutes of Mental Health provides a comprehensive booklet about anxiety disorders, covering topics such as symptoms and treatments, ways to get help, and types of anxiety disorders. The booklet can be printed out (since it is provided in .PDF format) or can be ordered free as a hard copy:

http://bvtlab.com/874Gm

Do I have an anxiety disorder?

This website from the Anxiety and Depression Association of America has many links to screening tools for disorders such as generalized anxiety disorder, obsessive-compulsive disorder, panic disorder, PTSD (post-traumatic stress disorder), social anxiety disorder, phobias, and depression. The screening tools are arranged so that you can take the screening test, and then print out your results to take to a health-care professional.

http://bvtlab.com/fPa64

Do I have symptoms of ADHD?

The Adult ADHD Self-Report Scale (ASRS-v1.1) is a quick screening quiz that has just the six questions that have been found to be most predictive of symptoms consistent with ADHD. This short quiz is available here:

http://bvtlab.com/87uba

Depression

<u>What Is Depression?</u>   Depression is an illness that involves one's mood. Sadness can often be confused with the illness of depression. Although everyone experiences times of sadness in their life, typically these episodes of sadness are time-limited. That is, you may feel sad for a day or two—or even for longer periods in the case of losing someone close to you—but this sadness gets better with time and does not linger or stay with you for weeks or months. Sadness is part of being human. It is a response to loss, and the result of having feelings about those you love and about things that happen to you. Moving to college and away from all your friends, family, and familiar support systems can cause feelings of sadness and loss for anyone.

Sadness can sometimes be accompanied by other symptoms. Things like loss of (or excessive) sleep, a change in appetite, an inability to feel happy about anything, and frequent crying or tearfulness are all symptoms that can occur alongside sadness. When you are sad, these symptoms might come and go, or might remain for a few days at a time. However, these symptoms should decrease over time and should not stay with you for weeks or months. All of these feelings are common among college freshmen. Remember these important ways to help yourself when you are feeling sad:

1. Do things that make you feel better during the day.

2. Assess the level of sadness you are experiencing.

3. Seek help if your sadness persists or if it causes you to change your daily behaviors—such as to miss classes, to stay in bed, to take drugs or drink alcohol excessively, or to avoid doing things with friends.

Don't ever hesitate to use counseling services on campus—they are a wonderful resource for you while you are in college. Almost all colleges have a counseling center that provides individual and group help for students who are experiencing sadness.

How Can I Tell If I'm Depressed?

If you are experiencing the illness of depression, the symptoms of sadness described above (loss of or excessive sleep, change in appetite, inability to feel happy about anything, frequent crying or tearfulness, etc.) persist over time and become chronic (long-lasting). You may find yourself feeling these symptoms for weeks or months at a time. If so, you need to get help from your counseling center immediately. If you are depressed, you will often notice changes in your daily activities. You might become withdrawn, stay in your room, avoid other people, and isolate yourself. You might stop following your daily hygiene routine (such as bathing, brushing your teeth, washing your hair, etc.). You may skip classes or stop doing homework. As soon as you recognize these changes, you need to get help from your counseling center.

How Is Depression Treated?

Depression is often treated with a combination of talk therapy (talking with someone on a regular basis) and medication. There is a wide range of medications that are helpful in reducing or totally removing depressive symptoms. Depression is a very treatable disease, so do not wait to get help. Try and get help as soon as possible when you notice symptoms. Seek out help from your counseling center if you are unsure about your level of sadness, or if you know that you are feeling depressed. Don't wait too long, because there are treatments that can help you before your depression begins to affect your daily activities and grades.

This chapter is not designed to provide medical advice for depression. The very best way to handle the sadness or depression that you might be feeling is to go to the college counseling center where you can talk with someone who can assess your level of depression, and provide therapy, medications, or both, if needed.

In regard to self-help, the following websites are reliable, helpful, and useful if you feel you may be experiencing depression in college or if you are concerned about a friend who is depressed.

Want to learn more? Try these resources.

This excellent webpage from the National Institute of Mental Health (NIMH) deals with answers to frequently asked questions about college depression—such as what depression is and how it affects college students—as well as information about different types of depression, including signs and symptoms, causes, and treatments:

http://bvtlab.com/C45Y8

Do I have a mental health issue right now?

This website from Mental Health America provides a test that screens for depression, anxiety, bipolar disorder, and post-traumatic stress disorder. The screening tool provides you with a number that will help you and your doctor understand if you have a treatable mental health disorder. The assessment report that you get when you have completed the test provides a scale indicating how disruptive your symptoms are, your risk for various disorders, and a section on recommended action. The assessment can either be printed or emailed to you.

http://bvtlab.com/6hu68

Reading Comprehension Question 9.3
(Inferential Comprehension)

Every college student should know that depression is _____.

a. a normal response to stress
b. not curable
c. a state of just feeling sad
d. a highly treatable disorder

Eating Disorders

Who Has Eating Disorders?   Eating disorders are a real mental illness—not a choice—and they affect both men and women of college age. Although they are less common in men than in women, they appear to display strikingly similar features in affected individuals of the two genders.[15] The rate of eating disorders among college men ranges from 4 percent to 10 percent, and a recent study on a large university campus found that the female-to-male ratio was 3–1.[16]

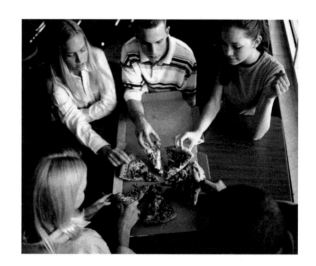

Between 28 percent and 68 percent of normal-weight young men think that they are underweight and want to increase their muscle mass through dieting and strength training.[17] One in five women struggle with an eating disorder; of those, 90 percent are between the ages of 12 and 25. Four out of ten people either have an eating disorder or have known someone who does.[18]

What Are Eating Disorders?   Eating disorders include anorexia nervosa, bulimia nervosa, and binge eating disorder. In addition to the symptoms listed in Table 9.1, severe distress or worry about body weight or shape and extreme behaviors designed to manage weight or food intake may also be characteristic of eating disorders. In the end, all eating disorders revolve around unhealthy eating and weight regulation. There are many adverse or negative effects psychologically, physically, and socially. An eating disorder can start with an individual merely eating smaller or larger amounts of food, but in order for it to be a disorder, at some point things must get worse—to the point that daily living is disrupted.

Eating disorders are real, treatable, medical illnesses. People with eating disorders often suffer from other illnesses such as depression, substance abuse, or anxiety disorders.[19] Symptoms of some eating disorders can be life-threatening if treatment is not provided; anorexia nervosa is associated with the highest mortality rate of any psychiatric disorder. Usually, eating disorders first appear during the teen years or in young adulthood, but they may also develop in childhood or in later life.[20]

Table 9.1

Symptoms of Eating Disorders

Anorexia Nervosa	Binge Eating Disorder	Bulimia Nervosa
• Very low body weight • Severe food restriction • Intense fear of gaining weight • Lack of menstruation in females • Distorted body image (belief that the body is bigger than it is) • Denial of the seriousness of low body weight • Unwillingness to maintain a normal/healthy weight	• Loss of control over eating • Periods of binge eating not accompanied by compensatory behaviors (e.g., purging, excessive exercise, fasting) • Often involves being overweight or obese	• Recurrent and frequent episodes of eating unusually large amounts of food • Feeling a lack of control over such episodes • Binge eating followed by behavior that compensates for the overeating, such as forced vomiting, excessive use of laxatives/diuretics, fasting, excessive exercise, or a combination of these behaviors • Usually able to maintain a normal weight; may be slightly overweight • Fear of gaining weight • Being unhappy with body size and shape

What Is the Treatment for Eating Disorders?   Treatment goals often include restoring nutrition, getting weight to a healthy level, reducing excessive exercise, and stopping bingeing and purging behaviors. For treating specific disorders, talk therapy has been shown to be helpful in some cases. Some antidepressant medications have also been found to help in the treatment for bulimia nervosa and may also be helpful for treating co-occurring anxiety or depression for other eating disorders.

Treatment plans for eating disorders often include one or more of the following:

- Individual, group, or family therapy

- Medical care and monitoring

- Nutritional counseling

- Medications (for example, antidepressants)

In some cases, hospitalization may be necessary to treat malnutrition or to ensure that the patients eat enough if they are underweight. Although sometimes difficult, eating disorders are treatable, and recovery is possible.

If you are experiencing the symptoms listed in Table 9.1, you may have an eating disorder or be at greater risk for developing one. It is a signal that you need to get some help with your eating and the way you feel about your body. If you think that you might have an eating disorder, you need to see a counselor as soon as possible. It may be helpful for you to tell a close friend what is happening with you. Perhaps a friend can accompany you to the counseling center. There, you could have an assessment done and talk with a counselor.

Remember that in college, your community is the campus and you need to reach out and seek help from that community. Some college students also maintain contact with their physician in their home town. You may wish to make an appointment there if you have insurance coverage. You may also wish to share your symptoms with your parents. For those who have experienced an eating disorder in the past, in some cases the stress of college can cause the disorder to come back. If you are already familiar with your eating disorder, you may be able to tell when symptoms could be getting out of hand. Monitor yourself, seek support from friends and family, and get to a counseling center as soon as possible in order to have the best outcome in treatment.

<u>What Should I Do If I Think One of My Friends Has an Eating Disorder?</u>   If you suspect that one of your friends has an eating disorder, or if someone has shared with you that he or she has an eating disorder, you should first be supportive. This friend is having a very difficult time and is suffering from an illness that needs to be treated. Behaviors that might lead you to suspect that your friend has an eating disorder include:

- Adherence to strict dieting, regardless of weight

- Regular trips to the bathroom immediately after eating

- Secretly bingeing on large amounts of food

- Hoarding large amounts of food

- An increase in taking laxatives, diuretics, or diet pills

- Exercising compulsively, more than the healthy amount

- Using prescription medications or illicit stimulant drugs to limit appetite

- Withdrawal from friends and family

- Avoidance of meals or situations where food may be present

- Preoccupation with weight, body size and shape, or specific aspects of one's appearance

- Obsessing over calorie intake and calories burned via exercise, even as one may be losing significant amounts of weight

You can best support someone with an eating disorder by being supportive and talking with your friend about what you are observing; conveying respect and concern for what he or she is going through; suggesting that she or he seek help at the counseling center on campus; offering to accompany her or him to the counseling center when she or he goes; and asking how she or he is doing after seeking treatment.

If you or a friend is experiencing the symptoms of an eating disorder, seek help immediately. Your college counseling center is a great place to start.

Want to learn more? Try these resources.

The following website comes from the National Association of Anorexia Nervosa and Associated Disorders and covers many eating disorders, including signs and symptoms and true, inspirational stories of recovery:

http://bvtlab.com/676E4

Do I have an eating disorder?

The following website, from the Center for Eating Disorders at Sheppard Pratt, provides a brief online assessment of eating disorders. If your answers suggest that you may have an eating disorder, there is a phone number to call to speak with a member of the Center for Eating Disorders staff, or you can fill out a form to have someone contact you. The site also provides additional links to learn even more about eating disorders.

http://bvtlab.com/86a8E

Reading Comprehension Question 9.4 (Analysis)

The main reason why there is a chapter on trying to maintain balance in your life while in college is _____.

a. because most students are not able to manage themselves in college

b. because most students are unaware that it is important to maintain balance in their lives during their college careers

c. because most students do not realize that maintaining balance will ensure that they have all the money they need and enable them to get high grades in college

d. because most parents never teach college students about how to avoid stress in college

9.4 Summary

In this chapter you learned some important principles about trying to maintain balance in your life during college. Four kinds of balance are physical, psychological, academic, and financial balance. Some tips on how to maintain balance in these four areas were discussed and websites were provided for you to explore additional information about these areas. Maintaining a successful balance in your life is, indeed, a key to student success.

Name: _____

Study Guide | Goal 1

The student will be able to define *balance* and list the important elements of overall balance as well as the characteristics of a balanced student.

Questions	Answers & Notes

Name: _____

Study Guide | Goal 2

The student will be able to discuss four reasons why balance is important in college.

Questions	Answers & Notes

Name: _____

Study Guide | Goal 3

The student will be able to list three common psychological problems faced by college students.

Questions	Answers & Notes

Name: _____

Study Guide | Goal 4

Students will be able to discuss one common way in which they can help themselves if they experience psychological problems during their college years.

Questions	Answers & Notes

Study Guide | Preparing for Class

Use this page to record questions or insights to discuss in class.

_____

_____

_____

_____

_____

_____

_____

_____

_____

_____

_____

_____

_____

_____

_____

_____

_____

_____

_____

_____

_____

_____

_____

_____

_____

_____

_____

_____

_____

_____

_____

_____

_____

Review Questions 9.1

Instructions

Following are five true-false statements taken from the information in this chapter. First, try to answer them without looking back at the chapter. Then review the chapter to see how well you did.

Question & Answer	Rationale
Circle true or false for each of the following statements.	Write an explanation stating why each statement is true or false.
1. Being "in balance" means that you do not have any illnesses. True or False	Your Rationale:
2. Stress is a normal part of the college experience. True or False	Your Rationale:
3. Psychological balance consists of behaving and feeling in ways that maximize your success in college. True or False	Your Rationale:
4. Depression is a state of sadness that resolves in a day or two. True or False	Your Rationale:
5. Eating disorders result from a person's desire to be thin and from his or her wish to overeat. True or False	Your Rationale:

Name: _____

Assignment 9.1

Maintaining Balance in Life During College

Goal

The purpose of this activity is for the student to understand the concept of maintaining balance in life while taking college courses and to have a plan in place for doing so.

Objective

The student will work toward an overall plan for maintaining balance while in college.

Instructions

Read the chapter to make sure that you understand why you should be concerned about balance in life; then follow these steps to create your plan.

Follow These Steps

Step 1: Outline the four major areas in which balance is important (academic, psychological, physical, and financial).

Step 2: Identify ways in which you can cope effectively to maintain overall balance while you are in college.

Step 3: Identify a plan for coping with stress in your own life during your freshman year. Share your plan for maintaining balance with a friend or mentor to get ideas for improving your plan.

Step 4: Assess whether or not your plan is working by evaluating how you are behaving and feeling during your first semester of college.

Step 5: If you find you are not in balance in some aspect of your life, reassess and seek help to get assistance in recovering your balance and maintaining it. Discuss at least two resources (locations, phone numbers, websites) on campus where you can seek help in recovering your balance.

Notes

_____
_____
_____
_____
_____
_____
_____
_____
_____
_____
_____
_____
_____
_____
_____
_____
_____
_____
_____
_____
_____
_____
_____
_____
_____
_____
_____
_____

Chapter Roadmap 10

Introduction

One way in which students must maintain balance while in college is physically. Proper diet, exercise, and sleep, and healthy perspectives on drug and alcohol use, as well as on sex and romantic relationships, are important in order for a student to maintain balance regarding physical health.

This chapter roadmap page presents the formal learning goals for this chapter and a checklist that you should follow as you read and study the chapter.

Student Learning Goals

After completing this chapter you should be able to do the following:

1. Define *physical balance* and list four important elements of physical balance as well as the characteristics of a physically balanced college student.

2. Discuss four reasons why it is important to maintain physical balance in your first year of college.

3. List five food groups recommended by the USDA.

4. List five tips for good bedtime behaviors.

5. List pros and cons of being involved in romantic relationships while in college.

6. Discuss how alcohol and drug use can cause harm to students while they are in college.

Chapter Checklist

You will benefit most if you complete the activities in the order that they are listed.

❑ **Target Date/Deadline:** _____
Complete Critical Thinking Activity 10.1.

❑ **Target Date/Deadline:** _____
Convert the student learning goals to questions that you can answer as you read the chapter. Write your questions on the study guide pages near the end of this chapter.

❑ **Target Date/Deadline:** _____
Read the chapter.

❑ **Target Date/Deadline:** _____
Try to answer the reading comprehension questions as you come to them in the chapter. Check each answer by comparing it to the list of correct answers in the back of the book. If any answer was not correct, then review the passages preceding the question to see why you missed the question.

❑ **Target Date/Deadline:** _____
Answer the student learning goal questions you created. These answered questions will be your study guide.

❑ **Target Date/Deadline:** _____
Write down any questions, insights, or comments as you read so that you can bring them up in class (if applicable).

❑ **Target Date/Deadline:** _____
Complete Review Questions 10.1.

❑ **Target Date/Deadline:** _____
Complete Assignment 10.1 (Maintaining Physical Balance During College).

❑ **Target Date/Deadline:** _____
Review what you have learned from this chapter.

Critical Thinking Activity 10.1

Before you read this chapter and without looking up any information about the topic on the Internet or elsewhere, use the space provided on this page to write your answers to the following questions.

1. When you think of physical balance, what comes to mind?

2. Have you experienced a time when you considered yourself to be in physical balance? If so, how did that feel?

3. Have you ever experienced a time when you considered yourself *not* to be in physical balance? If so, how did that feel? How was it different from when you were in balance?

4. Are there things that you do regularly to keep yourself in physical balance? If so, describe them below. If not, think of what you can do to achieve and maintain physical balance.

Physical Balance:

An Apple a Day

10

"Wisdom is your perspective on life, your sense of balance, your understanding of how the various parts and principles apply and relate to each other."

— Steven R. Covey[1]

As you may have heard, "An apple a day keeps the doctor away." There is an undeniable relationship between diet and health. Diet is one of the key components of maintaining physical balance in your college years. This is just one of the elements of physical balance that we will discuss in this chapter.

10.1 Elements of Physical Balance

A student who is balanced physically feels good, has energy to accomplish his/her short- and long-term goals, and is physically fit. Often weight (or body mass index—also known as BMI) is considered to be a measure of physical fitness and overall health.

This is not to say that a person who has an illness—either immediate (like a head cold) or chronic (like diabetes)—cannot be considered to be physically balanced. Physical balance implies that an individual, whether ill or not, has the necessary energy to accomplish not just daily activities but overall life goals, as well. So physical balance often carries with it the notion of functional ability, not just health status.

Reading Comprehension Question 10.1 (Knowledge)

Susan was diagnosed with diabetes when she was 5 years old. Which of the following statements is true of Susan?

a. She will never be in physical balance because she has a chronic illness.

b. Susan's illness will never impact her physical balance.

c. If Susan eats a candy bar, she will no longer be in physical balance.

d. If Susan has energy, feels good, meets her life goals, and maintains a proper diet and a healthy range of blood sugar levels, she could be considered to be in physical balance.

Striving to maintain balance physically involves four key practices:

1. Eating a diet that is healthy and adequate for you

2. Engaging in exercise and sleep regimens that help you to maintain your health

3. Maintaining healthy practices in your sexual and romantic relationships

4. Maintaining a healthy perspective on drug, nicotine, and alcohol use

Maintaining a Healthy Diet

Keeping your body in good working order includes eating a diet that is healthy for you and that helps you to maintain a body weight that is appropriate for your height, age, and activity level. Body mass index is a measure of body fat that is based on height and weight and is appropriate for adult men and women. You can calculate your own BMI and learn about the results at the following website: http://bvtlab.com/7C7Jp.

Your daily diet is important in maintaining a healthy weight. There are thousands of diets out there, and it may be the case that you have tried a few. However, as you probably know, fad diets rarely lead to healthy or permanent weight loss. Some diets are reasonable, lead to appropriate weight loss, and allow you to keep the weight off over time. If you are that rare person who can eat pretty much what you like and still maintain an appropriate body weight, you are lucky. However, even people who are at the right body weight can have a diet that is not necessarily good for them in the long run.

The U.S. Department of Agriculture[2] has outlined the five food groups that are the building blocks for a healthy diet (see Figure 10.1).

There is also a program specifically for college students, called "My Plate on Campus," that has many tips and ideas for eating healthy on a college campus.[3] If you are asking yourself, "How can I improve my eating habits?" the answer is simple:

1. Pay attention to what you are eating and drinking now.

2. Find out what you should be eating and drinking.

3. Take little steps toward improving your diet.

Some quick tips for healthy eating on campus include:

- Make half your plate fruits and vegetables.

- Enjoy your food, but eat less.

- Avoid oversized portions.

- Make at least half your grains whole.

- Drink water instead of sugary drinks.

- Watch the amount of sodium (salt) in your foods.

- Switch to fat-free or lowfat (1 percent) milk.

Figure 10.1

Building Blocks for a Healthy Diet

Source: U.S. Department of Agriculture

Want to learn more? Try these resources.

The USDA provides tips and information about diet and eating healthy.
http://bvtlab.com/W7HYW

The following website features downloadable posters that provide everyday tips about eating well. You could post these in your kitchen as reminders to eat healthy.
http://bvtlab.com/7c8QV

For a guide to eating in college, please visit:
http://bvtlab.com/66M98

For a guide to eating for sports, please visit:
http://bvtlab.com/r8p8q

The following website offers a questionnaire to help you determine whether or not you are eating in a healthy manner. The first nine questions of this tool will test your ability to make healthier choices when faced with a variety of options. The last five questions will test your knowledge of nutrition. At the end, you'll receive a score and a summary of your results.
http://bvtlab.com/9W5Ff

Reading Comprehension Question 10.2 (Literal Comprehension)

Which of the following is NOT one of the USDA-recommended five food groups?

a. fruits

b. vegetables

c. desserts

d. dairy

Maintaining Proper Exercise and Sleep Regimens

Maintaining Proper Exercise for Health

Maintaining proper exercise is critical to your well-being during your college years. Exercise helps you to keep fit and to stay as healthy as you can in many areas of your life. As a general goal, you should try to get at least thirty minutes of exercise each day. You might need more exercise if you are trying to lose weight or to meet some other fitness goal. If you are battling any chronic health problems (such as arthritis or diabetes) you should check with your doctor prior to beginning a new exercise program. Exercise is defined as any action that enhances body movement for a specific period of time—such as swimming, rowing, running, riding a bicycle, walking, or using exercise equipment. You can tell you are doing something that qualifies as exercise if you experience an increased heart rate or break a sweat.

There are multiple benefits from maintaining a healthy exercise regimen in college. Not only can you meet new friends by going to the campus gym, but exercise can also help you to maintain a healthy weight. Exercise is also known to boost your energy and immune function. Additionally, it can improve your mood and also promote good sleep!

There can also be negative consequences for *not* exercising. Many researchers have found that lack of physical exercise, heavy smoking, and alcohol use are associated with stress, anxiety, and depression.[4–7] One study by Seo and colleagues found that college students who smoked, perceived their weight as being higher, and consumed less fruit were also less likely to engage in physical exercise than were students who didn't smoke, perceived their weight as being lower, and consumed more fruit.[8] This demonstrates how a pattern of unhealthy habits, and perhaps low self-esteem, can cause you to continue to make poor choices regarding your physical well-being. Even if you have some of the unhealthy habits listed above, or others that aren't listed, you should still try to make good choices. Health is not an all-or-nothing deal! Every step toward better physical balance, no matter how small, is a good thing.

Want to learn more? Try these resources.

The following website provides a test to help you determine whether or not you are doing enough physical exercise to keep you fit: http://bvtlab.com/4cK89

To learn more about the benefits of exercise in college, please visit: http://bvtlab.com/7hd8X

In college, there are many activities that you can do to keep yourself healthy. First, set a weekly goal for exercising. Then, grab a friend for companionship and spend some quality time together. Have fun! Choose something that you enjoy to keep yourself interested. See Figure 10.2 for some suggestions.

Figure 10.2

Achieving Maximal Effect: Ways to Incorporate Exercise into Your Campus Life!

AT HOME

Do stretches or exercises like yoga or jumping jacks while watching TV. Use household items such as soup cans to do biceps curls during study breaks.

ON CAMPUS

In between classes, take a brisk ten-minute walk or bike ride. Join an intramural team, club team, or gardening group. Take a dance class for non-majors.

DURING FREE TIME

Sign up for a class at your campus fitness center or gym. Play games like basketball, soccer, or kickball with your friends on the weekend.

Good Sleep Habits

Your sleep habits are a very important part of overall physical health. You should try to maintain a regular sleep and wake cycle—meaning that you go to bed and wake up at the same time each day of the week. You should also spend an appropriate amount of time sleeping—not too much or too little.

When you are in college, disruptions to your sleep and wake cycles might be difficult to avoid. With so many classes, social events, and other activities, it is easy to find yourself going to bed at different times and for different lengths of time each night, thus disrupting your normal routine. It's important for you to keep track of your routine and to notice whether you are changing your routine and length of sleeping time. Take note of your sleeping patterns and try to determine whether you are maintaining a "normal" schedule. If you find yourself drifting into an unhealthy pattern of sleep, make the necessary corrections to create a healthy environment for yourself.

Try implementing these five good bedtime behaviors:

1. Try not to nap during the day.

2. Have a regular routine at bedtime that is relaxing.

3. Make your bed a place where you sleep, and not a place to watch TV or do homework.

4. Arrange your bedroom so that it is pleasant and makes you feel relaxed and happy.

5. Try not to consume food or alcohol, or stimulants like caffeine or nicotine, within a couple of hours before bedtime.

Want to learn more? Try these resources.

The following is an excellent website on sleep needs during college. It offers information about why we need sleep, the benefits of sleep, the need for sleep during college, and sleep and physical health issues:

http://bvtlab.com/7YvJD

For tips on how to design the ideal sleep-friendly bedroom (or dorm room), see:

http://bvtlab.com/Ya389

Reading Comprehension Question 10.3 (Inferential Comprehension)

How can you best remain physically balanced in college?

a. Monitor yourself so that your activities, exercise, sleep, and food intake all contribute to a sense of well-being.

b. Focus on the grades you are earning in each of your courses.

c. Purchase anything you want to in order to make yourself feel better emotionally.

d. Help your friends who may be experiencing difficulty in their college experience before you help yourself.

Sex and Romance in College

Sex and romance are often a part of college life. Students who are between the ages of 18 and 25 are learning how to date, how to develop romantic relationships, and how to choose an appropriate mate. Perhaps you came to college not having dated very much. Or maybe you dated throughout high school and are familiar with some of the positive and negative aspects of dating. Contraception and protection from sexually transmitted diseases (STDs) and sexually transmitted infections (STIs) are critical issues if you are having sexual relationships in college.

Many colleges have contraceptives and other protective devices available at the student health center. You should make an appointment to visit the student health center as soon as possible if you plan on dating. There are many instances in which dating and romantic relationships can interfere with students' daily activities, including studying and attending classes. If you feel you are having problems in school or in life that stem from an issue in a romantic relationship, remember that your counseling center can provide resources that will help you with this issue.

Sometimes young men and women find themselves engaging in "casual" sex during college, something they may not have done in high school. This type of relationship can have positive and negative consequences, depending on the characteristics of the individuals involved. Studies have shown that depression can be related to engaging in casual sex for young women.[9] In addition, researchers have found that higher levels of guilt and anxiety, and lower self-esteem, are related to casual sex among college women.[10] College-aged women are often seeking greater social connectedness and positive relationships, but they are trying to do so in an environment that is full of heavy drinking and casual sex. As Pompeo and colleagues put it, "This combination of interpersonal and environmental influences creates psychological distress in women, yielding depressive symptoms and low self-esteem."[11] Basically, this means that college women can begin to feel bad about themselves, and to experience depression, as a result of the campus social environment.

Want to learn more? Try these resources.

This website, *Hot Topics! College Students and Relationships*, covers practical issues about what constitutes a "healthy" relationship, how to tell if you may be in an unhealthy relationship, and five steps to setting limits in a relationship:

http://bvtlab.com/9m6w8

Many topics about sex are covered by the following website:

http://bvtlab.com/7qQ77

This site, from the Princeton University Counseling Center, is a reliable and user-friendly guide to all topics relating to health:

http://bvtlab.com/5cM8V

This site, from *Everyday Health* (an email newsletter), is a user-friendly guide to relationships in college and includes decision-making tips about sex in college as well as forms of birth control:

http://bvtlab.com/9dBTN

This website from the American College of Obstetrics and Gynecology answers all the questions you could have about birth control pills:

http://bvtlab.com/6pa78

From the Emerson College Center for Health and Wellness, this site offers information about various types of birth control:

http://bvtlab.com/9NmAt

Not all college relationships are casual. Some college students choose to pursue a romantic relationship. This can have a positive effect. A 2013 study reported that, during the college years, being involved in a romantic relationship (compared to being single) was related to fewer depressive symptoms for college women (but not for men).[12] Both male and female college students who were in committed relationships reported less overall problems with excessive drinking than did single students. These findings are echoed by several other studies about young adult relationships.[13,14] It is clear that different studies have found different results when it comes to college dating. It is important that each person recognizes and understands what effect college dating is having on him or her, individually.

Sexual Identity

Some students struggle with their sexual identity while attending college. Unfortunately this is a topic that is not always discussed freely in our society. Some students find themselves feeling isolated, fearful, and confused about their sexual identity. If these stresses become overwhelming, they can disrupt one's balance and interfere with academic performance. It is important that you seek help if you are struggling with your own sexual identity and that you are sensitive to the fact that new friends you make in college might be struggling with theirs. Remember that your college counseling center usually has resources that can help students with this issue.

Want to learn more? Try these resources.

This website, from the Wright State University, discusses self-acknowledgment, disclosure decisions, and research on coming out as a significant experience in college:

http://bvtlab.com/77BhU

San Jose State University offers this website about gender identity, including defining terms, coming out, and navigating your gender identity, as well as a goldmine of links to obtain further information and self-help about this topic:

http://bvtlab.com/5n8aP

Reading Comprehension Question 10.4 (Analysis)

Does it matter if students are aware of their sexual and romantic needs during college?

a. No, sex and romance are best left until after you graduate.

b. Yes, sex and romance can have both positive and negative consequences in college.

c. Yes, sexual relationships in college usually lead to negative academic consequences.

d. Yes, romantic relationships are difficult to navigate and eventually always lead to depression in college women.

Drug, Alcohol, and Nicotine Use in College

It is very common to use drugs, alcohol, and cigarettes during college. Many students interpret their freedom in college as a chance to do whatever they wish—sometimes in excess. Many students get into trouble with this philosophy. Students who have not been educated on the pitfalls and dangers of these activities may inadvertently harm themselves and those around them; they can even find themselves jeopardizing their success in college, or their future in general. It is wise to give the use—and abuse—of drugs, alcohol, and cigarettes the attention it deserves in order to avoid running into trouble in your first year of college.

Drug Use in College

Many different drugs have become available to college students in the past few decades. On any given college campus, you will find people who can supply you with drugs; some may even approach you about it without being asked. You can find a chart at the following website that illustrates common drugs of abuse including commercial and street names and selected acute effects and health risks: http://bvtlab.com/Nw7qQ. It is an excellent reference if you would like to learn more detailed information about drugs and their abuse. If you choose to use drugs in college, it is important that you consider the effects of these drugs upon both your body and your mind, as well as upon your academic achievement. Remember that your counseling center is an excellent resource for you and your classmates if you need help with understanding, or with treatment for, drug abuse.

Alcohol Use in College

Some people can have a drink or two and can stop there. Others find that they cannot stop after one or two drinks, even if it would be better for their health if they did. Alcoholism is a disease that is partly genetic and partly environmental. Many college students may not know whether or not they are alcoholics until they are in the college environment, where alcohol is easy to get.

Alcoholics find that, the more they drink, the more alcohol they need to consume the next time to achieve the same feeling. This is called tolerance. Your body builds up a tolerance to the alcohol, and before long, you need to drink twice the amount you originally drank in order to feel the same "buzz." Alcoholism can sneak up on you before you realize that it is having an effect on your body and your behavior. If you notice that your drug or alcohol use is affecting your daily living, you may have a problem. This is not uncommon. Your college counseling center can provide services to help you understand and deal with college drinking problems.

There can also be negative consequences to drinking, in general—even among non-alcoholics—and specifically on college campuses. While not all students drink, drinking (and, to a lesser extent, binge drinking) does happen on college campuses nationwide.[15,16] What's more, about one-quarter of all college students report having faced academic consequences from their drinking. These consequences included missing classes, falling behind, doing poorly on exams or papers, and making lower overall grades.

The following website provides information on many of the harmful consequences of alcohol use in college: http://bvtlab.com/8PB8S. The consequences of alcohol use, especially in excess, can include, but aren't limited to:

- Physical injury

- Assault (both physical and sexual)

- Unsafe consensual sex (which can lead to unwanted pregnancy and sexually transmitted diseases and infections)

- And even death

Additional webpages with excellent information about alcohol and alcoholism for college-aged students are provided in *Want to learn more? Try these resources.*

Want to learn more? Try these resources.

There are many websites that deal with drug and alcohol use in college. The following websites are trustworthy and have information that can help you to deal with your or a friend's alcohol or drug abuse.

If you wish to explore whether you have a drinking problem, you may want to consider taking the Michigan Alcohol Screening Test (MAST), available here:

http://bvtlab.com/77266

If you wish to explore whether you have a drug use problem, you may want to consider taking the Drug Abuse Screening Test (DAST), available here:

http://bvtlab.com/J8K6m

This website, created by the National Institute on Alcohol Abuse and Alcoholism (NIAAA), is "your one-stop resource for comprehensive research-based information on issues related to alcohol abuse and binge drinking among college students." With resources for students, faculty, parents, and others, it is also replete with links to additional information:

http://bvtlab.com/nB2qf

What Peer Educators and Resident Advisors Need to Know about College Drinking is a comprehensive and informative website that covers multiple topics: the scope of the college-drinking problem, the effectiveness of intervention programs currently used by schools and communities, and recommendations for college presidents and researchers on how to improve these interventions and prevention efforts:

http://bvtlab.com/8phb8

The NIAAA presents this webpage, entitled, "Tips for Cutting Down on Drinking":

http://bvtlab.com/s8867

Do I have a problem with alcohol, drugs, or both?

There are many screening tests online to assess alcohol and drug use. The following two are brought to you by the National Council on Alcohol and Drug Dependence and are research-based and dependable. When you take the online test, it provides you with a numeric score that is explained, as well as a summary of your test. These materials can also be printed.

http://bvtlab.com/7Q9TV

http://bvtlab.com/f776m

Nicotine Use in College

If you are a user of nicotine—one of the chemicals in cigarettes—you may wish to explore your smoking habits and think about quitting. Perhaps you have tried to quit smoking in the past or maybe you don't really know if you are addicted to nicotine. Beyond the traditional cigarette, electronic cigarettes have become popular in recent years. Whether you are smoking a cigarette or vaping (with a mod), you are taking in nicotine. There is some limited research about vaping versus smoking (see *Want to learn more? Try these resources.* below), however, the jury is still out on the safety of vaping.

If you are unsure if you are addicted to nicotine, there is a quiz available at www.smokefree.gov. The results will tell you how much you depend on nicotine, and the website can also provide helpful tips on how to reduce your cravings. The following feature provides several additional online sources of information that may be helpful to you as you consider your use of this highly addictive and often lethal drug.

Quitting the use of nicotine may be the one most powerful thing you can do for your health while you are in college. Reach out and try to find a healthier way to relieve stress, and you will find that it can enhance your daily life—and lengthen that life, as well.

Want to learn more? Try these resources.

For more information on the potential dangers of vaping, see the following website:
http://bvtlab.com/Y6768

For eighteen ways that nicotine affects your health, please see:
http://bvtlab.com/4m89C

For tips on how to quit smoking, please visit the following website:
http://bvtlab.com/489m5

10.2 Summary

In this chapter you learned some important principles for maintaining physical balance during college. You learned about maintaining a healthy diet, proper exercise and sleep, sex and romance, and drug and alcohol use in college. After reading chapter, you should now understand why maintaining physical balance is important—as well as some practical ways to maintain your physical balance during college.

Name: _____

Study Guide | Goal 1

The student will be able to define *physical balance* and list four important elements of physical balance as well as the characteristics of a physically balanced college student.

Questions	Answers & Notes

Name: _____

Study Guide | Goal 2

The student will be able to discuss four reasons why it is important to maintain physical balance in the first year of college.

Questions	Answers & Notes

Name: _____

Study Guide | Goal 3

The student will be able to list five food groups recommended by the USDA.

Questions	Answers & Notes

Name: _____

Study Guide | Goal 4

The student will be able to list five tips for good bedtime behaviors.

Questions	Answers & Notes

Study Guide | Goal 5

The student will be able to list pros and cons of being involved in romantic relationships while in college.

Questions	Answers & Notes

Name: _____

Study Guide | Goal 6

The student will be able to discuss how alcohol and drug use can cause harm to students while they are in college.

Questions	Answers & Notes

Study Guide | *Preparing for Class*

Use this page to record questions or insights to discuss in class.

Name: _____

Review Questions 10.1

Instructions

Following are five true-false statements taken from the information in this chapter. First, try to answer them without looking back at the chapter. Then review the chapter to see how well you did.

Question & Answer	Rationale
Circle true or false for each of the following statements.	Write an explanation stating why each statement is true or false.
1. Body mass index (BMI) is a measure of weight and can be used to determine whether or not you are physically healthy. True or False	Your Rationale:
2. Fruits, vegetables, grains, protein, and dairy are five food groups that are essential for overall dietary health. True or False	Your Rationale:
3. Proper exercise can help you to fight off disease and promote good physical health. True or False	Your Rationale:
4. The most important sleep habit is to always have warm milk before bedtime. True or False	Your Rationale:
5. College students rarely drink alcohol. True or False	Your Rationale:

Name: _____

Assignment 10.1

Maintaining Physical Balance During College

Goal	Notes

The purpose of this activity is for you to understand the concept of maintaining physical balance while taking college courses and to have a plan in place for doing so.

Objective

You will work toward a plan for maintaining physical balance while in college.

Instructions

Read the chapter to make sure that you understand why you should be concerned about physical balance; then follow these steps to create your plan.

Follow These Steps

Step 1: Discuss each of the four major areas that contribute to physical balance (healthy diet, proper exercise and sleep, sex and romance, drug and alcohol use).

Step 2: Determine what activities most suit you when it comes to maintaining physical balance while you are in college.

Step 3: Share your plan for maintaining physical balance with a friend or mentor to get ideas for how to improve it.

Step 4: Evaluate whether or not your plan is working by assessing how you are feeling during your first semester of college.

Step 5: If you find you are not in physical balance, seek help recovering your physical balance and maintaining it.

Chapter Roadmap 11

Introduction

In this chapter you will examine the challenges and opportunities that come with managing your finances. This information will be useful to you both while you are in college and in the future as you begin your career.

This chapter roadmap page presents the formal learning goals for this chapter and a checklist that you should follow as you read and study the chapter.

Student Learning Goals

After completing this chapter you should be able to do the following:

1. List at least two things that make an education valuable.

2. Identify at least three ways to obtain financial aid for college and include multiple potential sources.

3. Distinguish between *wants* and *needs* and discuss inexpensive ways to supply your needs while in college.

4. Define terms related to credit card debt, including credit, interest, and debt, and list the pros and cons of credit card debt.

5. Define identity theft and list ways to avoid it.

6. Discuss tips for managing your money during college.

Chapter Checklist

You will benefit most if you complete the activities in the order that they are listed.

❑ **Target Date/Deadline:** _____
Complete Critical Thinking Activity 11.1.

❑ **Target Date/Deadline:** _____
Convert the student learning goals to questions that you can answer as you read the chapter. Write your questions on the study guide pages near the end of this chapter.

❑ **Target Date/Deadline:** _____
Read the chapter.

❑ **Target Date/Deadline:** _____
Try to answer the reading comprehension questions as you come to them in the chapter. Check each answer by comparing it to the list of correct answers in the back of the book. If any answer was not correct, then review the passages preceding the question to see why you missed the question.

❑ **Target Date/Deadline:** _____
Answer the student learning goal questions you created. These answered questions will be your study guide.

❑ **Target Date/Deadline:** _____
Write down any questions, insights, or comments that you have as you read so that you can bring them up in class.

❑ **Target Date/Deadline:** _____
Complete Review Questions 11.1.

❑ **Target Date/Deadline:** _____
Complete Assignment 11.1 (Monthly Budgeting).

❑ **Target Date/Deadline:** _____
Review what you have learned from this chapter.

Critical Thinking Activity 11.1

Identifying Lifetime Goals and Objectives

As a way to begin thinking about your personal financial balance, make a list of your goals and objectives using Table 11.1. In the second column make a list of your academic goals and objectives. In the third column list your career goals and objectives. In the fourth column, list your financial goals and objectives. The first column specifies the time period in which you intend to complete each goal. Examples of each type of goal are written in the Table 11.2.

A *goal* is an overarching principle that guides your decision making. *Objectives* are specific, measurable steps that can be taken to meet your goals. One method for coming up with powerful goals and objectives is to use the SMART mnemonic,[1] which stands for:

S = Specific

M = Measurable

A = Attainable

R = Relevant

T = Time-bound

Try to give some serious thought to what your individual and unique goals and objectives are for these areas of your life and write at least one goal and one objective for each.

Table 11.1

	Goals and Objectives		
	Academic	**Career**	**Financial**
This Semester	Goal: Objective:	Goal: Objective:	Goal: Objective:
Right After Graduation	Goal: Objective:	Goal: Objective:	Goal: Objective:
Lifelong	Goal: Objective:	Goal: Objective:	Goal: Objective:

Table 11.2

Example Goals and Objectives

	Academic	Career	Financial
This Semester	Goal: End the semester with a GPA of 3.5 or above. Objective: Earn at least a B+ on the next PSY 101 test.	Goal: Complete the required coursework in my discipline of choice. Objective: Become knowledgeable about the basics of economics by the end of ECON 101.	Goal: Complete the semester with the least debt possible. Objective: Obtain all of the required reading materials by the time they are due for my courses without using a credit card.
Right After Graduation	Goal: Explore options for continuing my education. Objective: Investigate at least two certifications that can help me in my career in the first sixth months after graduation.	Goal: Obtain full-time work in my area of expertise. Objective: Register with a job search company and post my résumé online for a full-time position in my area at least six months prior to graduation.	Goal: Become financially stable with a realistic budget. Objective: Plan a detailed budget for living expenses and income during the first year after graduation.
Lifelong	Goal: Be a life-long scholar. Objective: Find at least three ways I can continue my education while working full-time during the three years after graduation.	Goal: Become an expert in my field of interest. Objective: Learn as much as possible about my position and its requirements for maximum expertise by the fifth year of employment.	Goal: Be able to retire while having an income that will support my budget in retirement. Objective: Explore at least two options for long-term retirement income planning at least ten years before retirement.

Managing Your Money:

Cashing in on the College Experience

11

"Money is a great servant, but a bad master."
— Francis Bacon[2]

"Don't tell me what you value; show me your budget, and I'll tell you what you value."
— Joe Biden[3]

"An investment in knowledge pays the best interest."
— Benjamin Franklin[4]

Money management is both a necessary evil and a wonderful opportunity for the college student. It is especially important to get a handle on your finances in college because financial worries can easily distract you from your studies and can undermine your most important college goals. It is also important because it will give you the opportunity to avoid the problems that many people face when they enter the workforce.

You may be a student who is living on your own away from home for the first time. You now find yourself responsible for a larger portion of your own finances than you did before you left your parents' home. Or perhaps you are a student who is beginning college after having been out on your own for some time. While you may be used to managing your own finances, college can still present a unique—and even daunting—financial challenge. In any case, knowing how to manage your finances will serve you well for the rest of your life.

In this brief chapter, we can't hope to provide you with every piece of information necessary to manage your finances. However, we can bring to your attention a few key issues that will make a big difference in your personal experience. In this chapter we will discuss money as a motivation for college, finding money for college, using money in your everyday experience, and using money wisely to build a better future for yourself.

Reading Comprehension Question 11.1 (Knowledge)

Which of the following best describes the goal of this chapter?

a. To provide you with every piece of information you might ever need to know to manage your finances

b. To help you get a handle on your finances in college

c. To explain why money is important

d. To convince you to avoid student loans

11.1 The Value of a College Education

A college education is primarily valuable for the learning experience. But it is also valuable because of the greatly increased earning power your college degree will give you.

First of all, people with a degree are more likely to be employed than those without a degree. And the higher your degree, the more likely it is that you will be able to find full-time employment year round. The National Center for Education Statistics reported that, for 2012, 73 percent of young adults with a bachelor's degree worked full time, year round, while only 60 percent of young adults with a high school diploma or equivalent worked full time.[5] (*Full time* is defined as working more than thirty-five hours per week.)

Second, the more education you acquire, the more money you are likely to earn. Figure 11.1, based on information from the U.S. Bureau of Labor Statistics,[6] shows the increased earnings a college degree can give you. The increase in pay associated with higher levels of education is impressive.

Looking at Figure 11.1, you can see that if you get an associate degree, you will earn about $100 more per week than you would with a high school diploma alone. If you get a bachelor's degree, you will likely earn greater than $400 more per week than you would with a high school diploma. Keep in mind that the incomes reported in this figure are higher than your take-home pay would be because they haven't yet factored in taxes and other deductions. In addition, remember that these figures are for established employees working full-time. They do not account for the fact that, right after graduation, you may make less money than you will after having been employed for a longer period of time.

While you should avoid loans if possible, it is easy to see that a very low interest school loan could be a wise investment if it enables you to earn a college degree. Even a $20,000 school loan could be repaid quickly if your new degree led to an income increase greater than that amount, annually. That said, you should try to develop realistic expectations about how much money you are likely to make after graduation if you work in the field of your major. Exact figures for specific careers are not listed in this chapter because there is so much variation. However, you should seek information about the earning power associated with your choice of career; that information is available from the U.S. Bureau of Labor Statistics (see http://bvtlab.com/8aSBs).

Figure 11.1

2014 Median* Weekly Earnings by Education Level

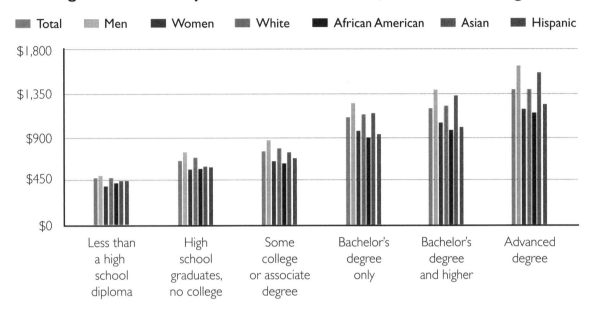

Median usual weekly earnings of full-time wage and salary workers age 25 and older by educational attainment, 2014 annual averages

Source: U.S. Bureau of Labor Statistics.

* The data in these figures are the median earnings. *Median* means the middle number out of all the different earning amounts. So for each category listed in the bar chart, exactly half of the people earned less than the median number and exactly half of the people earned more than the median.

Reading Comprehension Question 11.2 (Literal Comprehension)

Based on recent national data, which of the following is NOT true about earnings?

a. If you get a good job, you are likely to earn just as much as anyone else, regardless of your education level.

b. People with a degree are more likely to be employed than those without a degree.

c. Low-interest school loans may be a wise investment because the earnings you get from having a higher degree will likely be greater than the amount owed on the loans.

d. Those with an associate degree are likely to make more than those with a high school diploma.

Want to learn more? Try these resources.

If you want to know more about the income rewards associated with higher education and what levels of income are expected for various types of careers, you can access the following websites.

Digest of Education Statistics (Table 502.30)

Here you will find a table that displays the median annual earnings for about a decade. You will be able to examine differences in income in general, differences in income by education level, differences in income by sex, and differences in income by various racial categories including white, black, Hispanic, and Asian.

http://bvtlab.com/P8967

Annual Earnings of Young Adults

This link will let you download a four-page report examining the annual earnings of young adults ages 25 to 34. Comparisons are made between various levels of educational attainment. The information in this report is based on the table above.

http://bvtlab.com/YP2Ra

11.2 Money for College

Scholarships

The biggest advantage of scholarships is that you don't have to pay them back. Some scholarships are awarded based on merit (e.g., your grades), some are awarded based on minority status, and some are awarded to encourage entrance into a particular field (e.g., nursing). Many are available for a variety of interest areas. Some scholarships are nationwide, and some are available only on a particular campus. While the national scholarships might provide a larger amount of money, you are probably more likely to get a local scholarship because you will be competing against fewer people. You should check out the scholarships available on your campus.

On some campuses you will find an office that deals exclusively with the scholarships that are available to students. On others it may be difficult to find exactly who can help you with scholarships. However, if you inquire at your financial aid office, someone should be able to direct you to the appropriate place. You can also search the web for scholarships based upon your characteristics and interests. The following website may help you in this search: http://bvtlab.com/uXc57.

Some states offer scholarships for students who are residents of the state and meet certain other requirements (such as a certain high school grade point average). For example, Georgia offers the HOPE Program (Helping Outstanding Pupils Educationally). The National Association of Student Financial Aid Administrators (NASFAA) website lists organized links to information about aid in every state (http://bvtlab.com/D4sqv).

Many scholarships are connected to academic achievement—for example, a very high SAT score. You may also be asked to submit an original essay along with your application, or to appear before a panel to answer questions. The scholarship is then awarded to the highest-ranking applicants. Also, keep in mind that athletic scholarships should not be overlooked. There are many students who excel in athletics who would qualify for a number of scholarships on that basis.

There are also many scholarships that are not based solely on academic performance, some of which may be sponsored by corporations or may have been created in honor of influential community members. You should not overlook these scholarship opportunities because even scholarships with smaller dollar amounts can go a long way toward helping you pay for your education.

Financial Aid

Free Application for Federal Student Aid (FAFSA)

Federal Student Aid, a part of the U.S. Department of Education, is the largest provider of student financial aid in America. They process over twenty-two million FAFSA applications each year. As stated in the name, this application is free and every student should take the time to fill one out. The form is available online, and you might also be able to get it from the financial aid office at your college or university. Each state has a different deadline, and each college may have a different deadline, so it is imperative that you look up the deadline for your location and college. See *Want to learn more? Try these resources.* below for more information.

Want to learn more? Try these resources.

You can find out more information about FAFSA and obtain the form at the following website:
http://bvtlab.com/5869d

There is also a free financial aid calculator that the Federal Student Aid office provides at the following website:
http://bvtlab.com/CX8X7

There are deadlines for filing the FAFSA form are listed for each state here:
http://bvtlab.com/68vP3

For videos about the process of submitting a FAFSA, and more information about financial aid, go to the following address:
http://bvtlab.com/m53gc

Loans

Unlike scholarships, loans need to be paid back—usually with interest. Interest is money charged on top of the loan for the period of time between when you take out the loan and when you finish paying it back. The lowest interest is usually available on government student loans. Private loans can be taken out from a bank, but these are usually higher interest loans. In some cases private loans have very high interest rates; so if you must use a loan, you should investigate all of the options and compare them very carefully before you commit to one. You should use a loan only as a last resort to pay for college. If you do resort to loans, be sure that you understand your obligations.

When it comes to federal loans, there are two general types. These are called Direct Subsidized and Direct Unsubsidized Loans. The main difference between the two has to do with how interest is handled. Subsidized loans are more forgiving when it comes to interest, but there are also greater restrictions on who is eligible. For more information, you can visit: http://bvtlab.com/gGcq7.

Loan Forgiveness   You should also check out loan forgiveness programs. These are usually offered to students in order to entice them to work in areas that have limited resources. For example, a nursing student might obtain a loan from a local hospital with the provision that he or she work at that hospital for three years after graduation, at which time the loan would be forgiven—meaning the student would no longer be responsible for paying that money back.

Loan Consolidation   Consolidating loans can be done when you have taken out several different loans from different sources. For federal loans, a Direct Consolidation Loan allows you to combine multiple federal education loans into one loan. The result is a single monthly payment instead of multiple payments. There are pros and cons to consolidation; so if you are considering it, you need to be sure you understand all of the consequences.

Want to learn more? Try these resources.

For more information on loan consolidation, go to:
http://bvtlab.com/DPpK6

Here are some websites with important information about scholarships and loans:
U.S. Department of Education
http://bvtlab.com/796dM

Federal Student Aid
http://bvtlab.com/8W682

FinAid!®—The Smart Student™ Guide to Financial Aid
http://bvtlab.com/96D8Y

11.3 Money for Every Day: Buying Goods and Services

We have considered some ways to get money for college. Now let's entertain some strategies that will help you stretch your funds and keep from spending them too fast. When it comes to spending, you need to develop your ability to distinguish wants from needs and look for creative and inexpensive ways to supply your needs.

Distinguish Wants from Needs

Most of us are guilty of wanting extravagant things from time to time. Perhaps it's a new videogame console, cell phone, or tablet. Perhaps it's a pair of designer shoes, shaped like cats, with a price tag over $2,000. Whatever luxury you're craving, keep in mind that it's not worth the sacrifice. In order to buy that "must have" item, you may have to

Source: Kobi Levi Footwear Art, www.kobilevidesign.com

forfeit paying for something truly essential—like your electric bill, rent, or college textbooks. This will certainly have an impact not only on your daily life (it's hard to function without working lights!) but on your academic performance, as well. In order to avoid these consequences, it's important to recognize when that "must have" pair of shoes really isn't "must have" at all. Electricity, on the other hand, is certainly something you can't do without! There is a strong connection between academic success and finances—and the pursuit of something that you want but really cannot afford can lead to a negative impact on your grades.

When discussing things that we want, we often treat the terms *want* and *need* as synonymous, when, upon closer examination, it is easy to see that our wants are not really needs, after all. Of course, social definitions of wants and needs change over time. A paper published in the *College Student Journal* pointed out that "Americans' definition of what constitutes a 'need' has clearly changed from generation to generation."[7] It is easy to imagine that in the 1960s, computers were hardly a need; but in 2015, they would certainly be considered a need for the average college student. That being said, it's important to make a distinction between the things that you need to have in order to do well in college, and the things you want to have simply for the sake of having them. We often see things that we wish were needs, but that we simply can't afford. Most of us must prioritize our wants and needs in order to maintain financial balance. Can you identify your own needs and wants?

338

College Success: A Concise Practical Guide

Think About This

Take a few minutes to examine your own needs and wants. To better visualize them, create a chart like the one shown below.

Step 1. Make a list of your needs first. Don't try to identify any wants yet. Look over your list of needs and think about them carefully. Are any of them really wants masquerading as needs? Are any of them half need and half want? For example, if you were to write down "Need new shoes (designer brand)," that would be partly a need and partly a want. Let's assume that you really do need some new shoes. Then reasonably priced shoes would be a need, but a pair of super-expensive cat-shaped shoes would be a want.

Step 2. Now cross through any wants that were masquerading as needs and write them in the wants column instead. Think about other wants that you would like to add to your list. Just because they are not needs doesn't mean they aren't still attainable. If you are patient and save your money, you may be able to buy them in the future. No one said you can't have your needs and your wants, too!

Step 3. After you have filled out your lists, consider how you want to pursue each item. Write your decision in the Plan of Action column.

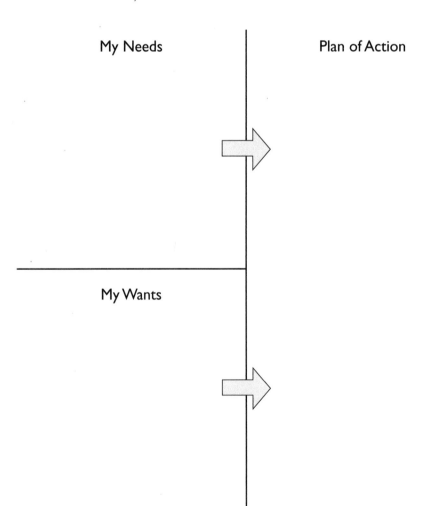

Inexpensive Ways to Supply Your Needs

Now that you have a better understanding of what your needs are, let's explore some cost-saving measures for things that most college students need. Among these are goods and services, such as textbooks, food, and daily supplies; health and recreation needs; entertainment, technology needs; and a little something extra.

Textbooks

It is fair to say that in almost all of your classes, buying or otherwise acquiring a textbook for the course is not a want—it is a need. Suppose that, during the first month of classes, you had enough extra spending money to purchase a textbook, but you really wanted to use it to buy a new cell phone, instead. In this day and age, a cell phone certainly seems like a need—but if your current phone still works, upgrading to the newest model then becomes a want. In this case, your extra spending money should go toward getting the textbook you really need; later, if you find yourself with spending money again, you can reconsider getting that shiny new phone. Don't be afraid to think creatively about how you can acquire a textbook for each of your classes. Textbooks are a need when it comes to academic success!

Food and Other Day-to-Day Goods and Services

Let's say you have a two-meal-a-day plan for the college cafeteria, but you only ever eat lunch. Instead of going to the cafeteria for breakfast, which would require getting up early, you instead buy junk food at the vending machines on campus on your way to class. There are two financial considerations to keep in mind in a case like this. First, those small vending machine charges can add up—fast. Even $5 a day winds up totaling $150 over the course of a month! The second consideration that you may have missed is that, by not using the second cafeteria meal each day, you are essentially losing money. That meal is already paid for, so not eating it is hardly any different from buying it and immediately throwing it in the trash.

Food, in the form of a nutritious, balanced diet, is certainly a *need;* but junk food from the vending machines on campus is purely a want. There are some economical food choices that you can make that could save you lots of cash and still provide you with a healthy diet. For example, instead of buying most of your food at restaurants (fast food or otherwise), buy some nutritious groceries to eat at home or in your dorm room. Even if you don't have a kitchen where you live, there are many fresh fruits, vegetables, nuts, and whole grains that you can enjoy at home. If you do have a kitchen (even just a freezer and microwave), you can really save by eating groceries instead of restaurant food. It is true that sometimes a restaurant salad is cheaper than buying all of the fresh ingredients needed to make one, so break out your calculator and make a wise decision on a case-by-case basis.

Health and Recreation

One of the great things about attending a college or university is that there are usually a plethora of services and resources on campus that students can use for free. Many campuses have health centers, fitness centers, tennis courts, gyms, nature trails, and even pools for students to enjoy. One of the authors of this book was a young father when he attended Kent State University. He took his kids to the indoor pool on campus two or three times a week. It was a great resource for regular exercise, plus it was fun bonding time. He taught them to swim in that pool, and they later went on to join the swim team and to set state records.

These kinds of campus resources are already covered by your student fees, so it would be silly—perhaps even financially irresponsible—not to take full advantage of them!

Entertainment

Entertainment (movies, plays, concerts, etc.) can be expensive these days. However there is still a wide variety of entertainment options that are low cost or even free. For example some campuses have movie screenings that are a fraction of the cost of movies in public venues. Many campuses also offer free concerts, plays, and other events. Off campus you can take advantage of local or natural attractions, such as state parks or points of interest like the local museum. If you take the time to look you can find entertainment options that still fit within your college budget. Many places also offer student discounts if you bring a valid campus ID!

Reading Comprehension Question 11.3 (Inferential Comprehension)

What is the main idea of the section on inexpensive ways to supply your needs?

a. If you are careful and plan ahead, you can supply your needs during college without going into an unmanageable amount of debt.

b. You must learn how to live on a shoestring budget to get through college.

c. Every college student spends in excess of his or her monthly income.

d. College is a protected place where you can have all your wants and needs met with minimal stress, financial or otherwise.

11.4 Managing Money

You will need to do more than find bargains on everyday needs to be successful in maintaining financial balance. You will also need to manage your money. In order to manage your money you will need to have a budget that you can review and revise on a regular basis. To do this you need to know certain things about your financial status. You may be surprised to learn how few college freshmen are prepared to manage their own money. One study of 1,150 university freshmen in Arkansas[8] found that:

- 42 percent of the students did not keep their money in the bank.

- 40 percent of the students did not know how much student loan debt they had.

- 43 percent of the students didn't know how much credit card debt they had.[8]

Let's explore how knowing these things will help you better manage your money.

Banks

An important step toward managing your money is having a bank account—also known as being banked. People who don't have a bank account are sometimes called *unbanked*. The *underbanked* are people who have a bank account but who still rely on alternative financial services to manage their money. Alternative financial services include things like nonbank money orders, nonbank cashing, nonbank remittances, payday loans, pawn shops, refund anticipation loans, rent-to-own services, and auto title loans. If you rely on these kinds of services, you will likely have to pay a significant amount of money in fees or interest just to access your own funds.

The Federal Deposit Insurance Corporation (FDIC) sponsored a survey conducted by the U.S. Census that revealed some interesting things about people without bank accounts.[9] Specifically, if you don't have a bank account, you will likely pay fees (from 2 percent to 5 percent of the amount of your check) for cashing checks and for money orders, you may face greater financial risks (since there is nothing to be done when cash is lost or stolen), and you may not be building a *financial identity* through consumer and credit reporting agencies. Figure 11.2 illustrates some of the pros of being banked and cons of being unbanked.

Figure 11.2

Banked Versus Unbanked

Banked

- You use a bank to manage your money.

- You are building your credit history if you have a savings account and checking account that have never bounced.

- As a student, you likely have access to free checking and savings accounts.

- The bank will look upon you more favorably because of your credit worthiness, and you may be able to obtain personal loans for school needs.

Unbanked

- You do not have a bank account, savings account, or checking account to help you manage your money.

- It will cost you more because you have to pay for cashing checks.

- You will not get a reference for good credit from the bank.

What type of bank account do you need? You should probably start with at least a savings account and a checking account with a debit card. A savings account will give you a safe place to keep money that you don't plan to spend right away (you ought to at least have an emergency fund), and the bank will pay you interest on the money as long as you keep it in the account. Remember: A dorm room is not a secure location.

A checking account will give you a place to put your income where you can use it readily to pay bills and make purchases. A debit card looks like a credit card—and it offers all the same conveniences. The difference is that when you use the debit card, you are not borrowing money; instead you are using your own money directly from your checking account.

For the purposes of this chapter we will not discuss every type of financial institution. However one of the more popular options is the credit union, and it bears further discussion.

Credit Unions

Credit unions are not-for-profit organizations that exist to serve their members rather than to maximize corporate profits. They offer many of the same services as banks—like savings accounts, checking accounts, debit cards, and ATMs. They also allow members to make deposits and get loans. But to have an account there you will have to become a member. Luckily the requirements for membership are often as simple as opening a savings account with a small deposit (sometimes as low as $25). Due to the nonprofit status of credit unions, in many cases they will pay higher interest on your deposits than a bank and charge lower interest on your loans.

Savings

Don't think, "I can't have a savings account when I have no money left after my monthly expenses." Instead remember that savings can start very small. Even if you add only very small amounts to your account each month, over time, it will grow. Any savings is better than no savings at all. Since different banks offer different interest rates, you might want to shop around for where to keep your savings.

Most students need at least some emergency savings. Emergency savings are exactly what they sound like: savings to be used in case of an emergency. Usually they are kept in a savings account where you try to maintain a certain dollar amount. Even if you think you are covered in the case of an emergency, it is important to have extra money available. It is also a good practice to have a general savings account. This account is the beginning of your efforts to build wealth for yourself. To start, it could simply be an extension of your emergency savings. Finally, it is never too early to begin a tax-sheltered retirement account, such as a *Roth IRA*. The value of this type of savings is twofold. First, since it is a tax-sheltered account, you will not be taxed for the money you put into it until you withdraw it after retirement. The second and most important value of this type of savings is that the sooner in your life you begin making contributions, the greater potential it has to grow. If you started putting money into retirement at age 18, you could have three or four times more money in your account by the time you retire than you would if you started saving at age 28. The sooner you start, the better.

Checking

You should shop around for a financial institution that offers free checking. Some banks offer free checking to students even if they do not offer it to the general public. The *free* part is important because the nonfree versions sometimes come with hefty fees. According to a 2014 survey conducted by MoneyRates.com, the average checking account now costs $154.44 a year to maintain.[10]

Even with a free account, you will need to be very careful not to write checks that bounce. A check will bounce if you write checks that together exceed the balance in your account; a check that bounces has been rejected by the bank and will be returned to the person or business to which you wrote it. In this case, the bank may charge you an overdraft fee (usually around $30). You must keep a strict record of each check that you write (in your check register) and always subtract the amount of the check from the amount in your account. This way you will be unlikely to overdraw.

Most banks now allow you to view your accounts online. However you should not depend solely on the online tool to know if you have enough money in your account to make a purchase. The information you see online represents only those checks that have already cleared. Sometimes a check may take a while to clear, making it appear that you have more money in your account than you actually do. For a good reference on checking accounts for college students, go to: http://bvtlab.com/b6eQg.

Debit Cards and ATMs

Some students avoid having to pay for paper checks altogether by using debit cards to access the funds in their checking accounts. A debit card can be used to make purchases pretty much anywhere a credit card could be used. Debit card purchases clear the bank faster than checks, but you will still need to keep a strict record of your debit card purchases, just as you would with checks, because sometimes a debit card purchase may take several days to show up in your account online.

Want to learn more? Try this resource.

Visit the following website to calculate your savings goals: http://bvtlab.com/eb885

Your Budget: Credit Versus Debit (Income Versus Expenses)

A budget is simply a record of your income (credits) and expenses (debits) that you can use as a spending guide and continually adjust over time. Assignment 11.1 will walk you through the process of creating a simple budget. Figure 11.3 illustrates the cycle of budgeting. When you use a budget, you will be able to see exactly where your money is going and make necessary adjustments. In this chapter you have read many ideas about minimizing your expenses each month. Try some of them out and you will see how much they can affect your monthly budget for the better. Monitoring your budget is one of the most powerful habits you can develop when it comes to managing your money during your college years. Doing so can help you avoid many of the pitfalls students encounter while in college. If you manage your money in the most efficient way possible, when you graduate, you can begin your career in a positive financial position.

It is an excellent practice to use a table or spreadsheet to keep track of your credits and debits each month. There are a wide variety of budget plans available to you in books and online. However instead of using a static copy of a budget plan, try going to http://bvtlab.com/RTc6T, as described in Assignment 11.1. There you will find an excellent fill-in-the-blank budget worksheet that you can use to track your finances. Alternatively you can create your own budget using spreadsheet software, some of which is even available for free. Once you have created your monthly budget, print it out and review it. Be sure to keep up with it each month and make adjustments as needed. Keep it handy so that when you do your monthly bills, you will have ready access.

Figure 11.3

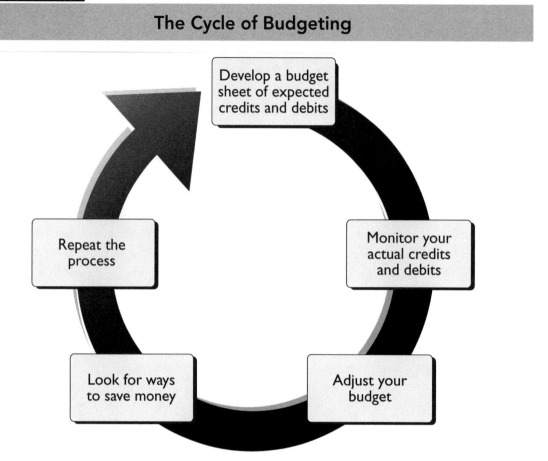

The Cycle of Budgeting

- Develop a budget sheet of expected credits and debits
- Monitor your actual credits and debits
- Adjust your budget
- Look for ways to save money
- Repeat the process

Identity Theft

Identity theft is when someone uses information about you without your permission, and it's a serious crime. A thief could use your name and address, credit card or bank account numbers, social security number, medical insurance account numbers, or other such personal information to make purchases or to take out a line of credit or a loan in your name without you even knowing. This can have consequences beyond just the loss of your money. An identity thief can seriously damage your credit score and can get you into trouble with debt collection agencies. You may have to pay for what the thief bought even if you did not condone, and were not even aware of, the purchases.

Are you safe if you check your accounts regularly? Yes and no. There could still be bills that you are completely unaware of. For example the thief could get a new credit card using your name and then change the address. The bills would then go to the thief's address, but she or he might never pay them. The credit card company would then blame *you* for the debt, even though you neither asked for the card nor saw a single bill!

That would hurt your credit score, which would make it more difficult to get a job or a place to live, set up utilities, or get a line of credit. An identity thief can use your name and information to do a variety of things, including buying goods and services with your credit cards; getting new credit cards; opening a phone, electricity, or gas account; stealing your tax refund; getting medical care on your insurance; and even pretending to be you if they are arrested.

How can you protect yourself from identity theft? By protecting your personal information (see Figure 11.4).

Figure 11.4

Tips on Preventing Identity Theft

AT HOME

- Keep your financial records and social security card in a safe place.

- Don't give your personal information to someone who calls you or emails you.

- Shred papers that include your personal or medical information.

ON THE COMPUTER

- Use passwords that are not easy to guess; be sure to use upper and lower case letters, numbers, and symbols in your passwords.

- Don't respond to emails or other messages that ask for personal information.

- Don't put personal information on a computer in a public place, like the library.

11.5 Managing Credit and Debt

What Is Credit?

Simply put, credit involves:

- Borrowing money with a credit card or loan in order to buy goods and services

- Buying goods and services with that borrowed money

- Paying back the money later, usually with *interest*

What Is Interest?

When you repay borrowed money, more often than not you will need to pay extra money (called *interest*) to whoever gave you the credit card or loan. The interest is the money you are charged for the service of borrowing. Lenders publish the amount they charge to allow you to borrow as a rate, usually called an *APR (annual percentage rate)* or *APY (annual percentage yield)*.[11] These rates are used to indicate the interest rate you will pay for borrowing money from that source. For more information, please see: http://bvtlab.com/v7nK8 and http://bvtlab.com/J8pg9.

You may like to know how the interest on your credit card is calculated. Since there is some variation between credit card companies, you should read the fine print on your statement to see how you are affected by interest. However, in general, the steps to calculate your interest for the month would be 1) figure out your *average daily balance,* 2) figure out your *periodic interest rate,* 3) multiply your periodic interest rate by your average daily balance, and 4) multiply your answer by the number of days in the *cycle.* For more information on interest and how it is calculated, please see *Want to learn more? Try these resources.* later in this chapter.

The Credit CARD Act of 2009 (Credit Card Accountability Responsibility and Disclosure) requires credit card statements to include a section that clearly outlines how long it will take you to pay off your card if you only pay the minimum balance. Some statements also show what amount you would have to pay monthly to completely pay off the debt in just three years. You will save a lot of money if you follow the three-year plan instead of just making the minimum payment.

What Is Debt?

When you owe money to someone, you are in debt. You might have a loan. You might use a credit card. Even a home mortgage is an example of debt.

You may ask, "Is debt always bad?" Debt is only bad when you owe money that you cannot pay back. In such a situation, debt collectors may start calling you. You can even run into legal problems if you cannot pay back the money you owe. Sometimes debt can hurt your credit history—for example if you owe a lot of money on credit cards, if you pay your bills late, if you cannot pay the minimum amount due, or if you skip payments. On the other hand consistently paying your bills on time can actually help your credit score, even if you aren't completely debt free.

Debt-to-Income Ratio

A *debt-to-income ratio (DTI)* is the percentage of a person's monthly *gross* (or total) *income* that goes toward paying debts (and sometimes other things like taxes, fees, and insurance premiums, among others). Many lenders use your DTI to calculate how large a loan you can handle. For example a mortgage lender will use your DTI to figure out what size mortgage payment you can afford after all your other monthly debts are paid. To calculate your DTI, divide your monthly debt by your monthly income, then multiply by one hundred.[12] Credit card limits are often based on your credit score and your DTI. You can use the following information to interpret your DTI.

- **36% or less:** This is the healthiest debt load for most people, but you should avoid incurring more debt.

- **37%–42%:** Not bad, but you should start reducing your debt to get into a better financial position.

- **43%–49%:** You are heading toward—or already in—financial trouble; start paying debts now to prevent debt overload.

- **50% or more:** *Danger!* Aggressively pay off your debts and don't hesitate to seek professional help.

Credit Card Debt

Credit cards are a critical part of any discussion regarding financial survival in college. Too often students get carried away with credit card spending as if that money actually belonged to them, not taking into consideration they will have to pay in addition to the money borrowed. Some institutions offer special cards for students. It is important to understand the specific terms of any card that you use, as well as the general consequences of using credit cards, to begin with.

First, it is important to note that charge cards are not the same as credit cards. Nor are they debit cards. Primarily issued by American Express, these cards require cardholders to pay off the balance each month. There are no interest rates or hard-and-fast spending limits on a charge card. However they come with their own costs and limitations. And when it comes to the effect on your credit score, there is no difference between a credit card and a charge card.

You may be surprised to learn that, according to researchers, most college students (84 percent) spend irresponsibly and have unhealthy amounts of debt. Undergraduate college students have an average of almost five credit cards each.[7] A lot of debt can build up across that many cards! It is clear that students need to be educated on the pitfalls of excessive credit card use in one's college years.

Why do college students have so much credit card debt? Many factors come together to make it very easy to get into excessive debt in college. First, it is considered by many to be normal. Credit card debt is so common that sometimes we forget that it's a serious problem. Second, the cards are easy to get. Banks are willing to take risks with college students because they assume students will only pay the minimum balance; this means the bank will then earn money on the interest. Students end up paying interest, on average, for fifteen years after the money is initially borrowed.[13] Third, many students view credit cards as a symbol of adulthood. Some researchers have suggested that "credit cards are one of the many ways of proclaiming … freedom from Mom and Dad."[13] Fourth, many students are financially ignorant. This is not an insult. It's simply the unfortunate truth: Many students do not know enough about finances to realize that the excessive use of credit cards is a deep financial trap from which it is very difficult to escape.

So what should you do? There are several things you can do to avoid excessive debt—and, more specifically, excessive credit card use—in college.

1. *Set goals for yourself that are higher than the expectations of our society today.* You may know many people with credit card debt, but that doesn't mean it's a good idea to follow in their footsteps.

2. *Refuse to be lured into credit card debt by clever commercials, offers of gifts, or offers of instant gratification.* It is better to save your money and wait to buy something you want than it is to buy something immediately with a credit card and run the risk of paying for it four or five times over through interest payments before you are debt free again.

3. *Realize that the real symbol of adulthood is taking responsibility for your budget.* Carrying a credit card is not a sign of independence. In fact, it's quite the opposite. Ask anyone who has struggled with debt—debt can control your life far more than your parents ever did.

4. *Educate yourself about your personal finances.* Get the full scoop on any transactions or commitments you make before you sign up for any kind of financial services—whether it's a checking account or a credit card.

Reports You Can Obtain About Your Credit

Credit Report and Credit Score

Your credit report is a comprehensive listing of all of your debts, current and past. It includes lots of information about each debt, including the lender, address, loan amount, and payment history; it also includes an overall *credit score.* The three major credit reporting agencies are Experian, Trans Union, and Equifax. You are entitled to a free credit report from each of the three agencies every twelve months. You can get your free copies by contacting one central source online at AnnualCreditReport.com, by phone at 877-322-8228, or by mail. Please keep in mind that AnnualCreditReport.com is the *only* federally authorized website for getting your free credit report. Many scam websites were created afterward using similar names or even deliberate misspellings of the legitimate web address. *Be very careful*—at best, these websites want to con you out of your money, and, at worst, they can have identity theft or other serious crimes as their primary goal.

Your credit score is a number that is used in many ways, mostly to do mortgages, car loans, and the like. It is used by lenders to determine whether or not you qualify for a loan. Your credit score is calculated using several financial indicators, including how much of your available credit you are using, the number of accounts you have and of what kind they are, your bill-paying history, how long you've had your accounts open, your recent credit activity, and whether you have ever had a debt referred for collection, a foreclosure, or a bankruptcy. Your credit score is a three-digit number, typically between 300 and 850, and it represents your credit worthiness—how much you can be trusted to pay back what you owe. The three credit reporting agencies all use similar methods to calculate a credit score, but the formulas are not exactly the same and your credit score will vary from agency to agency.

Want to learn more? Try these resources.

If you want to know more about managing your money, you can access the following websites:

Annual Percentage Rate (APR) and Effective APR

Many credit cards advertise an annual APR that is actually less than what the customer is charged in a year. In these cases, the actual method for calculating the interest is to compound a daily interest rate 365 times. This video explains compounding.

http://bvtlab.com/37e97

Calculating Interest

For more information on interest, and instructions on how to calculate it yourself, please visit:

http://bvtlab.com/J8pg9

How to Set Up a Budget

This video presents six steps for creating a budget:

http://bvtlab.com/a79QC

Reading Comprehension Question 11.4 (Analysis)

What is the main purpose of this chapter on finances during college?

a. To demonstrate that as a student, you will be unable to manage your finances on your own during college

b. To provide education about finances because education is one of the most important factors in effective money management among students

c. To illustrate just how difficult and complicated it is to manage your own budget

d. To provide you with information on how to avoid paying for college

11.6 **Summary**

In this chapter you learned about the value of a college education, ways to pay for college and for everyday expenses, and credit card debt. You also learned how to obtain your own credit report and found out about identity theft and how to avoid it. Finally you learned about developing a budget and tracking your income and expenses each month as a way to manage your money efficiently during college.

Education about finances is one of the most important determining factors when it comes to college students successfully managing their own money; and managing your money wisely during college is one of the most important ways to ensure that, when you graduate, you can begin your new life with a financially healthy and secure future.

Name: _____

Study Guide | Goal 1

The student will be able to list at least two things that make an education valuable.

Questions	Answers & Notes

Name: _____

Study Guide | Goal 2

The student will be able to identify at least three ways to obtain financial aid for college and include multiple potential sources.

Questions	Answers & Notes

Name: _____

Study Guide | Goal 3

The student will be able to distinguish between *wants* and *needs* and discuss inexpensive ways to supply needs while in college.

Questions	Answers & Notes

Study Guide | Goal 4

The student will be able to define terms related to credit card debt, including credit, interest, and debt, and list the pros and cons of credit card debt.

Questions	Answers & Notes

Study Guide | Goal 5

The student will be able to define identity theft and list ways to avoid it.

Questions	Answers & Notes

Name: _____

Study Guide | Goal 6

The student will be able to discuss tips for managing money during college.

Questions	Answers & Notes

Study Guide | Preparing for Class

Use this page to record questions or insights to discuss in class.

_____

_____

_____

_____

_____

_____

_____

_____

_____

_____

_____

_____

_____

_____

_____

_____

_____

_____

_____

_____

_____

_____

_____

_____

_____

_____

_____

_____

_____

_____

_____

_____

Name: _____

Review Questions 11.1

Instructions

Following are five true-false statements taken from the information in this chapter. First, try to answer them without looking back at the chapter. Then review the chapter to see how well you did.

Question & Answer	Rationale
Circle true or false for each of the following statements.	Write an explanation stating why each statement is true or false.
1. People without a college degree are more likely to be employed than those with a degree. True or False	Your Rationale:
2. Scholarships must be paid back, with interest, after you graduate. True or False	Your Rationale:
3. Many campuses have health centers, fitness centers, tennis courts, gyms, nature trails, and even pools for students to use for a fee. True or False	Your Rationale:
4. Undergraduate college students have an average of ten credit cards each. True or False	Your Rationale:
5. You are entitled to as many free credit reports from each of the three agencies as you would like. True or False	Your Rationale:

Name: _____

Assignment 11.1

Monthly Budgeting

Instructions

This assignment will help you to learn how to plan a monthly budget. Follow the steps below and be ready to discuss with the class how the process went for you.

Follow These Steps

Step 1:   Go to the following website:

http://bvtlab.com/RTc6T

(Alternatively, you could use spreadsheet software.)

Step 2:   Plug in your monthly credits and debits to make up a monthly budget sheet.

Step 3:   Print out your budget sheet. Make comments about each section and discuss whether or not the debits you have listed are *wants* or *needs*.

Step 4:   Write a short paragraph about what it was like to do your budget. Do your credits balance with your debits? Did you list needs that would more accurately be labeled *wants?* Make notes on what you might do to make your monthly budget more balanced.

Notes

Chapter Roadmap *12*

Introduction

In this chapter you will learn about the typical requirements for graduation from college, including core curriculum requirements and the requirements of a particular major. We will discuss some practical information about selecting courses and planning when to take them. For a follow-up assignment you will use the information in this chapter along with information from your college to plan which courses you will take next semester and also to design your long-term graduation plan.

This chapter roadmap page presents the formal learning goals for this chapter and a checklist that you should follow as you read and study the chapter.

Student Learning Goals

After completing this chapter you should be able to do the following:

1. Understand the general requirements for graduation from college.

2. Identify which courses are required for graduation within a chosen major.

3. Calculate a grade point average.

4. Design a long-term graduation plan that includes a list of all of the courses needed to graduate.

5. Prepare a semester registration plan based on a long-term graduation plan.

Chapter Checklist

You will benefit most if you complete the activities in the order that they are listed.

❑ **Target Date/Deadline:** _____
Complete Critical Thinking Activity 12.1.

❑ **Target Date/Deadline:** _____
Convert the student learning goals to questions that you can answer as you read the chapter. Write your questions on the study guide pages near the end of this chapter.

❑ **Target Date/Deadline:** _____
Read the chapter.

❑ **Target Date/Deadline:** _____
Try to answer the reading comprehension questions as you come to them in the chapter. Check each answer by comparing it to the list of correct answers in the back of the book. If any answer was not correct, then review the passages preceding the question to see why you missed the question.

❑ **Target Date/Deadline:** _____
Answer the student learning goal questions you created. These answered questions will be your study guide.

❑ **Target Date/Deadline:** _____
Write down any questions, insights, or comments that you have as you read so that you can bring them up in class.

❑ **Target Date/Deadline:** _____
Complete Review Questions 12.1.

❑ **Target Date/Deadline:** _____
Complete Assignment 12.1 (Design Your Long-Term Graduation Plan).

❑ **Target Date/Deadline:** _____
Complete Assignment 12.2 (Plan Semester Registration).

❑ **Target Date/Deadline:** _____
Visit your advisor for registration (if applicable).

❑ **Target Date/Deadline:** _____
Review what you have learned from this chapter.

Critical Thinking Activity 12.1

Consider the following questions related to planning for your graduation from college. Put a check mark in the appropriate column, depending on whether or not you know the information necessary to answer the question. Check the YES column if you are very confident that you know the information. Check the NO column if you don't know the information—or if you think you know, but are not completely confident.

Information of Importance	YES (Confident)	NO (Not Sure)
1. What are the courses that you are required to take for a degree in your major?		
2. How many credit hours are required to graduate from your university?		
3. How many credit hours should you take each semester? Why?		
4. How do you calculate your GPA?		
5. How does your GPA affect graduation?		
6. Should you take an online course?		
7. Exactly when and where should you submit your application for graduation?		

Analysis		
A. How many checks are in the YES column?	+	
B. How many checks are in the NO column?		−
C. Subtract the number of NO checks from the number of YES checks. This is your score for this exercise.		

Reflection
If your score for this exercise is less than 4, then your lack of knowledge about these issues puts you in greater danger of not graduating. The good news is that this chapter provides the answers for all of these questions.

Planning Your Future:

What Courses Should I Take?

12

"It is as difficult to achieve a goal that you don't have as it is to come back from a place that you have never been."

— Zig Ziglar[1]

Why are you attending college? The answer to this question depends, in part, on what kind of college you are attending. Some students go to a two-year college and plan to graduate with an associate degree. Other students who start at a two-year college plan to earn the necessary credits to transfer to another institution—perhaps a four-year college or university—to obtain their final degree.

Most students who go straight to a four-year college plan to graduate from that same college, earning a bachelor's degree. Some of these students also plan on continuing their education beyond the bachelor's level. It is becoming more and more common for students who have completed a bachelor's degree to continue their education by pursuing a master's degree or a doctorate (PhD). You may pursue an advanced degree (a master's, PhD, or a professional degree—such as a medical or law degree) at the same university where you got your bachelor's; but it is more likely that you will move to a new institution. After obtaining a PhD, many graduate students go on to pursue postdoctoral research, almost always at a new institution. The question is, "How do you get there from here?" This chapter is designed to answer that question by helping you to plan for graduation at the bachelor's-degree level.

One of the most important things you have learned from reading this book is that planning is a major key to success. To design your long-term graduation plan, you will need to understand both the core curriculum requirements (courses required for all majors) and the requirements for your chosen field of study. This chapter will describe, in some detail, the core curriculum and other requirements for graduation. We will include some practical information about how courses and credit work in college, how to calculate your grade point average (GPA), how to decide which courses to take, and how many courses to take each term. You will be able to use the information in this chapter along with information from your college (usually found in the college catalog) to design your long-term graduation plan.

Reading Comprehension Question 12.1 (Knowledge)

To design your long-term graduation plan, you will need to do which of the following?

a. Understand the core curriculum requirements as well as the requirements for your chosen field of study

b. Know all the courses that are offered in your college system

c. Use a software program called "Plan It" on your college's website

d. None of the above

12.1 Graduation Requirements

Many students begin college with only a vague idea about how to proceed past the first semester. You may realize that you are here to take a lot of classes and then graduate. That is a good start. However, sometime during your first semester you need to pay attention to the specifics of what you are going to do each semester between now and graduation.

Most likely, when you were a high school freshman, you didn't have to worry too much about exactly what you would do and which courses you would take as a sophomore, junior, and senior. With the exception of a few choices, the school probably took care of most of that for you—and it's possible that your parents helped figure out the rest. Alternatively, perhaps you are entering college during a different phase of your life. For those who have not recently attended school, the task of figuring out graduation requirements can at first seem daunting. Colleges help you a little by setting up programs of study for specific majors and publishing those requirements in the college catalog. However, in college, you have many more choices, and it is mostly up to you to create and follow through with a plan for graduating with the degree you want.

Let's explore some background information that you need to know before you create your own graduation plan. What courses do you have to take? When, and in what order, should you take them? How many of them should you take at once? Which courses should you avoid? How can you monitor your progress toward graduation?

The Core Curriculum

In most colleges, there are certain courses that everyone must take, regardless of your major area of study. These courses are often referred to as the **core curriculum**. These usually include some introductory courses from a variety of disciplines that are designed to help you become a well-rounded liberal arts graduate. Everyone with a college degree, regardless of the major, is expected to have some command of the humanities, the field of mathematics, the natural sciences, and the social sciences. In the United States, the federal government mandates a basic knowledge of U.S. history and government, so you can expect to take some required courses related to those topics as well. Most of the core courses are completed during the first two years of college. This makes planning during the first two years a little easier since all students will have to take courses from these categories regardless of major.

Core requirements may vary somewhat from college to college, but there is a general consistency that makes transferring easier. Many students begin their college experience at a two-year college where they complete their core requirements, and then transfer to a four-year college or university to complete the second half of their baccalaureate, or bachelor's, degree.

You will enjoy courses related to your chosen major during the second two years of a four-year program. Some private colleges may have a core regimen that looks different, at least in terms of the course titles, from the core curriculum found in their public counterparts. However, the courses usually still offer a foundation in the same variety of disciplines. If this is the case at your college, it is critical that you work with your advisor in order to develop an enrollment plan that will ensure your successful completion of a college degree in an appropriate time frame.

The College Catalog

It is wise to consult the college catalog during your first semester and use it to create a list of the courses you plan to take from the first semester until graduation. Of course, this plan can be adjusted along the way as new courses become available, and you should *check course offerings every term* to see if a new class is available that fulfills one of your existing requirements. (Course offerings will also vary more between terms for some majors than others.)

The college catalog usually provides a list of the core curriculum and the additional courses that are required for graduation in each major. This information is typically organized by department and then by specific majors. A large university may organize the catalog by college, then department, and finally by major. In the U.S., a *university* is defined as a *collection of colleges* (for example, the College of Arts and Sciences, the College of Engineering, the College of Nursing, and so on).

If your college catalog does not list the information you need, then be sure to learn where to find it. Course descriptions and the list of courses required for graduation from your specific college should be available somewhere—perhaps online or through your advisor. Many colleges have abandoned the paper hard copy of the catalog and provide, instead, a catalog in electronic format online.

It would be beneficial to talk with your advisor to determine what resources your college provides for specific majors to plan for graduation. Some campuses offer various "worksheets" that can help you come up with a plan, or track your progress toward graduation. You should take full advantage of whatever resources your school provides. For any resources they lack, you can create your own by using your college catalog and the generic worksheet provided in Assignment 12.1 at the end of this chapter.

Courses and Credit

Most college courses are measured in units called **credit hours**. The number of credit hours assigned to a course is usually related to how much time, per week, that class spends meeting. For example, fifty minutes of class time is usually worth one credit hour. Therefore, an English composition course that meets for fifty minutes three times a week would be worth three hours—or credits, for short. Exceptions to this pattern include courses with labs, or something like a physical education course that meets twice a week but earns only one credit hour. Once you determine which courses you need to take and understand the credit hour scheme at your own college, you will be ready to plan your course load for each semester.

Your **academic program** is the series of courses that are required in order to earn your college degree. Exactly which courses are included in the list differs depending on your major area of study (sometimes called your program of study). You need to create a **long-term graduation plan** in order to ensure that you take all the courses that are required for a degree in your chosen major.

Courses to Avoid

There are so many choices in college. It seems like there are courses on every topic imaginable. As a new college freshman, you may be attracted to many of the courses that you see listed in the catalog; however, you are not truly free to take just any course. You have to take the courses that are required for your particular major, and you should plan on doing so over a set period of time (typically four years). This means that your time for extra classes—classes that don't advance you toward your degree—will be limited, if you have any at all.

Some majors allow a limited number of elective courses; but even then, you will likely have to choose your electives from a list of courses that are approved for your major. If you are an art major, then you could probably use a pottery course for your major. It may even be a required course for an art major. But if you are a business major, it is unlikely that you will be allowed to use a pottery course on your graduation application. When considering any course, you must ask yourself, "Does this course fit into my graduation plan?"

Does this mean that the college won't allow you to take a studio art course if you are a business major? No, of course not! As long as you pay your tuition, meet the course prerequisites (which will be discussed later in this chapter), and are a student in good standing, most colleges will let you take any course. The more important question is not "Can I take this course?" but "Should I?" A business major could take a pottery course merely for personal growth, but the credits earned for the pottery course would likely not count toward graduation with a business degree. No matter what extra courses you take, you have to earn all of the credits required for graduation using approved courses. Too many extra courses and not enough required ones can lead you to overstay your welcome in college—a costly and time-consuming consequence.

There is one more thing that you should know about extra courses. Remember that all of the courses that you take, whether they count toward graduation or not, will be used to calculate your *cumulative grade point average.* (Only courses actually listed on your graduation application will be used to calculate your *graduation or major GPA,* but all courses are used for the *cumulative GPA.*) In addition, when you transfer to another institution, the college will forward all of your grades to the receiving institution—not just those that you used for your degree. Additional information about this appears later in this chapter under the heading "How to Calculate Your GPA."

If you are interested in an extra course but you do not want to receive a grade for it on your transcript, then you can often **audit** the course without receiving a grade. A student once told me that he audited a golf course every semester in college because he loved to play golf. He didn't need those physical education credits, but as a student on a budget, auditing the course was less expensive than the green fees he would have had to pay to play on his own.

Online Courses

Online courses are becoming common in colleges around the country. Many colleges even offer entire degree programs online. Who should take an online course? The answer to this question varies. Your level of experience, level of comfort around technology, and level of maturity all influence your likelihood of success in an online class.

During college, you are likely to experience at least one of the *three basic types of online course work:*

1. The online course, taught entirely online

2. The hybrid course, taught partially online and partially in a classroom

3. The online-supported course, taught face-to-face in a classroom but with handouts, study guides, and/or other support tools provided online

Following are six things that you should know about online classes:

1. Online classes may be more convenient than face-to-face (F2F) classes; however, they require just as much time as, if not more than, the same course in a F2F format.

2. Online courses often have strict deadlines throughout the semester. Just because it is online does not mean that the students can submit assignments for a grade anytime they wish before the end of the semester.

3. Online courses often require more writing than would the same course in a F2F format.

4. Online courses require that the student is mature and disciplined enough to work independently in order to be successful.

5. Online courses require that the student has an Internet connection at home or otherwise has unlimited access to a computer and the Internet.

6. Online courses require that the student knows how to use the computer and the Internet. This usually involves, but is not limited to, using email, attaching files, using word processing software, reading and writing in a discussion board, taking timed quizzes, uploading, downloading, and performing simple operating system functions like copy, cut, and paste.

Want to learn more? Try this resource.

Here is an online questionnaire that will help you decide if online courses are right for you:

The Smarter Measures Tool
http://bvtlab.com/hw79p

Reading Comprehension Question 12.2 (Literal Comprehension)

Which of the following topics does this book cover?

a. The requirements for graduation at your particular college

b. How to earn a bachelor's degree in under four years

c. How to develop a long-term plan for graduation

d. All of the above

Planning Your Semester Course Load

How many credit hours should you take each semester? The answer to this question varies, based on the needs of each student.

Keep in mind that different colleges may have different credit hour requirements. You will need to determine what the specific requirements are at your college. To illustrate the process in this book, we will use the semester system scheme.

In the typical semester program, a course load of about sixteen credit hours per semester is considered normal. To be considered a full-time student (which is often necessary for financial aid purposes), you must typically be enrolled in at least twelve credit hours. These two numbers are different because the federal government, rather than the college, determines the definition of *full-time* for federal financial aid. Thus, twelve credit hours are required if you are to be considered a full-time student for financial aid (grants or loans), but sixteen credit hours is considered "normal" because you would have to take an average of sixteen credit hours per semester to graduate with a bachelor's degree within four years.

Attending less than full time does not always prevent a student from receiving financial aid, but it may still affect the amount of aid received. Some students also need to take at least twelve credit hours to satisfy the requirements of scholarships, to receive discounts on auto insurance or to remain as dependents on their parents' health insurance policy, to be allowed to live in a dorm on campus, or to be allowed to play for a campus sports team.

Most colleges also specify a maximum number of credit hours (usually seventeen or eighteen) in which the student can enroll without receiving special permission. You should check your college's policy if you are interested in taking more than the maximum number of credits in one semester. Usually, an academic official—such as the dean or the vice president for academic affairs—must grant the permission. You should not enroll in more credit hours than you are able to keep up with and still earn high grades.

In the typical semester system program, students are required to earn about sixty credit hours to graduate with a two-year degree and about one hundred and twenty credit hours to graduate with a four-year degree. In either case, the normal course load for a semester is fifteen credit hours (four semesters at fifteen credits each adds up to sixty; eight semesters at fifteen credits each adds up to one hundred and twenty).

Many colleges require a few extra courses in the core curriculum beyond the credit hours required for a degree. These are courses that the institution feels are necessary for a well-rounded education and may be only one or two credit hours each. Examples of such courses include health, first aid, and physical education courses. If your college requires an additional four credit hours total for these types of courses, then the normal course load would be sixteen credit hours for each semester. Table 12.1 illustrates this scenario.

Alternatively, you could complete the sixty-four credits for a two-year degree by taking twelve credits each fall, twelve credits each spring, and eight credits each summer, as is illustrated in Table 12.2.

Table 12.1

Credit Hour Scenario for the First Two Years (Without Summer Courses)			
	Fall Semester	**Spring Semester**	**Summer Semester**	**Total Credits**
Year One	16 credits	16 credits	Zero credits	
Year Two	16 credits	16 credits	Zero credits	= 64 credits

Table 12.2

Credit Hour Scenario for the First Two Years (with Summer Courses)			
	Fall Semester	**Spring Semester**	**Summer Semester**	**Total Credits**
Year One	12 credits	12 credits	8 credits	
Year Two	12 credits	12 credits	8 credits	= 64 credits

Don't be discouraged if you do not graduate within two years for an associate degree or within four years for a bachelor's degree. *Very few people do.* According to the U.S. Census, the average number of years that it took students to complete a bachelor's degree in 2004 was 6.5 years, and the average number of years it took to complete an associate's degree was 4.4 years.[2] What matters most is that you do, in fact, finish the program of study and graduate. Those students who have many time-consuming, non-academic responsibilities (work, children, etc.) may choose to enroll in less than a normal load in order to maintain good grades while juggling those additional responsibilities. You must also keep your grade point average high in order to graduate. Take as many courses as you can responsibly handle. You must devote enough time to each course to learn the material and to be able to demonstrate what you have learned.

When you are planning which courses to take, keep in mind that it is not a good practice to take all easy classes (or classes that are easy for you) in one semester because that means that in the future you will likely have a semester with all difficult classes. Instead, select a balanced course load with some classes that you will find easy and some that you will find challenging. A balanced schedule will make it easier for you to maintain the required GPA necessary for graduation. Since you must maintain a certain grade point average in order to graduate, you need to know how to calculate your GPA.

How to Calculate Your GPA

This section of the chapter is included because your GPA sometimes affects which courses you select for a particular semester. GPA is the number of *grade points* earned divided by the number of *credit hours* attempted.

Suppose that a student took five classes that added up to twelve credit hours, total. How would you calculate the GPA for those courses? First, you would need to determine how many grade points the student earned. The number of grade points earned for each credit hour is as follows:

A = 4 grade points

B = 3 grade points

C = 2 grade points

D = 1 grade point

F = 0 grade points

You multiply each class's credit hours by the grade points earned according to each letter grade to determine the grade points earned (according to the letter grade) in order to determine the grade points earned for each class. (In the example below, for the health class, 2 credit hours × 4 grade points [for an A] = 8.) Then you can determine the sum of credit hours attempted. Finally, divide the sum of the grade points earned by the sum of credit hours attempted to find the grade point average.

For example, suppose Charlie earned the following grades for the semester:

Course	Credit Hours	Grade Earned	Grade Points Earned
Composition 101	3	C (= 2)	3 × 2 = 6
Algebra 1A	3	C (= 2)	3 × 2 = 6
Sociology 101	3	C (= 2)	3 × 2 = 6
Health	2	A (= 4)	2 × 4 = 8
Student Success	1	A (= 4)	1 × 4 = 4
TOTALS	**12**	—	**30**

His GPA would be 2.5 because the total grade points (30) divided by the total number of credit hours attempted (12) equals 2.5.

Many colleges calculate two types of GPA: the graduation GPA and the cumulative GPA. Only courses that count toward graduation are used to calculate the graduation (sometimes called "major") GPA. Those are the courses that the student needs to graduate and that are listed on the graduation application. However, all of the courses that a student has taken are used when calculating the *cumulative* GPA. If a student has taken the same course twice, both grades will be used to calculate the cumulative GPA. It is the cumulative GPA that is usually transferred to other colleges since all of the courses on your transcript are sent to the receiving institution. Check your college catalog to see if this is the rule at your college. There may be some variation of policy from college to college.

Reading Comprehension Question 12.3 (Inferential Comprehension)

Why would you need to know how to calculate your GPA?

a. Because sometimes your GPA may determine which courses you might need to take in a given semester

b. Because doing math is important for college students

c. Because your GPA will determine how much you get paid, regardless of your job, after graduation

d. All of the above

Graduation Application

You cannot just go along from year to year taking courses until one day the college calls you and says, "You are graduating this semester, so remember to show up for the ceremony … and wear a robe." Instead, graduation is an event that is planned well in advance and usually involves the completion of some paperwork by the student. Some colleges call this paperwork a graduation application, and there is usually a small fee for submitting it.

What is on the application? It usually asks for your name, student ID, address, major, name of your advisor, and a checklist of the courses required for your major, along with a space to indicate the grade earned in that course and the date that the course was taken. The graduation application form may have a place for you to list your name *as you want it to appear* on your diploma, so be careful about how you fill it out. If you write a nickname like "Butch" on the form, you might be very disappointed at graduation to receive a diploma with Butch Williams engraved on it, rather than David Alexander Williams Jr., as you expected.

A graduation application form can usually be downloaded from your registrar's webpage. At most colleges, you must submit a completed graduation application to the registrar by a *deadline during the semester before your last semester of classes.* Suppose you were planning to graduate after the end of the spring semester of 2020. In that case, you probably need to submit your graduation application before the deadline during the middle of the fall semester of 2019. Check your college's official calendar (usually online) to determine the deadline, or call the registrar's office.

The graduation application usually requires several signatures—your signature as well as those of some other academic officials (such as your academic advisor and possibly the chair for the department or division of your academic major). Therefore, when the appropriate semester comes, make an appointment with your advisor early in the semester so that he or she can help you get the form signed and submitted on time. You need to start thinking about that graduation application during your very first semester in college. You need to plan ahead as much as you can for which courses you will take and in what order. In other words, you need a long-term graduation plan.

12.2 Designing Your Long-Term Graduation Plan

Now that you know some of the basic information about course credits, course loads, and GPA requirements, you are ready to design your long-term graduation plan.

The long-term graduation plan is really very simple. It is *a list of all of the courses that you plan to take, arranged in the order that you plan to take them.* You can use the form provided in Assignment 12.1 to create your own plan. The form provides a series of boxes representing each semester from your first semester until the term you plan to graduate. You should label each box with the date of the semester and list titles of the courses that you plan to take that semester in the box.

In order to design the plan, you will need to determine a few things:

- Which courses are required for your program of study (major)?

- Do any of these courses have *prerequisites* (other courses you must have already completed in order to enroll in this course)?

- How many credit hours would you like to take each semester?

- Would you like to take classes in the summer?

Step 1: Select an Academic Major

You should select an academic major as soon as possible because it will help you to be more effective in your planning. Experts who study issues related to higher education have suggested that the students who are most likely to be successful in college are those who choose a program and stick with it.

One benefit of working toward a particular major is that you will know exactly which courses you need to take. As previously stated, a list of courses associated with each major is usually found in the college catalog. There are certain courses specified in the list that are required, not optional. The required major courses usually account for only a portion of the course credits required to graduate. The additional credits will be earned by taking elective courses. Elective does not mean that you can select any course that you wish, but rather that you may select any course within a specified list of elective courses. These elective courses are also listed in the college catalog and depend on which major you have chosen. You may have a bit of fun browsing that list and antici-pating some of those courses.

You should know that there are some (but not many) majors that allow little or no elective choice. For example, in one college where I taught, the education major had very few elective choices. This was simply because there were so many courses required by that state's accrediting agency that were considered essential for anyone who planned to teach; by the time you took them all, you had enough credits for a degree and no room left for anything extra.

If you choose a major during your freshman year but later change your mind, you can change your major. Changing your major during the first two years of college is not usually problematic because most of the courses you will take during those years are core courses that can be used for any major. If you do happen to take a course that can only be used for your initial major, then you would not be able to use that course on your graduation application after switching majors.

In most colleges, when you choose a major or change your major, you will need to complete and submit some type of form (for example, a "Change of Program of Study" form) to the registrar in order to make your choice official. These forms are usually available on the webpage for the registrar or in the office of the registrar.

You can still work on a graduation plan even if you have not decided which program of study you would like to pursue. Simply insert a placeholder for those courses into your long-term plan. For example, you could write, "major area course #1," "major area course #2," and so on. Plan as best you can. Then, when you decide on a major, you can replace those placeholders with the appropriate course titles. Obviously, the placeholder strategy is not the best method because it leaves you with a lot of unknowns in your long-term plan—but it is still better than having no plan at all.

If you are interested in two or three different majors and are having trouble deciding, you may also wish to complete more than one graduation plan worksheet (one for each major). Then you can compare them side-by-side and easily identify which courses they all have in common and how they differ. First, take the courses that your favorite majors have in common. That will give you a little more time to think about which major you want to ultimately pursue.

The U.S. Census Bureau provides some data about how many Americans graduate with each type of major. There is also census data about what types of jobs people are doing who have graduated with a certain major and how much money they earn. In general, the data show that the higher the education people have, the greater their earning potential. It also suggests that people with college degrees in some majors earn more than people with degrees in other majors. If you are looking for the major that has the most earning power, then you will be interested in that aspect of the data. Keep in mind, however, that earning power may not be the only criteria that you want to use when deciding your career. As is often said, *"pick a job that you enjoy doing, and you will never have to go to work."*

One final note about majors and their relationship to your career: The data show that many people end up in jobs or careers that are not directly connected to their undergraduate college major. Choosing a major does not determine your career path for the rest of your life. It is merely one step on a journey that will feature many unexpected twists and turns.

Step 2: Identify Prerequisites

In order to create a graduation plan, you will need to determine if there are prerequisite requirements that are associated with any of the courses you plan to take. A **prerequisite** is a requirement that must be met before you are allowed to take the course. A common type of prerequisite is prior completion of another course.

As an example, suppose that Composition I, Composition II, and World Literature are all required for your major. Now, let's say that Composition II is a prerequisite for World Literature. You cannot enroll in World Literature until you have successfully completed Composition II. Composition II also has a prerequisite: Composition I. Therefore, when you are planning which humanities courses to take over several semesters, you should start with Composition I, then plan to take Composition II during the following semester, and finally plan to take World Literature during the semester after that. If you wait until the semester before you graduate to take the Composition II course, then you would have to hang around an additional semester to take the remaining required World Literature course.

Often an introductory-level course will be a prerequisite for a higher-level course in the same discipline. For example, in many colleges, the Introduction to Sociology course must be taken prior to any higher-level sociology course, such as Marriage and Family or Classical Sociological Theory. This is because there is information in the introductory level course that you will need to understand before you attempt to tackle the higher-level course.

The main point here is that you must *plan ahead.* By the end of your first semester in college, you should have planned what courses you will take (and when) for your entire first two years of college, at least.

Step 3: Determine When Specific Courses Are Available

Another important question to address when designing your plan is, "In which semesters will my college be offering the courses that I need?" Every course is not offered every semester. Some courses are offered only in fall, whereas others are offered only in spring. In many colleges the summer schedule changes from year to year depending on budget issues and the availability of instructors. And for some majors, course offerings vary so that each term, new courses are available to fulfill the same requirement. (Be sure to consult your advisor about the requirements for your specific major.) However, most colleges publish a list of course offerings well in advance and allow you to view the list of course offerings for future semesters via a link on your college website. Your advisor may also be able to help you discover when and with what frequency a particular course is offered.

Step 4: Record When You Plan to Take Each Required Course

Follow the instructions provided with Assignment 12.1 to create a table that shows when you plan to take each of the courses that are required for your major. On the following pages you will find a partial example of a completed "Long-Term Graduation Plan." There is also an explanation of the different aspects of the example.

The example in Figure 12.1 is for a student who wishes to graduate in four years and who does not wish to take classes during the summer. If you were planning to take classes during the summer, then you would need to record the titles of those courses in the column for summer.

Figure 12.1

Partial Example of a Graduation Plan Worksheet

1 FALL (Year: 2016)	**1** SPRING (Year: 2017)	**1** SUMMER (2017)
2 English Composition I (3 credits)	**2** English Composition II (3 credits)	
2 4 Pre-calculus (3 credits)	**2 4** Calculus I (3 credits)	
U.S. History (3 credits)	U.S. Government (3 credits)	
Public Speaking (3 credits)	Social science elective: Sociology (3 credits)	
College Success (3 credits)	Other required course (3 credits)	
Fitness Walking (1 credit)	Other PE course (1 credit)	
TOTAL CREDITS = 16	TOTAL CREDITS = 16	

Partial Example of a Graduation Plan Worksheet *(Cont.)*

1 FALL (Year: 2017)	**1** SPRING (Year: 2018)	**1** SUMMER (2018)
2 World Literature (3 credits)	Humanities elective: Intro to Art (3 credits)	
2 3 4 First required science (4 credits)	**2** Second required science (4 credits)	
Social science elective: Psychology (3 credits)	Other required course (3 credits)	
Other required course (3 credits)	Other required course (3 credits)	
Other required course (3 credits)	Other required course (3 credits)	
TOTAL CREDITS= 16	TOTAL CREDITS = 16	

1 FALL (Year: 2018)	**1** SPRING (Year: 2019)	**1** SUMMER (2019)

1 FALL (Year: 2019)	**1** SPRING (Year: 2020)
Note: Submit graduation application.	Graduate!

Examine the plan. Is a strategy apparent? Note the following characteristics of the example worksheet (these descriptions match the number labels on the example):

1 Record the appropriate dates for each semester in the header for each box.

2 Note how this student planned courses with prerequisites in order—thus, the prerequisites will be taken prior to the courses that require them for the humanities sequence, the mathematics sequence, and the science sequence.

3 This student used a placeholder, "First required science," because she has not yet decided which science course she prefers. Since some science courses must be taken in sequence (i.e., Biology I before Biology II), she has planned accordingly.

4 Note that this student has planned to take the required mathematics courses in the first year and then the required science course in the second year. This is because the student is aware that having a stronger mathematics background before you take science may help you perform better in the science class. (Some science courses may have a math course as a prerequisite.)

12.3 Summary

In this chapter you learned about the value of a long-term graduation plan and how to design such a plan. In order to design an effective plan, you need to understand the core curriculum requirements, requirements for the major you wish to pursue, how to determine an appropriate semester course load, and how to determine if online courses are appropriate for you, as well as how to calculate your GPA.

The things you learned in this chapter will enable you to create a long-term academic plan that lists all of the courses you are required to take in college in the order in which you plan to take them. Once you have done this, you will be prepared to plan your schedule for next semester. These tasks will be easier if you have selected a major because you will know exactly what courses you need to include in your plan. Take time to create your long-term academic plan and to complete your semester registration planning form *before* you visit your advisor. Take the completed forms with you when you visit your advisor so that you can talk with your advisor about them. Visit your advisor as soon as possible (you will have to make an appointment) when registration starts. In most colleges, the most popular courses and courses offered at the time of day most preferred by students tend to fill up quickly. If you wait too late to register, then you may find that your first choices have filled up and are closed.

You will benefit most from this chapter if you do the following:

1. Select a major early

2. Create a written long-term graduation plan

3. Complete a semester registration planning form based on the information in the long-term plan

4. Make an appointment with your academic advisor as soon as possible *before* registration and register for the courses specified in the long-term plan

5. Save the "Long-Term Graduation Plan" template that is provided in Assignment 12.1 below, and use it every semester to keep a record of the courses that you have completed along with your grades (keeping in mind that you must repeat required courses in which you did not receive a passing grade)

6. Calculate your GPA after each semester and consider the effect that it will have on your future course load

7. Complete and submit a graduation application form to the registrar's office on time

Reading Comprehension Question 12.4 (Analysis)

Why is it important for you to understand this chapter?

a. It provides information to guide you in designing your entire academic program at college.

b. It is only important for those who know their major ahead of time.

c. It is not important for all students, only those who plan to transfer to a four-year college.

d. None of the above

e. All of the above

Name: _____

Study Guide | Goal 1

The student will be able to understand the general requirements for graduation from college.

Questions	Answers & Notes

Name: _____

Study Guide | Goal 2

The student will be able to identify which courses are required for graduation within a chosen major.

Questions	Answers & Notes

Name: _____

Study Guide | Goal 3

The student will be able to calculate a grade point average.

Questions	Answers & Notes

Name: _____

Study Guide | Goal 4

The student will be able to design a long-term graduation plan that includes a list of all of the courses needed to graduate.

Questions	Answers & Notes

Name: _____

Study Guide | Goal 5

The student will be able to prepare a semester registration plan based on a long-term graduation plan.

Questions	Answers & Notes

Study Guide | *Preparing for Class*

Use this page to record questions or insights to discuss in class.

Name: _____

Review Questions 12.1

Instructions

Following are five true-false statements taken from the information in this chapter. First, try to answer them without looking back at the chapter. Then review the chapter to see how well you did.

Question & Answer	Rationale
Circle true or false for each of the following statements.	Write an explanation stating why each statement is true or false.
1. If a student plans to graduate with an associate degree within two years from a college that uses the semester system without taking summer courses, then he or she will have to take sixteen credit hours worth of courses each semester. True or False	Your Rationale:
2. You don't really need to know how to calculate your GPA because there is no reason to know what your GPA is until you are ready to graduate. True or False	Your Rationale:
3. It does not matter which semester you plan to take a specific course because all of the courses are always offered in both fall and spring semester. True or False	Your Rationale:
4. According to experts, students are more likely to be successful if they pick a program and stick with it. True or False	Your Rationale:
5. A long-term academic plan will lead you to successful completion of your academic program. True or False	Your Rationale:

Name: _____

Assignment 12.1

Design Your Long-Term Graduation Plan

Goal

The purpose of this activity is for the student to understand the course requirements for a particular program of study and to create a long-term graduation plan.

Objective

The student will construct a long-term graduation plan.

Instructions

Read the chapter to make sure that you understand why you should create your long-term graduation plan and then follow these steps:

Follow These Steps

Step 1: Select a major program of study.

Step 2: Determine what courses are required for graduation under your program of study.

Step 3: Determine when (which semesters) the courses are offered and whether any of them have prerequisites.

Step 4: Write the titles of the courses that you plan to take in the space provided on the **Long-Term Graduation Plan Worksheet** provided on the next page.

Step 5: Show your plan to your academic advisor when you visit him or her for registration. Ask your advisor to confirm that your plan is sound.

Notes

_____
_____
_____
_____
_____
_____
_____
_____
_____
_____
_____
_____
_____
_____
_____
_____
_____
_____
_____
_____
_____
_____
_____
_____
_____
_____
_____
_____

Long-Term Graduation Plan Worksheet

FALL (Year: _____)	SPRING (Year: _____)	SUMMER (Year: _____)
TOTAL CREDITS =	TOTAL CREDITS =	TOTAL CREDITS =

FALL (Year: _____)	SPRING (Year: _____)	SUMMER (Year: _____)
TOTAL CREDITS =	TOTAL CREDITS =	TOTAL CREDITS =

FALL (Year: _____)	SPRING (Year: _____)	SUMMER (Year: _____)
TOTAL CREDITS =	TOTAL CREDITS =	TOTAL CREDITS =

FALL (Year: _____)	SPRING (Year: _____)	SUMMER (Year: _____)
TOTAL CREDITS =	TOTAL CREDITS =	TOTAL CREDITS =

Name: _____

Assignment 12.2

Plan Semester Registration

Goal

The purpose of this activity is for the student to plan a schedule in time to participate in early or regular registration.

Objective

The student will construct a schedule for his or her next semester based on his or her **Long-Term Graduation Plan** for a specific program of study and take it to his or her academic advisor for early or regular registration.

Instructions

Use information from the chapter and your **Long-Term Graduation Plan** to complete the **Semester Registration Plan** form provided on the next page. Then follow these steps:

Follow These Steps

Step 1: Determine which courses you need based on your **Long-Term Graduation Plan.**

Step 2: Search the course catalog at your college to find schedule information about the courses that you need.

Step 3: Complete the **Semester Registration Plan** form.

Step 4: Make an appointment with your advisor for early or regular registration. Take your completed **Long-Term Graduation Plan** worksheet and your completed **Semester Registration Plan** form to your advisor for approval and registration.

Notes

_____

_____

_____

_____

_____

_____

_____

_____

_____

_____

_____

_____

_____

_____

_____

_____

_____

_____

_____

_____

_____

_____

_____

_____

_____

_____

_____

_____

Semester Registration Plan

Take the following steps in preparation to meet with your advisor:

1. Log onto your college website and view the course schedule for next semester.

2. Observe which courses are offered and at what times they are offered.

3. Make sure that you meet the prerequisite requirements before attempting to enroll in the course.

4. Use the table below to record your first and second choices for courses. Be sure to include the computer code (usually a number) for the course if necessary.

5. Take this completed form with you and show it to your advisor when you meet.

Name: _____ Student ID: _____

Major: _____ Advisor: _____

First Choices			
Course	Computer Code	Meeting Days & Time	Credits
Total Credits:			

Second Choices			
Course	Computer Code	Meeting Days & Time	Credits
Total Credits:			

Appendix

Answer Key for Reading Comprehension Questions

Background

The reading comprehension questions found throughout this textbook have been designed to assess the following four major aspects of reading: 1) vocabulary, 2) literal comprehension, 3) inferential comprehension, and 4) analysis.

Following are descriptions for each category:

Vocabulary entails identifying the meanings of words as they are used in passages. The student may use context clues, structural analysis, and/or a general understanding of the meaning of the passage to determine the meaning of a word.

Literal Comprehension entails recognizing information and ideas presented explicitly within the passages. Literal comprehension questions require a student to recognize one or more of the following: 1) the important details or facts, 2) a sequence of events, 3) a comparative relationship, 4) a cause-and-effect relationship, or 5) the referent for which a word or group of words has been substituted in a passage.

Inferential Comprehension entails synthesizing and interpreting material that is presented in a passage. Inferential comprehension items involve the following skills: 1) identifying the main idea of a passage or paragraph, 2) inductive reasoning, 3) deductive reasoning, and 4) interpretation of figurative or other language.

Analysis is concerned with how or why a passage is written, rather than what a passage is about. In general, analysis items require inferences to be made about the style, purpose, or organization of a passage.

Follow-Up Analysis

If you score your responses to the reading questions and then tabulate how many questions you answered correctly for each of the four categories, you can gain some insight into which categories you need to work on in your reading. Use the following answer key to score your responses and then use the score analysis table to tabulate the number of correct answers for each category. There were twelve questions of each type. The higher your total, the stronger your reading skill is for that category. By comparing your scores for the different types of questions, you can identify areas of strength or weakness in your reading. If you work on overcoming your weaknesses, you will be able to read and learn more effectively. When you read and learn more effectively, you will naturally earn higher grades.

Answer Key for Reading Comprehension Questions

Q#	Type	Answer	Score	Q#	Type	Answer	Score
1.1	knowledge	d		4.1	knowledge	a	
1.2	literal comprehension	a		4.2	literal comprehension	a	
1.3	inferential comprehension	a		4.3	inferential comprehension	a	
1.4	analysis	d		4.4	analysis	b	
2.1	knowledge	c		5.1	knowledge	b	
2.2	literal comprehension	a		5.2	literal comprehension	e	
2.3	inferential comprehension	a		5.3	inferential comprehension	a	
2.4	analysis	c		5.4	analysis	a	
3.1	knowledge	a		6.1	knowledge	d	
3.2	literal comprehension	b		6.2	literal comprehension	e	
3.3	inferential comprehension	a		6.3	inferential comprehension	d	
3.4	analysis	a		6.4	analysis	b	

Q#	Type	Answer	Score	Q#	Type	Answer	Score
7.1	knowledge	c		10.1	knowledge	d	
7.2	literal comprehension	c		10.2	literal comprehension	c	
7.3	inferential comprehension	d		10.3	inferential comprehension	a	
7.4	analysis	e		10.4	analysis	b	
8.1	knowledge	c		11.1	knowledge	b	
8.2	literal comprehension	c		11.2	literal comprehension	a	
8.3	inferential comprehension	c		11.3	inferential comprehension	a	
8.4	analysis	b		11.4	analysis	b	
9.1	knowledge	e		12.1	knowledge	a	
9.2	literal comprehension	d		12.2	literal comprehension	c	
9.3	inferential comprehension	d		12.3	inferential comprehension	a	
9.4	analysis	b		12.4	analysis	a	

Score Analysis Table

Category	Number Correct	Strength or Weakness?
Knowledge (Vocabulary)		
Literal Comprehension		
Inferential Comprehension		
Analysis		

References

Chapter 1 *Adjusting to College*

1. Winston Churchill, "Searchquotes," retrieved February 20, 2014, http://www.searchquotes.com/search/Some+people+dream+of+success+while+others+wake+up+and+work+hard+at+it.

2. Montgomery College website, Montgomery, Alabama, http://cms.montgomerycollege.edu/edu/.

Chapter 2 *Connecting to Resources*

1. Bill Gates, "BrainyQuote," retrieved February 25, 2014, http://www.brainyquote.com/quotes/quotes/b/billgates384628.html.

2. Henry Ward Beecher, "BrainyQuote," retrieved May 1, 2012, http://www.brainyquote.com/quotes/quotes/h/henrywardb383333.html.

3. Shelby Foote, "Goodreads," retrieved February 25, 2014, http://www.goodreads.com/quotes/126013-a-university-is-just-a-group-of-buildings-gathered-around.

4. ERIAL (Ethnographic Research in Illinois Academic Libraries) project, retrieved January 19, 2014, http://www.erialproject.org/.

Chapter 3 *Learning and Grades*

1. Mahatma Gandhi, "Goodreads," http://www.goodreads.com/quotes/2253-live-as-if-you-were-to-die-tomorrow-learn-as.

2. T. A. Angelo, " A Teacher's Dozen: Fourteen General, Research-Based Principles for Improving Higher Learning in Our Classrooms" [electronic version], *AAHE Bulletin* 45, no. 9 (1993): 3–13.

3. G. T. Doran, "There's a S.M.A.R.T. Way to Write Management's Goals and Objectives," *Management Review* (AMA FORUM) 70, no. 11 (1981): 35–36.

4. L. W. Anderson, ed., D. R. Krathwohl, ed., P. W. Airasian, K. A. Cruikshank, R. E. Mayer, P. R. Pintrich, J. Raths, and M. C. Wittrock, *A Taxonomy for Learning, Teaching, and Assessing: A Revision of Bloom's Taxonomy of Educational Objectives* (New York: Longman, 2001). Retrieved November 22, 2015, http://www.celt.iastate.edu/pdfs-docs/teaching/RevisedBloomsHandout.pdf.

5.   J. Michaels and T. Miethe, "Academic Effort and College Grades" [electronic version], *Social Forces* 68, no. 1 (1989): 309–319.

6.   H. M. Shelby, "Exploring Cramming: Student Behaviors, Beliefs, and Learning Retention in the Principles of Marketing Course" [electronic version], *Journal of Marketing Education* 30, no. 3 (2008): 226.

7.   N. Entwistle, "A Model of the Teaching-Learning Process," in *Student Learning: Research in Education and Cognitive Psychology,* eds. J. T. E. Richardson, M. W. Eysenck, and D. Warren Piper (Milton Keynes, UK: Open University Press & SRHE, 1987).

8.   L. Norton, "Assessing Student Learning," in *Handbook for Teaching and Learning in Higher Education,* 132–150 (London: Taylor & Francis Group, 2009).

9.   J. Biggs, *Teaching for Quality Learning at University: What the Student Does,* 2nd ed. (London: Society for Research into Higher Education & Open University Press, 2003).

10.   G. Gibbs, ed., *Improving Student Learning: Theory and Practice* (Oxford: The Oxford Centre for Staff Development, 1994).

11.   R. W. Tyler, *Basic Principles of Curriculum and Instruction* (Chicago: University of Chicago Press, 1949).

12.   K. Wiesenfeld, "Making the Grade: Many Students Wheedle for a Degree as If It Were a Freebie T Shirt" [electronic version], *Newsweek* 16, no. 16 (1996).

Chapter 4   *Learning Preferences*

1.   M. Horner, "The Quotations Page," retrieved March 24, 2014, http://www. quotationspage.com/quote/3010.html.

2.   D. H. Schunk, *Learning Theories: An Educational Perspective,* 6th ed. (Boston: Pearson, 2012).

3.   R. M. Felder and R. Brent, "Understanding Student Differences" [electronic version], *International Journal of Engineering and Education* 94, no. 1 (2005): 57–72; R. M. Felder and L. K. Silverman, "Learning and Teaching Styles in Engineering Education" [electronic version], *International Journal of Engineering and Education* 78 no. 7 (1988): 674–681.

4.   R. M. Felder and B. Soloman, "Learning Styles and Strategies," retrieved February 25, 2014, http://www4.ncsu.edu/unity/lockers/users/f/felder/public/ILSdir/styles.htm.

5.   R. M. Felder and J. E. Spurlin, "Applications, Reliability, and Validity of the Index of Learning Styles" [electronic version], *International Journal of Engineering and Education* 21, no. 1 (2005): 103–112.

Chapter 5 *Getting Organized*

1. H. MacKay, "Harvey MacKay Quotes," retrieved May 17, 2009, http://thinkexist.com/quotation/time-is-free-but-it-s-priceless-you-can-t-own-it/366011.html.

2. Ellen DeGeneres, "The Quotations Page," retrieved September 22, 2015, http://www.quotationspage.com/quote/38477.html.

3. S. Nist and J. P. Holschuh, "Timely Tips: The ABC (&D)'s of Time Management," 71–83, in *College Rules!* (Berkeley, CA: Ten Speed Press, 2002).

4. A. J. Hoffman, *What Every Student Should Know About Procrastination* (New York: Pearson Prentice Hall, 2008).

Chapter 6 *Listening and Taking Notes*

1. C. Tucker, actor, and B. Ratner, director, *Rush Hour* [motion picture, 1998] (United States: New Line Cinema). Retrieved May 3, 2009, http://www.imdb.com/title/tt0266915/quotes.

2. Dante Alighieri, *The Divine Comedy,* "The Quotations Page," retrieved February 25, 2014, http://www.quotationspage.com/quote/24494.html.

3. Deb Peterson, "Studying—Active Listening: Active Listening Is Where Studying Begins," About Education website, retrieved May 1, 2009, http://adulted.about.com/od/intro/qt/activelistening.htm.

4. J. Fodor, "Suggestions for Active Listening," retrieved February 25, 2004, http://www.studygs.net/listening.htm; R. G. Nichols, "What Can Be Done About Listening," *The Supervisor's Notebook* 22, no. 1 (1960): 1–3; P. Stewart, "Listening," California Polytechnic State University, Academic Skills Center website, retrieved February 25, 2014, http://sas.calpoly.edu/asc/ssl/listening.html.

5. F. Scott Fitzgerald, *The Crack-Up,* "The Quotations Page," retrieved February 25, 2014, http://www.quotationspage.com/quote/90.html.

6. J. Macionis, *Sociology,* 9th ed. (Upper Saddle River, NJ: Prentice Hall, 2002).

7. C. Nunn, "Discussion in the College Classroom: Triangulating Observational and Survey Results" [electronic version], *The Journal of Higher Education* 67, no. 3 (1996): 243–267.

8. E. Leonard, *College Success Simplified,* 2nd ed. (New York: Longman, 2008).

9. E. Leonard, *What Every Student Should Know About Study Skills* (New York: Pearson Longman, 2007).

Chapter 7   *Reading Textbooks*

1. Atwood Townsend, "Goodreads," retrieved September 22, 2015, http://www. goodreads.com/author/quotes/4619811.Atwood_H_Townsend; Austin Phelps, "Goodreads," retrieved September 22, 2015, http://www.goodreads.com/ quotes/1628-wear-the-old-coat-and-buy-the-new-book.

2. M. Nagaraju, *Teaching Reading to College Students* [slideshow], retrieved April 22, 2012, http://www.slideshare.net/lionnagaraju/teaching-reading-to-college-students.

3. S. D'Agostino, S. "Students Don't Read Textbooks," QED Insight (blog), April 8, 2011, retrieved March 15, 2012, https://qedinsight.wordpress.com/2011/04/08/ students-dont-read-textbooks/.

4. P. Babcock and M. Marks, "The Falling Time Cost of College: Evidence from Half a Century of Time Use Data," *The Review of Economics and Statistics* 93, no. 2 (2011): 468, retrieved February 25, 2014, http://ideas.repec.org/p/nbr/nberwo/15954.html.

5. D. Jairam and K. A. Kiewra, "An Investigation of the SOAR Study Method" [electronic version], *Journal of Advanced Academics* 20, no. 4 (2009): 602–629.

6. D. Jairam and K. A. Kiewra, "Helping Students Soar to Success on Computers: An Investigation of the SOAR Study Method for Computer-Based Learning" [electronic version], *Journal of Educational Psychology* 102, no. 3 (2010): 601.

7. K. A. Kiewra, "How Classroom Teachers Can Help Students Learn and Teach Them How to Learn" [electronic version], *Theory Into Practice* 41, no. 2 (2002): 71–80.

8. K. A. Kiewra, *Learn How to Study and SOAR to Success* (Upper Saddle River, NJ: Pearson, 2005).

9. University of Nebraska-Lincoln, "College Undergrads Study Ineffectively on Computers, Study Finds: Students Transfer Bad Study Habits from Paper to Screen," *Science Daily,* August 10, 2010. Retrieved April 29, 2012, http://www.sciencedaily.com /releases/2010/08/100810094617.htm.

10. Academic Skills Center, "SQ3R Method", Dartmouth College Academic Skills Center website, retrieved April 22, 2012, http://www.dartmouth.edu/~acskills/docs/sq3r_ method.doc.

11. Francis Pleasant Robinson, *Effective Study* (New York: Harper & Row, 1970).

12. K. T. McWhorter, Guide to College Reading (New York: Pearson, 2006).

13. J. D. Novak and A. J. Canas, "The Theory Underlying Concept Maps and How to Construct and Use Them" (Technical Report IHMC CmapTools 2006-01 Rev 2008-01, Institute for Human and Machine Cognition, Pensacola, Florida), retrieved December 7, 2015, http://cmap.ihmc.us/docs/theory-of-concept-maps.

Chapter 8   *Writing College Papers*

1. Stephen King, "Goodreads," retrieved September 22, 2015, http://www.goodreads.com/quotes/tag/writing?page=6.

2. J. K. Rowling, "BrainyQuote," http://www.brainyquote.com/quotes/quotes/j/jkrowlin454020.html#MA2jKGtka40XLkjh.99.

3. J. Williams and L. McEnerney, "Writing in College: A Short Guide to College Writing," University of Chicago Writing Program website, retrieved September 22, 2015, http://writingprogram.uchicago.edu/resources/collegewriting/preparing_to_write_and_drafting.htm.

Chapter 9   *Psychological Balance*

1. G. B. Hinckley, "Goodreads," retrieved February 25, 2015, http://www.goodreads.com/quotes/144912.

2. Ellen DeGeneres, "Goodreads," retrieved February 25, 2015, http://www.goodreads.com/quotes/498361.

3. Deepak Chopra, "Goodreads," retrieved February 25, 2015, http://www.goodreads.com/quotes/382188.

4. Albert Einstein, "Goodreads," retrieved February 25, 2015, http://www.goodreads.com/quotes/29213.

5. American College Health Association, "American College Health Association—National College Health Assessment II" (Reference Group Data Report Spring 2011, American College Health Association, Hanover, Maryland).

6. E. Hollinger, "Help! College Scares Me!" *Campus Life* 52, no. 8 (1994): 5–6.

7. R. Dyson and K. Renk, "Freshman Adaptation to University Life: Depressive Symptoms, Stress, and Coping," *Journal of Clinical Psychology* 62, no. 10 (2006): 1231–1244.

8. I. R. Galatzer-Levy, C. L. Burton, and G. A. Bonanno, "Coping Flexibility, Potentially Traumatic Life Events, and Resilience: A Prospective Study of College Student Adjustment." *Journal of Social and Clinical Psychology* 31, no. 6 (2012): 542–567.

9. J. T. Sargent, J. Crocker, and R. K. Luhtanen, "Contingencies of Self Worth and Depressive Symptoms in College Students," *Journal of Social and Clinical Psychology* 25 (2006): 628–646.

10. R. P. Gallagher, *National Survey of Counseling Center Directors 2011* (Washington, DC: International Association of Counseling Services, 2008). Retrieved February 23, 2015, http://www.iacsinc.org/.

412

College Success: A Concise Practical Guide

11. A. M. Pompeo, L. Kooyman, and G. Pierce, "Counseling College Women: The Interplay of Psychological Development, Social Factors, Alcohol, and Sexual Risk-Taking," *Adult Span Journal* 13, no. 1 (2014): 15–29.

12. L. L. Frey, D. Beesely, and M. R. Miller, "Relational Health, Attachment, and Psychological Distress in College Women and Men," *Psychology of Women Quarterly* 30 (2006): 303–311.

13. L. L. Frey, J. Tobin, and D. Beesley, "Relational Predictors of Psychological Distress in Women and Men Presenting for University Counseling Center Services," *Journal of College Counseling* 7 (2004): 129–139.

14. D. M. Ackard, J. K. Croll, and A. Kearney-Cooke, "Dieting Frequency Among College Females: Association with Disordered Eating, Body Image and Related Psychological Problems," *Journal of Psychosomatic Research* 52 (2002): 129–137.

15. R. Olivardia, H. G. Pope Jr., B. Mangweth, and J. L. Hudson, "Eating Disorders in College Men" [electronic version], *American Journal of Psychiatry* 152, no. 9 (1995): 1279–1285.

16. D. Eisenberg, E. J. Nicklett, K. Roeder, and N. E. Kirz, "Eating Disorder Symptoms Among College Students: Prevalence, Persistence, Correlates, and Treatment-Seeking," *Journal of American College Health* 59, no. 8 (2011), doi: 10.1080/07448481.2010.546461.

17. M. P. McCabe and L. A. Ricciardelli, "A Longitudinal Study of Pubertal Timing and Extreme Body Change Behaviors Among Adolescent Boys and Girls" [electronic version], *Adolescence* 39 (2004): 145–166.

18. D. R. McCreary and S. W. Sadava, "Gender Differences in Relationships Among Perceived Attractiveness, Life Satisfaction, and Health in Adults as a Function of Body Mass Index and Perceived Weight" [electronic version], *Psychology of Men and Masculinity* 2 (2001): 108–116.

19. J. I. Hudson, E. Hiripi, H. G. Pope Jr., and R. C. Kessler, "The Prevalence and Correlates of Eating Disorders in the National Comorbidity Survey Replication" [electronic version], *Biological Psychiatry* 61, no. 3 (2007): 348–358.

20. U.S. Department of Health and Human Services, National Institutes of Health Publication No. TR 14-4901 (Washington, DC: NIH, revised 2014).

Chapter 10 *Physical Balance*

1. Stephen R. Covey, "Think Exist," retrieved February 26, 2015, http://thinkexist.com/quotation/wisdom_is_your_perspective_on_life-your_sense_of/297538.html.

2. U.S. Department of Agriculture, "Welcome to the Five Food Groups," retrieved February 26, 2015, http://www.choosemyplate.gov/food-groups/.

3. U.S. Department of Agriculture, "My Plate on Campus," retrieved February 26, 2015, http://www.choosemyplate.gov/MyPlateOnCampus/index.html.

4. S. J. H. Biddle and N. Multrie, *Psychology of Physical Activity* (London: Routledge, 2001).

5. N. Grant, J. Wardle, and A. Steptoe, "The Relationship Between Life Satisfaction and Health Behavior: A Cross-Cultural Analysis of Young Adults," *International Journal of Behavioral Medicine* 16 (2009): 259–268.

6. J. D. Kassel, L. R. Stroud, and C. A. Paronis, "Smoking, Stress, and Negative Affect: Correlation, Causation, and Context Across Stages of Smoking," *Psychological Bulletin* 129 (2003): 270–304.

7. D. A. Regier, M. E. Farmer, D. S. Rae, B. Z. Locke, S. J. Keith, L. L. Judd, et al., "Comorbidity of Mental Disorders with Alcohol and Other Drug Abuse," *JAMA* 264 (1990): 2511–2518.

8. D. C. Seo, E. Nehl, J. Agley, and S. M. Ma, "Relations Between Physical Activity and Behavioral and Perceptual Correlates Among Midwestern College Students," *Journal of American College Health* 56, no. 2 (2007): 187–198.

9. C. Grello, D. Welsh, and M. Harper, "No Strings Attached: The Nature of Casual Sex in College Students," *Journal of Sex Research* 43 (2006): 255–267.

10. E. Paul, B. McManus, and A. Hayes, "'Hookups': Characteristics and Correlates of College Students' Spontaneous and Anonymous Sexual Experiences," *Journal of Sex Research* 37 (2000): 76–88.

11. A. M. Pompeo, L. Kooyman, and G. Pierce, "Counseling College Women: The Interplay of Psychological Development, Social Factors, Alcohol, and Sexual Risk-Taking," *Adultspan Journal* 13, no. 1 (2014): 15–29.

12. S. W. Whitton, E. M. Weitbrecht, A. D. Kuryluk, and M. R. Bruner, "Committed Dating Relationships and Mental Health Among College Students," *Journal of American College Health* 61, no. 3 (2013): 176–183.

13. S. R. Braithwaite, R. Delevi, and F. D. Fincham, "Romantic Relationships and the Physical and Mental Health of College Students," *Journal of Social and Personal Relationships* 17 (2010): 1–12.

14. R. W. Simon and A. E. Barrett, "Nonmarital Romantic Relationships and Mental Health in Early Adulthood," *Journal of Health and Social Behavior* 51 (2010): 168–182.

15. Substance Abuse and Mental Health Services Administration, "Table 6.88B—Alcohol Use in the Past Month Among Persons Aged 18 to 22, by College Enrollment Status and Demographic Characteristics: Percentages, 2012 and 2013," 2013 National Survey on Drug Use and Health (NSDUH), http://www.samhsa.gov/data/sites/default/files/NSDUHDetTabsPDFWHTML2013/Web/HTML/NSDUHDetTabsSect6peTabs55to1072013.htm#tab6.88b.

16. Substance Abuse and Mental Health Services Administration, "Table 6.89B—Binge Alcohol Use in the Past Month Among Persons Aged 18 to 22, by College Enrollment Status and Demographic Characteristics: Percentages, 2012 and 2013," 2013 National Survey on Drug Use and Health (NSDUH), http://www.samhsa.gov/data/sites/default/files/NSDUHDetTabsPDFWHTML2013/Web/HTML/NSDUHDetTabsSect6peTabs55to1072013.htm#tab6.89b

Chapter 11   *Managing Your Money*

1. G. T. Doran, "There's a S.M.A.R.T. Way to Write Management's Goals and Objectives," *Management Review* (AMA FORUM) 70, no. 11 (1981): 35–36.

2. Francis Bacon, "Goodreads," http://www.goodreads.com/quotes/446478-money-is-a-great-servant-but-abad-master.

3. Joe Biden, "Goodreads," http://www.goodreads.com/quotes/10478-don-t-tell-me-what-you-value-show-me-your-budget.

4. Robert Berger, Forbes.com, http://www.forbes.com/sites/robertberger/2014/04/30/top-100-money-quotes-of-all-time/.

5. National Center for Educational Statistics (2014), retrieved September 22, 2015, http://nces.ed.gov/programs/digest/d12/tables/dt12_439.asp.

6. Bureau of Labor Statistics, U.S. Department of Labor, "Median Weekly Earnings by Educational Attainment in 2014," The Economics Daily, retrieved September 22, 2015, http://www.bls.gov/opub/ted/2015/median-weekly-earnings-by-education-gender-race-and-ethnicity-in-2014.htm.

7. Cliff A. Robb, and Mary B. Pinto, "College Students and Credit Card Use: An Analysis of Financially At-Risk Students," *College Student Journal* 44, no. 4 (2009): 823–835.

8. P. Tew and K. Tew, "First Year Students' Financial Decision-Making: The Good, Bad, and Ugly" (presentation made at the 34th Annual Conference on the First Year Experience, Dallas, Texas, February 8, 2015).

9. Susan Burhouse, K. Chu, R. Goodstein, Joyce Northwood, Yazmin Osaki, and Dhruv Sharma, 2013 FDIC National Survey of Unbanked and Underbanked Households, retrieved September 22, 2015, https://www.fdic.gov/householdsurvey/2013report.pdf; M. B. Gross, J. M. Hogarth, and M. D. Schmeiser, "Use of Financial Services by the Unbanked and Underbanked and the Potential for Mobile Financial Services Adoption," *Federal Reserve Bulletin* 98, no. 4 (2012), retrieved September 22, 2015, http://www.federalreserve.gov/pubs/bulletin/2012/pdf/mobile_financial_services_201209.pdf.

10. R. Barrington, "The Latest MoneyRates.com Update on Bank Fees," retrieved September 22, 2015, http://www.money-rates.com/research-center/bank-fees/.

11. J. Vohwinkle, "The Difference Between APR and APY," retrieved September 22, 2015, http://financialplan.about.com/od/savingmoney/qt/APRvsAPY.htm.

12. L. Irby, "How to Calculate Your Debt to Income Ratio," retrieved September 22, 2015, http://credit.about.com/od/reducingdebt/ss/dtiratio.htm.

13. Eric Hoover, "The Lure of Easy Credit Leaves More Students Struggling with Debt," *Chronicle of Higher Education* 47, no. 40 (2001): 35–36. Cliff A. Robb and Deanna L. Sharpe, "Effect of Personal Financial Knowledge on College Students' Credit Card Behavior," *Journal of Financial Counseling & Planning* 20, no. 1 (2009): 25–43.

Chapter 12 *Physical Balance*

1. Z. Ziglar, *See You at the Top* (Gretna, LA: Pelican Publishing Company, 2005).

2. U.S. Census Bureau, "What It's Worth: Field of Training and Economic Status in 2004," Facts for Features (data tables are available from U.S. Census Bureau, Survey of Income and Program Participation, 2004 Panel), retrieved September 22, 2015, http://www.census.gov/population/www/socdemo/education/sipp2004w2.html.

Index

College Success: A Concise Practical Guide